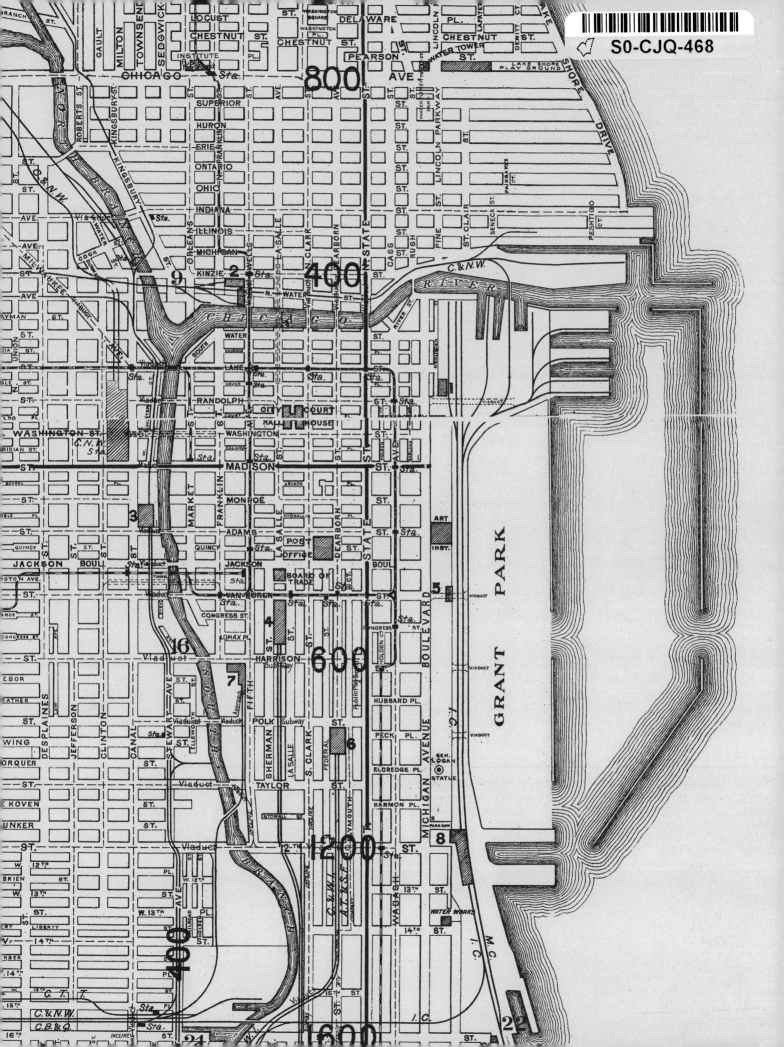

This volume is published in conjunction with the Chicago Historical Society's Bicentennial exhibition developed by Gail Farr Casterline, Staples & Charles, and the staff of the Chicago Historical Society. Publication was made possible in part by the Philip K. Wrigley Special Publication Fund.

Sketched & Drawn on Stone by PARSONS & ATWATER.   ENTERED ACCORDING TO ACT OF CONGRESS, IN THE YEAR 1874 BY CURRIER & IVES, IN THE OFFICE OF THE LIBRARIAN OF CONGRESS, AT WASHINGTON

DEXTER RACE COURSE   GREAT UNION STOCK YARDS   CANAL   ELEVATOR   BRIDEWELL   MICH SOUTHERN, C.R.I.&P DEPOT GRAND PRAIRIE HOTEL   WEST SIDE   CENTRAL PARK
                              BRIGHTON TROTTING PARK   SOUTH FORK OF RIVER   ELEVATORS, R.R.   ELEVATOR   NEW GOVERNMENT BLDG   RIVERSIDE PARK
        ENGLEWOOD   ST PAULS UNIVERSALIST CH.   GRACE EPISCOPAL CHURCH   FIRST BAPTIST CH.   AIKINS THEATRE   MCVICKERS THEATRE TRIBUNE BLDG   SOUTH BRANCH OF RIVER   P.F.W.&C.& ST LOUIS DEPOT   BRIDGE HOUSE
        SECOND PRESBYTERIAN CHURCH   GARDINER HOUSE   GREAT CENTRAL DEPOT FIELD LEITER & CO BLDG   KARNELLS BLDG   STARK DUTING BLDG TIMES BLDG
                                             LAKE MICHIGAN   LAKE PARK   CRYSTAL PALACE   PALMER HOUSE   CENTRAL ELEVATORS   CHAMBER OF COMMERCE CITY HALL, GERMAN HO.
                                                              SOUTH SIDE   ENTRANCE TO THE CHICAGO RIVER   REAPER BLOCK   TREMONT HOUSE   GALENA ELEVATOR

THE CITY OF CHICAGO

CHICAGO
Creating New Traditions

by Perry Duis

Chicago Historical Society
Chicago, Illinois, 1976

All illustrations, unless otherwise credited, are from the collections of the Chicago Historical Society.

Cover: A portion of the stenciled canvas used by Adler and Sullivan to decorate the trading room of the Chicago Stock Exchange Building, 1894.
Chicago School of Architecture Foundation

Endpapers: Downtown section of The Rand McNally New Standard Map of Chicago, 1911.

Frontispiece: Currier & Ives panorama, Chicago, 1874. Chicago on the eve of its era of greatest contributions to American life.
William McCormick Blair

Designed by Staples & Charles

Set in Mergenthaler VIP Baskerville by Carver Photocomposition, Inc. and in Typositor Comstock by Artisan Type, Inc.

Printed in the United States of America on Warren Patina by Garamond-Pridemark, Inc.

Library of Congress Cataloging in Publication Data

Duis, Perry, 1943-
    Chicago: Creating New Traditions.

    Bibliography; pp. 144; includes index.

    1. Chicago—Civilization. 2. Arts—Chicago.
3. Chicago—Social conditions. 4. Chicago—Commerce.
5. American literature—Chicago—History and criticism.
6. Cities and towns—Planning—Chicago. I. Chicago Historical Society.

F548.3.D84   977.3'11   76-45167
ISBN 0-913820-03-2
ISBN 0-913820-05-9 pbk.

The Chicago Historical Society is grateful to the following for providing financial support for this exhibition and publication.

The National Endowment for the Humanities
The Guild of the Chicago Historical Society
The Chicago Community Trust
The Field Foundation of Illinois, Inc.
Continental Bank Foundation
The First National Bank of Chicago Foundation
The Northern Trust Company Charitable Foundation
The Graham Foundation for Advanced Studies in the Fine Arts
The Illinois Bicentennial Commission
The Harris Bank Foundation
The Quaker Oats Foundation

Lenders to the Exhibition

Academy of Motion Picture Arts and Sciences
Alberta Government Telephones
The American Institute of Architects
The Art Institute of Chicago
The Donald Banovitz Family
Attractions, Inc.
Auditorium Theatre Council
Avery Library, Columbia University
Bill Birch
Blackhawk Films, Inc.
William McCormick Blair
Caedmon Records, Inc.
Chicago Architectural Photographing Company
Chicago Defender
Chicago Federation of Labor and Industrial Union Council
Chicago Joint Board, Amalgamated Clothing and Textile Workers Union, AFL-CIO
Chicago School of Architecture Foundation
Chicago Symphony Orchestra
Commission on Chicago Historical and Architectural Landmarks
Czechoslovak Society of America
Perry Duis
Alfreda M. Barnett Duster
Evanston Historical Society
Graham, Anderson, Probst and White, Architect-Engineers
Field Enterprises, Inc.
Wilbert and Marilyn Hasbrouck
Holabird and Root, Architects and Engineers
Illinois Institute of Technology
Jensen and Halstead, Limited; Architects, Engineers, Consultants
Laurette Wheeler Kenney
Krannert Art Museum, University of Illinois, Urbana-Champaign
Lake County Museum
Mr. and Mrs. John C. Lewe, Jr.
Milwaukee Journal
Library of Congress
Manuscript Collection, University of Illinois at Chicago Circle
Marshall Field & Co.
Moody Bible Institute
Montgomery Ward
The Newberry Library
Richard Nickel Committee
Northwestern University
Oak Park Public Library
Olmsted Associates, Inc.
Roosevelt University Archives
Carl Sandburg Home National Historic Site, National Park Service, U.S. Department of the Interior
Sears, Roebuck and Co.
The David and Alfred Smart Gallery, The University of Chicago
Smithsonian Institution
Southern Illinois University at Carbondale
Staples & Charles

State Historical Society of Wisconsin
Tribune Company Archives
University of Chicago Library
University of Pennsylvania Library
The Visiting Nurse Association of Chicago
WFMT-FM
WGN Continental Broadcasting Company
Joseph M. Williams
Woman's Christian Temperance Union
The Frank Lloyd Wright Home and Studio Foundation

Acknowledgments

Such a project as *Chicago* must be a collaborative effort. From the very beginning, when it was merely a vague idea, the Historical Society's president, Theodore Tieken, and the other members of the Society's Board of Trustees have been active and enthusiastic supporters of the project. As for the day-to-day work of actually locating and assembling the hundreds of objects, writing the exhibition captions, and carrying out the literally thousands of tasks which finally come together as a finished product, this work fell to Gail Farr Casterline, whose energy and imagination are visible everywhere in the exhibit. Professor Perry Duis, of the University of Illinois at Chicago Circle, willingly took on the task of helping to develop the humanistic framework of the exhibition and is directly responsible for the interpretive essays and captions in this book.

An exhibit is a very special medium, one that is the most basic means of communication for a museum. And this medium requires its own special skills. Throughout the process of developing *Chicago* we have had the pleasure and challenge of working with the firm of Staples & Charles, who were partners in the development of the concept and its transformation into a legible, imaginative, and informative exhibit environment. In addition, Elizabeth Chatain assisted in compiling a massive photographic record of exhibit possibilities throughout the city. Wilbert Hasbrouck was an enthusiastic and active collaborator in the field of Chicago architecture, and Dian Post, who edited the essays, captions, and exhibition labels, has made an invaluable contribution to the project.

The efforts of this group could not have been carried out without the informed resourcefulness and special talents of the entire staff of the Chicago Historical Society. Whether carrying out research, surveying their collections for appropriate materials, making photographs, reading copy, or actually installing the exhibit, every staff member has made a major contribution to *Chicago*.

Special thanks must also go to our colleagues in sister Chicago institutions: Courtney Donnell, Annette Fern, Jean Finch, Milo Naeve, and Esther Sparks of The Art Institute of Chicago; John Aubrey, Paul Banks, Diana Haskell, Joel Samuels, and James Wells of the Newberry Library; Robert Allison, John Cash, Judith Cushman, Sidney Huttner, Mary Janzen, Robert Rosenthal, and Albert Tannler of the Regenstein Library, University of Chicago; Mary Ann Johnson, Mary Lynn McCree, and Mary Lynn Ritzenthaler of the University of Illinois at Chicago Circle, for their suggestions, insights, and leads to new information or materials.

Our thanks also go to the following individuals who greatly assisted us in the development of *Chicago:* Barbara Ballinger, Oak Park Public Library; Stanley Balzekas, Jr., Balzekas Museum of Lithuanian Culture; Manny Banayo, Sears, Roebuck and Co.; Lois Baum, WFMT-FM; The Rev. Donald S. Bilinski, Polish Museum of America; James Breckenridge, Northwestern University; Joan Breitman; George Bushnell, Illinois Institute of Technology; Edith

Butler; A. W. Cashman, Alberta Government Telephones; George Chapman, Jensen & Halstead; Muriel B. Christison, Krannert Art Museum; Beverly Cox, National Portrait Gallery; John Craib-Cox, Chicago School of Architecture Foundation; Alexander Crary, Smithsonian Institution; Mikell Darling, Evanston Historical Society; Benjamin H. Davis, Carl Sandburg Home NHS; Margaret DeSchryver; Alice Donahue, Visiting Nurse Association of Chicago; William Dring, The Frank Lloyd Wright Home and Studio Foundation; Ken Duckett, Morris Library, Southern Illinois University at Carbondale; Gerald Eisel, Graham, Anderson, Probst and White; Eugene Feldman, DuSable Museum of African American History, Inc.; Jeanette Fields, Chicago School of Architecture Foundation; Terry Fisher, Oscar Mayer and Company; Roy Forrey, Commission on Chicago Historical and Architectural Landmarks; Thurmon O. Fox, State Historical Society of Wisconsin; Frances Freiwald, Northwestern University; William Grisham; James Goode, Smithsonian Institution; F. Gerald Ham, State Historical Society of Wisconsin; Richard Hartung, Rock County (Wisconsin) Historical Society, Walter Hass, The University of Chicago; Harold Haydon; James Henn, International Harvester Company; Tom Herriman, Chicago Joint Board, Amalgamated Clothing and Textile Workers Union, AFL-CIO; John Holabird, Holabird and Root; Harold Hutchings, Tribune Company Archives; Diane Ignasher, Midway Studios; Selma Jacobson, Swedish Pioneer Historical Society; Walker Johnson, Holabird and Root; Katherine Keefe, The David & Alfred Smart Gallery, The University of Chicago; Claudia B. Kidwell, Smithsonian Institution; Robert Kite, Chicago Federation of Labor and Industrial Union Council; Irwin Klass, Chicago Federation of Labor and Industrial Union Council; Robert Knox, Caedmon Records, Inc.; Frankie Kozuch, Roosevelt University Archives; Robert Kular, Chicago Symphony Orchestra; Gregory Lennes, International Harvester Company; Mr. and Mrs. Jack Lindahl, Attractions, Inc.; Bill Loupas, WCFL; Gordon Loux, Moody Bible Institute; D. T. McAllister, Michelson Museum, China Lake, California; John McGowan, Northwestern University; Mrs. Robert W. McLallen, Visiting Nurse Association of Chicago; Lee Major, Tribune Company Archives; Thomas Mapp, Midway Studios; Gordon S. Mark; Michael Mason, Southern Illinois University at Edwardsville; David Milberg, WBBM; Elena Millie, Library of Congress; Pat Miller, Marshall Field & Co.; Ken Munson, Lake County Museum; M. Frederick Nash, University of Illinois at Urbana-Champaign; David Norris; Leslie F. Orear, Illinois Labor History Society; Walter Osborn, Moody Bible Institute; George Pettengill, American Institute of Architects; Adolf Placzek, Avery Library, Columbia University; Sylvia Plotkin, Chicago Public School Art Society; Patrick M. Quinn, Northwestern University; Tom Ray, Field Enterprises, Inc.; Mary Frances Rhymer; Deborah Rodgers, Montgomery Ward; Chuck Schaden; Cathlyn Schallhorn; Richard Schock, Moody Bible Institute; Michael Sedlak, Northwestern University; Mildred Simpson, Academy of Motion Picture Arts and Sciences; James Smart, Library of Congress; David Sokol, The Frank Lloyd Wright Home and Studio Foundation; Mrs. John V. Spachner, Auditorium Theatre Council; Paul Spehr, Library of Congress; Mrs. Herman Stanley, Woman's Christian Temperance Union; William Stepen, Pilsen Butcher's Benevolent Association; Loring Stevenson, Montgomery Ward; William Surman, Graham, Anderson, Probst and White; Mary Sweeney, WCFL; T. J. Swigon, Museum of Science and Industry; Lenore Swoiskin, Sears, Roebuck and Co.; Margaret Symon, Marshall Field & Co.; George Talbot, State Historical Society of Wisconsin; Milton Thompson, Illinois State Museum; Dorothy Unger; Harvey Versteeg, Lake County Museum; John Vinci, Vinci and Kenney; Frank Vodrazka, Czechoslovak Society of America; Louise Wade, University of Oregon; Tim Walch, Society of American Archivists; Lois Walker, *Chicago Defender;* Warren R. Weber, Carl Sandburg Home NHS; Neda Westlake, University of Pennsylvania Library; William H. Wills, WGN Continental Broadcasting Company; Alfred Wood, Carter G. Woodson Regional Library.

Table of Contents

Preface

Chicago has always had a special place in the American experience. Its rapid growth, its size, its raw vitality, its diversity, have made it perhaps the most American of our great cities. In a lecture given in 1918, Frank Lloyd Wright referred to Chicago as the "national capital of the essentially American spirit." In this Bicentennial year, the Chicago Historical Society felt it important to develop both a major interpretive exhibit and a publication that would explore and interpret Chicago's role in the transformation of America from a rural, agricultural society into the urban, technological nation which we see around us today. What is striking about this transformation is the degree to which Chicago and Chicagoans were leaders in the process. For a time Chicago was not only a place but also a trademark for innovation and change. In the following pages and in our exhibition we explore Chicago's contributions in six important areas of American life: Architecture, Planning, Reform, Culture, Merchandising, and Literature. In each of these areas, innovations and reforms pioneered in Chicago to deal with the growing pains of a great urban metropolis had an impact and significance that went far beyond the city's boundaries. We see in Chicago the problems of every American city, while we see in its innovative response small revolutions in thought and action that have since become so much a part of American life that we hardly notice them.

But in the large brushstrokes of this story we should not forget to notice that the reforms and changes which developed in Chicago were the creation of real people. Again and again the names of Jane Addams, Frank Lloyd Wright, Harriet Monroe, Daniel Burnham, Graham Taylor, and others appear and reappear in different parts of our story. In an age concerned about the impersonality of urban society we should not forget that America's urban frontier had its own pioneers. It is amazing to note the number of these who were Chicagoans.

Chicago, then, is a reminder to us all of the long tradition of small revolutions that have characterized our national experience and a focus on Chicago's special place in these revolutions. We hope that not only Chicagoans, but everyone who sees this exhibition or reads the pages of this book, will be reminded of the exploring spirit that is reflected in *Chicago* and will realize that this spirit can be a harbinger of new frontiers of the American experience still to come.

Harold K. Skramstad, Jr.
Director

Architecture: Building for People

The *Chicago Tribune* had a complaint and a wish. In a long feature published on October 28, 1883, it criticized Chicagoans for the ugly homes and commercial buildings they had put up after the Great Conflagration of 1871. Most offensive was the ostentatious use of colored stone and the inappropriate styles, especially ersatz "Swiss chalets." Architects apparently followed the mere whims of their wealthy but unrefined clients, instead of striving to elevate their sense of aesthetics. Nevertheless, the *Tribune* anticipated something better:

> *All sorts of ambitious enterprizes and prodigious results are characterized as Chicago developments; why may there not be an additional style in the superb role which architecture has created, and which, known as Chicago style, may go down to posterity as honored, as novel, as full of harmony and beauty as the best of those which have come to be throughout the ages?*

The *Tribune* seems not to have realized it, but Chicago already was beginning to show a new departure in American architecture. The purely technological aspects such as the steel frame and the wide expanse of the "Chicago window" have since become well-known. But Chicago's contribution to architectural form was even greater. This was a refreshing response to human needs, a response that first borrowed what was useful from earlier styles and then attacked the whole idea of style as stifling to creativity. In a city where the practical outweighed the traditional, human needs shaped both the private and public buildings that architects designed. The motivations for this humanistic architecture were sometimes altruistic, though more often based on profit; but the result was something uniquely oriented toward people.

Reliance Building, D. H. Burnham, 1895. This aging skyscraper features windows that look remarkably modern.
Staples & Charles

St. Mary's Roman Catholic Church, 1833. Probably the first balloon-frame building in the world, this church was built at a cost of $400 by Chicago's first priest, Father John St. Cyr. Initially located near the corner of State and Lake streets, it was moved three times during the ten years it served as a church.

The Mixed Legacy of Balloon Frames

Chicago had barely been founded when its first major contribution to American architecture was forthcoming, the balloon-frame wall. Previously, housebuilders had been handicapped by slow, laborious construction techniques. While houses in more settled portions of the country were made of stone or brick, those on the frontier were often fashioned out of logs. Traditional frame buildings with walls of heavy timber held together by mortise and tenon joints required talented craftsmen and large quantities of building material. In a young boom-town both the skills and supplies were scarce. Chicago's earliest settlers included few professional builders. Clay for brick and limestone for mortar were miles away, and lumber was in short supply.

Convenience and necessity dictated a new approach to building in Chicago. By the mid-1830s a variation of the traditional wooden structure was becoming commonplace, the balloon frame. Lighter boards, some with a cross-section as small as two inches by four, replaced heavy timbers; this, in turn, allowed builders to substitute nails for interlocking mortise-work. To finish off the exterior they tacked thin, closely fitted boards over the frame, and the interior was sheathed with wood or plaster.

Nobody ever patented this idea, and so its exact origins remain clouded. We do know that a local builder named Augustine Taylor erected the first ballon-frame structure, St. Mary's Church, in 1833, and that within a few years there were hundreds of them. Chicagoans quickly discovered that the balloon frame was much cheaper than the traditional frame. It required far less lumber, while its light weight enabled a simple nailed construction which meant that anyone could become his own builder. One student of American domestic housing observed in 1869 that "a man and boy can now attain the same results, with ease, that twenty men could on an old-fashioned frame." The carpentry, which required no tools other than a hammer and saw, could be mastered simply by watching a neighbor. And, because it was so easy, a new house took days rather than weeks.

The result was an instant city whose growth was unhindered by a lack of building materials. As early as 1833, shortly after St. Mary's was finished, one sharp entrepreneur, Dr. W. B. Egan, put up "Egan's Row." This was the city's first subdivision. In later years builders marketed vast tracts of cheap houses. Because the balloon frame was a hidden part of the structure, designers discovered that they could create exteriors in just about any style. Soon the streets of the new city were lined with fanciful structures like Myrick's Castle, replete with tower and cupola. Diversity ruled—verandas and Norman windows, columns and Mansard roofs, Grecian and Italian forms. Owners could afford to experiment because the basic cost was so low.

The legacy of the balloon frame was mixed. Although the structural style was adopted in most parts of the world and has brought cheap housing to millions, it created problems in the city of its birth. The frame house was easily portable. While this enabled thousands of Chicagoans to move to a new neighborhood without having to pay for a new house, it also fostered the practice of moving old houses to the back of lots and then building new ones fronting the street. These concealed the old houses, which quickly became "rear-alley tenements." Wooden housing also proved less durable and less sanitary. A structure that once was someone's dream could become someone else's tragedy, and by the 1840s and 1850s Chicago already had extensive wooden slums.

It was in just such a slum, beginning on the night of October 9, 1871, that the most disastrous shortcoming of balloon frames became terribly clear. The Great Chicago Fire blazed for days, destroyed 18,000 buildings, and left thousands homeless. Although civic booster William Bross insisted that the cost of each house "was comparatively small, and they were quickly and cheaply rebuilt," the Fire left an indelible mark on Chicago. The City Council passed a new building ordinance that prohibited wooden frame structures within certain prescribed boundaries. Contractors rushed crews to the city who worked nonstop to rebuild. Torches illuminated their nighttime labors, while heating the concrete allowed pouring to continue throughout the winter. Ironically, the first Chicago building innovation had contributed to a catastrophe which opened the way to an era of stylistic and design innovation probably unmatched in all American history.

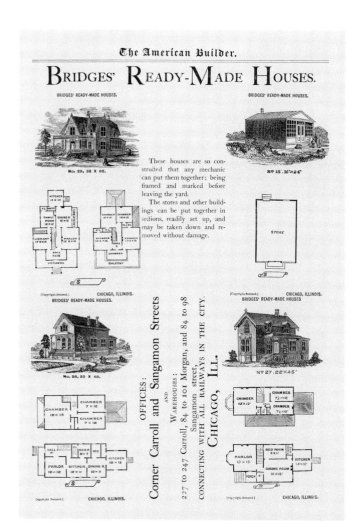

Prefabricated house, The American Builder, *January 1871. The portability of the balloon frame permitted pre-assembly of buildings in a variety of styles, and easy re-location as well. The balloon frame gave new meaning to the concept of mobility.*

Morgan Park, c1900. The balloon-frame technique made possible what amounted to assembly-line production of houses. In this Far South Side neighborhood carpenters are erecting the frame of one house, while another crew is installing shingle siding next door. The other houses have recently been completed.

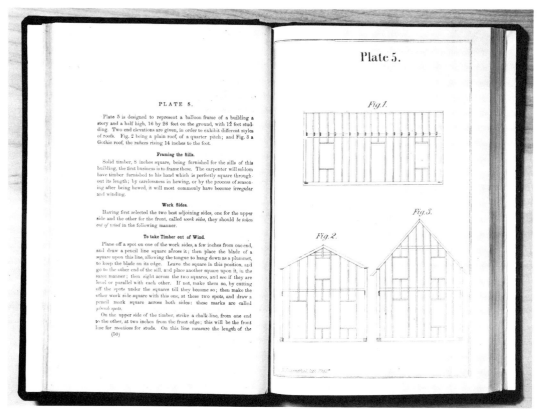

Early carpentry manual, 1857. The balloon frame enabled anyone to become an expert carpenter. This manual, written by a man from Ottawa, Illinois, was designed for "Amateurs who have felt the necessity of a faithful guide in house-building and other structures, especially in new settlements . . ." From William E. Bell, Carpentry Made Easy; or the Science and Art of Framing, or a New Improved System *(Philadelphia: Howard Challen, 1857). University of Illinois, Urbana-Champaign*

John M. Van Osdel (1811-91), c1890. Van Osdel was Chicago's first professional architect. Legend has it that as the spreading Chicago Fire approached the newly-completed Palmer House, Van Osdel rushed to the basement, dug a pit in the wet sand and clay, and buried his record books. Although he did not invent clay fire-proofing tile, the fact that his books escaped damage in the flames helped convince other Chicago architects of its virtues.

William LeBaron Jenney (1832-1907), c1890. Inventor of the steel frame, Jenney was a leader in the development of a Western style of architecture.

Daniel H. Burnham (1846-1912). Burnham profoundly influenced American architecture through the dozens of buildings he designed in Chicago and in the Midwest. His Plan of Chicago has been called the most important document in the history of modern city planning.

John Wellborn Root (1850-92), c1890. Some architectural historians believe that Root was the true creative genius behind the firm of Burnham and Root.

Dankmar Adler (1844-1900). Like many other Chicago architects, Dankmar Adler learned many principles of engineering during the Civil War.
The Art Institute of Chicago

Louis H. Sullivan (1856-1924), c1890. Sullivan spent his most productive years, 1879-1895, in partnership with Dankmar Adler, and together they designed many important buildings including the Auditorium Theater. Though idolized to the very end by young architects, he died virtu-ally pennyless in a cheap rooming house.
The Art Institute of Chicago

William Holabird (1854-1923), c1890. A popular figure among Chicago architects, Holabird and his partner Martin Roche designed many significant buildings, including the Tacoma, the Congress Hotel (origi-nally the Auditorium Annex), the Marquette, the LaSalle Hotel, and the Sherman Hotel.

Martin Roche (1855-1927), c1920. Though apprenticed to a cabinetmaker, young Roche was inspired by visits to the Art Institute and determined to be-come an architect. Ironically, when his partnership with William Holabird got off to a shaky start, Roche turned to designing cabinets to keep the firm together. He is credited with originat-ing the idea of the sub-basement, which added considerably to the underground floorspace in Loop buildings.
Holabird and Root, Architects and Engineers

The Emergence of the Professional Architect

Post-Fire rebuilding was carried out in great haste. Many new structures were little more than reincarnations based on salvaged plans and lingering memories. But some property-holders decided to make the most of the disaster by erecting larger structures more in keeping with Chicago's burgeoning growth. They crowded architect's offices which, in turn, soon began to resemble factories. In one year, the firm of John Van Osdel (first to have established himself as a professional architect in Chicago, in 1841) designed buildings that, if lined up side by side, would have totaled over a mile and a half of frontage. The immense task of rebuilding made Chicago a mecca for ambitious young draftsmen and designers. Even the severe depression that began in 1873 failed to stem the inflow of talent. This proved to be a turning-point for Chicago architecture—indeed, for American architecture. A nation's ideas about building were changed fundamentally.

The emergence of the new Chicago style of building was largely a product of one generation of architects supplanting another. The earlier group, which included men like Van Osdel and Augustus Bauer, had arrived before the Civil War. Their designs were relatively simple, based on building techniques that dated back centuries. They regarded architecture as a set of venerable traditions, classical styles, and a method that was virtually frozen. Their "practice" was just what the word implied, a set of techniques to be passed on generation after generation through apprenticeship.

The disruptive forces of the Civil War and the rapid growth of the city changed all that. While Van Osdel and Bauer lived on until the early 1890s, their work remained rooted in earlier concepts. The truly creative ideas came from younger professionals who had come to Chicago after the war, and who often started out as neophyte assistants to senior designers. During the last three decades of the nineteenth century, however, these young architects helped precipitate a major change in their growing profession, a change based largely on increasing specialization. Out of this emerged a new team relationship among designers, as well as a new kind of relationship between professionals and their clients.

The new professional architects reflected a great diversity of backgrounds. Their acknowledged leader, William LeBaron Jenney, had arrived just after the Civil War. Born in 1832 in Fairhaven, Massachusetts, he was the son of a prosperous shipowner. By the age of nineteen Jenney had sailed around Cape Horn, visited Manila, and completed three years of technical education in Massachusetts. But, for an engineer, Europe offered the best training, and so in June 1853 he enrolled at the École Centrale des Arts et Manufactures in Paris. He graduated three years later. Upon returning to America he became an engineer. Then, after two years he went back to Paris for more training. Within eighteen months he was home again, this time because of the imminent outbreak of the Civil War.

Military experience proved important to many young engineers and architects. Jenney soon found himself under the command of General William Tecumseh Sherman. Although General Sherman made use of his talents to construct forts, he found him more admirably suited to directing demolition work in conquered regions. Participating in Sherman's famous "March to the Sea," Jenney learned how to destroy bridges and buildings with great efficiency. More important, this experience taught him much about iron construction, foundations, and framing. After the war he returned east to work as a coal-mining engineer, but his true ambition was to build things above ground. In 1868 he decided that his greatest opportunities lay in the West, and he settled in Chicago.

Jenney established an architectural firm based on the division of tasks among specialists. This enabled undertaking several large projects at once. It also allowed "The Major," as Jenney was called, to concentrate his personal efforts on structural problems. This was really his forte. As Louis Sullivan pointed out, Jenney was not actually an architect, "except by courtesy of terms. His true profession was that of an engineer."

Jenney's staff included several young men who later established distinguished careers of their own, including Martin Roche and William Holabird. Roche had grown up in Chicago and had been educated in its public schools. When he was eighteen Jenney hired him as a draftsman to help relieve the backlog of post-Fire work. Holabird, a native of New York, had some formal training from West Point. Arriving in Chicago in 1875, he also went to work for Jenney. Five years later he left The Major to form his own firm. Roche joined him in 1881, and their firm, Holabird and Roche, went on to produce notable buildings for the next forty-six years.

Young Louis Sullivan also had been a member of Jenney's staff. Born in Boston in 1856, Sullivan was the son of an Irish immigrant who ran a dancing academy. When Louis was twelve his parents moved to Chicago, leaving him behind in Massachusetts with his grandparents. He entered M.I.T. at the age of sixteen, but lasted only a year. After a brief stint as a draftsman in Philadelphia, he moved west to Chicago where he found similar work with Jenney's firm. But he soon became bored with the routine of drafting, left for Paris, and in 1874 enrolled at the École des Beaux Arts. The following spring he was back in Chicago, this time on his own. He first designed the interiors of a Southside synagogue and the Moody Tabernacle on North LaSalle Street. It was through these efforts that he came to the attention of Dankmar Adler, who was twelve years his elder.

Adler had been born in Germany in 1844, the son of a cantor in a synagogue. At age ten he had come to the United States with his family, which first settled in Detroit and then, in 1861, in Chicago, where his father assumed the leadership of the Anshe M'ariv congregation. Young Adler wanted to be an architect, but after failing the entrance examinations at the University of Michigan he settled for a draftsman's job in Detroit. He soon returned to Chicago, however, to work for Augustus Bauer, one of the city's elder architects. Like Jenney, Adler served as an engineer during the Civil War. After the war he went back to Bauer's office, but only briefly—quitting after a dispute about the value of military engineering experience. In January 1871 he formed a partnership with Edward Burling, a builder whose work dated back to the 1840s. Burling's service on the Cook County Board and his participation in party politics earned him an appointment as director of the U.S. Customhouse, a building he had designed.

Subsequently, Adler was without a major partner for two years, then in 1881 he took on the twenty-five year-old Sullivan. The two made a splendid team. Although he was a competent stylist, Adler was more comfortable solving problems of structure, foundation, heating, and ventilating. It was Sullivan whose pencil sketched a building's shape and ornamental intricacies. The Adler-Sullivan partnership lasted until July 1895, when Adler became the architect for a large Chicago plumbing-supply manufacturer. He left after a year, and spent the remaining four years of his life in private practice.

The story of Adler and Sullivan had marked parallels to the city's other leading architectural partnership, that of John Wellborn Root and Daniel H. Burnham. These men were likewise from diverse backgrounds. Root, a native of Georgia, had been sent off to school in England at the outbreak of the Civil War. His home district had been devastated by General Sherman's army—ironically, with the help of Jenney, who would later become his close friend. Root studied at Oxford for a while, then returned to New York University to take engineering. Upon graduating in 1869 he became an apprentice to two New York firms, but left for Chicago after learning of the post-Fire opportunities there. Arriving in January 1872, he went to work for Peter Wight, another of the city's senior architects, and it was here that he met his future partner, Daniel H. Burnham.

Burnham had been born in New York in 1846, the son of a salesman. His family soon moved to Chicago, and young Daniel was educated in the city's public schools. Despite help from private tutors, he was unable to pass the Harvard entrance exams. The demoralized youth spent the next few years drifting from one unsatisfying job to another. Finally, he decided to become an architect. With the help of his father, by then a successful merchant, he was able to obtain apprentice positions, first under John Van Osdel and then under Peter Wight. Like many other architects, Wight was swamped with reconstruction work, and the skillful sketches and renderings that originated on Burnham's desk were of great value. When Burnham and Root left Wight's office to establish their own firm in 1873, Burnham's easy, outgoing personality proved to be a great asset in obtaining contracts. If Adler was the engineer and Sullivan the designer, then Root was the architect and Burnham the businessman.

The development of these firms was indicative of the evolution of architecture as a profession. Architects were no longer simply draftsmen like Van Osdel, who remained at his drawing board and turned out plans for his fellow builders. The division of labor evident in other businesses had become important in the architectural profession as well. Typically, one member of a firm was responsible for

obtaining contracts. In this new scheme of things a personable partner like Daniel Burnham was an essential asset. Another member became a firm's structural expert. Jenney, for example, kept young designers busy working on facades while he himself attended to engineering problems; Dankmar Adler performed much the same function in his office. Louis Sullivan, on the other hand, was fascinated with the finer details of decoration and design. Finally, each office employed many draftsmen and apprentices—180 of them at D. H. Burnham and Company by 1912—who toiled over drawings, dealt with contractors, and supervised actual construction. The confluence of many specialized skills yielded a department store of design, a multifaceted organization capable of solving almost any challenge.

Chicago architects also developed a keen sense of professionalism. This was difficult in the mid-nineteenth century when building techniques were simple. William LeBaron Jenney warned young architects that they should not bend too easily to the "whims of the client," even though he paid the bill. Part of an architect's job was to try and uphold the canons of good taste. Yet, at the same time, the architect had to fit a building to the owner's genuine needs. Coming to an accommodation would require a series of frank interviews. The daily habits of each member of a household or each department of a business would help determine the shape of the final work, which, in turn, ought to express the character of the owner or the activity carried on inside.

Chicagoans were also aware that they were developing an architecture different from that of the East. Whereas New York architects deliberately sought to emulate European "historic styles," Chicago architects enjoyed being iconoclasts. This sense of self-awareness was clearly evident in the periodical *Inland Architect*, founded in 1883. Its editor, Robert McLean, promoted the idea of a distinct professional organization as well, and the following year Jenney, Wight, Burnham, and Root founded the Western Society of Architects. Still another organization, the Chicago Architectural Club, appeared in the late 1880s and became a major arena for the exchange of ideas between young architects. The Club held frequent meetings, and, after 1898, sponsored annual exhibitions and competitions.

The Inland Architect & Builder
banner, 1884.

Forces Demanding Change

Chicago architects never tried to escape the realities of their situation in a fast-growing city. Their drawing boards were never isolated from the exigencies of the corporate boardrooms, the local politicos, and the crowds in the street. They realized that forces unknown to the general public often shaped the skyline. Sometimes determinants were obvious—an economic panic, say. But often they were peculiar and idiosyncratic—someone's conviction that one street was more convenient than another or that one type of building was more comfortable than another. These factors multiplied could result in major commissions or drive an architect into bankruptcy. Chicago architects paid heed to many signals, including those that explained why the Loop of 1880 was not only bigger than that of 1860, but qualitatively different as well.

Innovative architects realized that the process of urban evolution created a continuous demand for new ideas and techniques. The technological revolution that took place during the 1880s drew its stimuli from such diverse factors as the popular regard for the safety of public buildings and the emerging demand for the accommodation of large crowds in privately-owned buildings with public access. Chicago architects also understood the economic forces that shaped buildings, the effects that soaring land values had on income yield, and the factors underlying the need to replace old structures.

Central to all of these new demands on architects was a changing perception of space in urban society. Chicago was becoming more crowded, the era of rural independence was over, and almost everyone depended on others for food, water, clothing, education, entertainment, and other necessities. As urbanites began to spend more of their time away from home, the places they spent it assumed a different character. In most cases these facilities continued to be privately owned, but pressing crowds had, in effect, turned them into quasi- or semi-public places. Architects realized that the presence of surging masses had frequently all but eradicated the distinction between public and private spaces.

After the Fire the protection of lives and property became a key determinant of Chicago's architectural design. The ultimate goal, of course, was the fireproof building; the quest for this incidentally directed the attention of Chicago architects toward a style that was both innovative and utilitarian. Mansard roofs, once regarded almost as a necessity, fell into disfavor because their wooden construction helped spread flames from one rooftop to another. Moreover, what had once been considered the most advanced technology, cast-iron framing, was rejected because it buckled and snapped in intense heat. Some local builders returned to traditional building materials, limestone and brick. Others adopted a new form of fire protection first developed in New York. A hollow tile envelope built around an iron frame enclosed air space which provided insulation. If cast in long arch-shaped units, the hollow tile frequently had sufficient strength to constitute a fully fireproof floor. In-

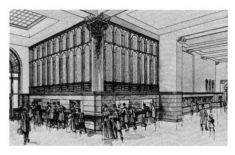

Grand Central Station, illustrations from promotional booklet, c1890. Designed by S. S. Beman, this spacious depot handled 10,000 passengers a day during the 1890s.

Fireproofing advertisement, Inland Architect and Builder, *April 1885. This illustrates the technique of encasing iron I-beams and vertical columns in hollow ceramic tiles. The same material was also cast into fireproof wall-brick and into elongated tiles that fitted together to form arched ceilings and floors.*

Auditorium Building, working drawings by Louis Sullivan, c1888. The ornamental as well as technological accomplishment of the Auditorium Building drew national attention. These drawings were for the ornamental plaster-work around the arched entrance to the hotel lobby.
The Art Institute of Chicago

Auditorium Building, 1888. While not even complete when the Republican Party staged its national convention here in June 1888, at least it provided the delegates shelter from the rain. On December 10, 1889, President Benjamin Harrison and Vice President Levi Morton came to Chicago to dedicate the building.
Auditorium Theatre Council

ventors and salesmen descended on Chicago to promote various kinds of fireproofing, but it was the Kendall Building, constructed on North Dearborn in 1873, that gained distinction as the first fireproof building in Chicago.

Architects could now build semi-public structures with confidence in their safety. Adler and Sullivan were the first to realize the full possibilities of the semi-public building, a field in which they produced some of their most distinguished work. Their Auditorium Theater was an outstanding example. A group of local promoters had been concerned about Chicago's lack of an appropriate place to stage operas and concerts. To contribute to operating revenues and keep ticket prices down, they had Adler and Sullivan design a structure with a hotel and offices surrounding the theater itself. Begun in 1886, the Auditorium Theater was a masterpiece. When President Benjamin Harrison arrived to dedicate it, Chicago received worldwide notoriety. Adler had so mastered the art of acoustics that someone speaking in a normal voice on stage could be heard even in the rear gallery. Sullivan had kept a free line of vision for every one of the 4,237 seats. The interior was ornately finished in gold and ivory, colors which blended well with the thousands of electric lights whose glowing yellow filaments themselves became part of the ornament. Finally, an elaborate circulation system passed incoming air through cooling sprays on the roof, making the Auditorium one of the first air-conditioned buildings.

Adler and Sullivan took a similar approach with other semi-public buildings. For example, the Schiller (later Garrick) Theater of 1891 was topped with an office tower to help generate revenue. Again they took great care with the acoustics and decoration. But the most magnificent

triumph was Sullivan's alone. Four years after Adler left the firm in 1895, Sullivan received a commission to design a new store for the firm of Schlesinger and Mayer. Because of difficulties in acquiring land, the building had to be erected in sections; when completed it covered a quarter of a square block. Later purchased by Carson Pirie Scott & Co., it has been justly recognized as one of the most important commercial structures ever erected.

This was Sullivan's response to the rise of the department store as a semi-public place. It was not simply an enlarged urban version of a country general store. First of all, the customers were likely to be women. To please their sensibilities Sullivan and his designer George Grant Elmslie created an elaborate lacework of iron trim around the entrance and show windows. Utilitarian fixtures such as radiators were humanized with iron ornament, as was a passageway to the elevated station. Large windows helped illuminate the merchandise, an important consideration in the days when electric lighting was weak. The grand entranceway was designed to lure customers in from the sidewalk and make them feel important. Finally, there were restaurants, nurseries, restrooms, a dispensary, and other conveniences. Sullivan knew that "shopping" had emerged as a form of entertainment as well as a requisite function of family life, and he tried to make it a pleasant experience. The principles of design, however, were not uniquely his, for every creative architect knew of Chicago's preeminent role in the creation of yet another kind of semi-public place. This was the skyscraper that held the vertical crowd.

There were numerous reasons why tall buildings seemed to develop so naturally in Chicago, and why Chicago so readily

Auditorium Theater interior, c1970. This magnificent hall held over 8,000 people when the huge stage was utilized for seating.
Richard Nickel for Commission on Chicago Historical and Architectural Landmarks

Auditorium Building, Adler and Sullivan, c1897. The entrance to the right, on Wabash Avenue, led to offices, while the entrance to the left, on Congress Street, led to the theater. The front door, leading to the hotel, faced Michigan Avenue.

adopted and refined subsidiary technologies that originated elsewhere. The elevator, a product of New York, was a rarity in the low buildings of pre-Fire Chicago. However, elevator technology had attained a high degree of refinement by the early 1870s, just when Chicagoans had begun to rebuild their city. Unhampered by the presence of an older technology, Chicago's new buildings had the advantage of starting out with the latest forms of vertical transportation. Thus, as late as 1890 the *Tribune* could boast that the city had elevators that were half-again as fast as those in New York, and more numerous than in any city in the world.

The rapid development of the Loop also fostered the development of tall buildings. Although there were no natural barriers to the city's residential expansion, the downtown was constricted on one side by the lake and on two sides by rivers. The constant opening of bridges for commercial vessels impeded access to the north and west sides, and old tunnels under Washington and LaSalle streets were inadequate. The result was a concentration of commercial activities within a limited area. This boosted land values which, in turn, prompted owners to construct buildings that would yield maximum revenue. The skyscraper became not only practical but also desirable economically.

This produced a second windfall for young architects. Dozens of five-story and six-story buildings constructed just after the Fire became obsolete during the last fifteen years of the century, and this helped precipitate one of Chicago's most extensive downtown renewals. Burnham and Root's Rookery (1886) replaced a small temporary City Hall whose water tank had been pressed into service as Chicago's first public library. The same firm's Ashland Block (1892) replaced a smaller building which was dismantled and moved

to another site. All the city's major architectural firms shared in the prosperity. Holabird and Roche's Tacoma (1889) replaced the four-story Schweizer Block (1872), while their seventeen-story Marquette Building of 1894 stood on the site of a six-story predecessor by the same name built twenty-two years earlier. On occasion, a firm like Adler and Sullivan might receive a commission to remodel an older edifice. In 1888 it added two floors and new cornices to the four-story Bay State Building (1872). These improvements helped enable the renting of offices to physicians and other professional people.

Tall buildings were also the indirect result of a gradual shift in the city's economic geography, and the emergence of specialized districts. Before the Fire the Loop had contained a fairly undifferentiated mixture of land uses, with wholesalers, retail stores, office buildings, and theaters scattered about indiscriminately. The upper floors, inconvenient for business use because of the absence of elevators, had a sizeable residential population. After the Fire, residential use ceased, and functional specialization became more apparent. State Street emerged as the leading retail street, while LaSalle Street, with the new Board of Trade Building, became the financial center. Nearby South Dearborn Street saw the growth of offices whose functions related to LaSalle Street and to the federal courthouse. Meanwhile, wholesalers moved to the riverfront at the north and west edges of downtown, and Randolph and Monroe streets became entertainment districts. Finally, with the construction of the Auditorium Theater, the Studebaker (now Fine Arts) Building, the Academy of Fine Arts (later the Art Institute), and Orchestra Hall, South Michigan Avenue became Chicago's cultural mecca.

Carson Pirie Scott & Co. (originally
Schlesinger and Mayer), Louis Sullivan, 1899, 1903-4. Sullivan shaped
the Chicago window into long horizontal bands and decorated the ground
level with frilly ornamental iron work.
Often called the highest achievement of
American commercial architecture, this
was his last major building.
Daniel Burnham designed one addition (1906) to conform to the original
plan, and Holabird and Root recently
added another (1960-1).
Staples & Charles

Chicago Stock Exchange, entrance
arch detail, Adler and Sullivan.
Richard Nickel Committee

Elevator grill detail, Chicago Stock
Exchange. This is typical of the way
Adler and Sullivan treated the utilitar-
ian features of office buildings.
Richard Nickel Committee

The Technological Triumph

Chicago architects responded to new social and economic patterns by creating a new style of architecture. It was different in many respects, both structural and aesthetic. But the technological revolution was also a response to the shortcomings inherent in Chicago's site. While ideally located as a trade center, the city was built on an impossible swamp. Many commentators expressed fear that large buildings would sink into the ground. Most traditional building methods employed in eastern cities were not feasible in the moist, sandy clay of Chicago. Thus, if architects were to meet the social and economic demands of a fast-growing city, they would have to create a new technology of building.

The first major innovation dates from 1873, when a local architect named Frederick Baumann published *The Art of Preparing Foundations for All Kinds of Buildings, With Particular Illustration of the Method of Isolated Piers as Followed in Chicago.* Baumann suggested that each pier, or major vertical member, should have its own foundation with the weight spread out on a pad that resembled a pyramid. Burnham and Root employed this method in their Montauk Block (1881-2), but found that the foundation literally filled the basement. Isolated piers could not support a building of more than eight or ten stories, so, when they designed their Rookery (1886), they substituted a system of criss-cross rails embedded in concrete. This spread the weight of the masonry walls over a wider area and freed the basement for heating equipment and elevator machinery.

Meanwhile, the team of Adler and Sullivan faced their own foundation problems. The site of their Auditorium was only a few hundred yards from the lakeshore. The basement under the stage was actually six feet below the lake level, and thus subject to flooding. Adler and Sullivan solved that problem by employing a new automatic pumping device developed by a New Yorker, an early version of the sump pump. But the foundation itself required applying their own ingenuity. Concrete, heavy wooden timbers, and steel beams were woven together to create an enormous platform on which the huge building literally floated, suspended by the soil and the pressure of water in the ground. The architects created an especially heavy foundation under the Auditorium's tower, so that it would settle at the

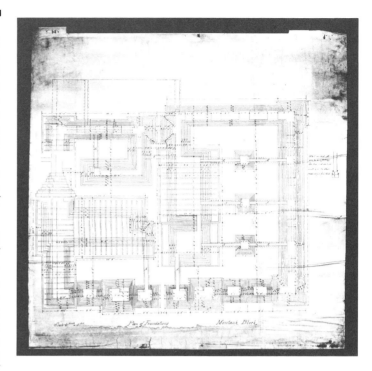

Pyramid foundation, Montauk Block, Burnham and Root blueprints, 1881-2. The metal frame of the skyscraper concentrated all the weight just beneath the columns. To distribute the weight over a larger area, Chicago architects devised several novel types of foundation. Here, columns rest atop pyramids made of alternating layers of concrete and stone.

Marshall Field Building sub-structure, D. H. Burnham & Co., c1909. Caisson construction reached through several layers of earth to the solid rock below. Placement of 252 concrete caissons beneath Marshall Field's allowed the store space to be extended several levels into the ground. Water, usually present in the soft Chicago soil, seeped into the ejector pit in which pumps were located.

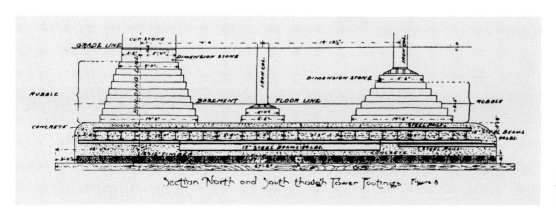

Auditorium Building foundation, Inland Architect and Builder, March 1888. Adler and Sullivan designed footings so that the tower would settle at the same rate as the rest of the building.

Panorama of Chicago as seen from the Monadnock, by George W. Melville, 1897.

The Monadnock, Dearborn between Jackson and Van Buren. Burnham and Root designed the right half of this building in 1889. It is the tallest structure ever built without a steel frame. The other half, designed by Holabird and Roche in 1893, is similar in appearance, but has a steel frame and was capped by a decorative cornice.

New York Life Insurance Building addition, Jenney and Mundie, summer 1898. The steel frame enabled rapid responses to unexpected real estate opportunities. In this case, one section of the building, twelve stories tall, had been completed in 1896; when adjacent land came on the market two years later, Jenney and Mundie built an addition blending the old and new facades.
Jensen and Halstead, Limited; Architects, Engineers, Consultants

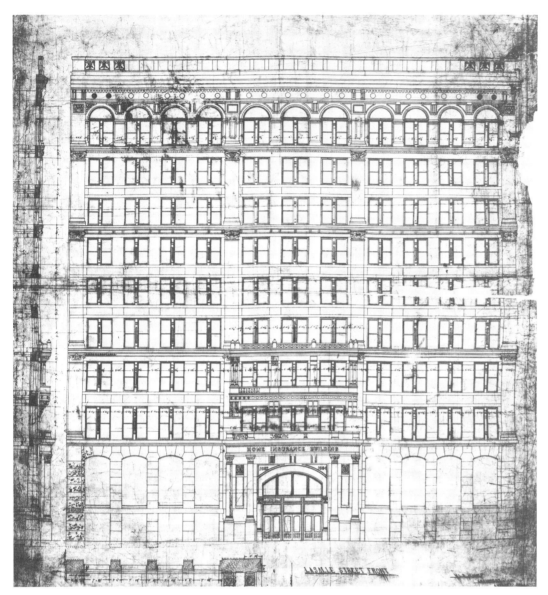

The Home Insurance Building, William LeBaron Jenney, blueprint for facade, 1885. The world's first steel-framed building stood on the northeast corner of LaSalle and Adams. As originally constructed it had nine floors and a partially-exposed basement; in 1891 two additional stories were added. Although the facade was not particularly noteworthy, the greenstone and polished grey stone columns used on the first floor made it colorful as well as historic. It was demolished in 1931 to make way for the Field Building, an Art Deco skyscraper.

Jensen and Halstead, Limited; Architects, Engineers, Consultants

Many critics disputed Jenney's claim that he invented steel skeleton construction, insisting that similar plans had been on drawing boards in other parts of the country. In 1896 a ship-building firm sought evidence to end the dispute, and Jenney could take satisfaction in its conclusions. A special committee, appointed to supervise the razing of the Home Insurance Building in 1931, confirmed Jenney's claim.

The American Institute of Architects

same rate as the rest of the building. Although the structure did sink into the soil as much as eighteen inches in some places, no damage to its masonry walls resulted. Nor was there much damage to the plumbing system, because Adler and Sullivan had introduced flexible pipe at points of potential stress.

Taller buildings, however, required more substantial foundations. Soil tests determined that there were layers of rock some fifty feet below the surface. Builders had used wooden piles in the construction of grain elevators along the river, but it was not until the 1890s that they began to consider using pilings under buildings some distance from the water's edge. Adler and Sullivan supported their Schiller (later Garrick) Theater (1892) on 770 wooden piles, but with their Stock Exchange Building of two years later they encountered a special problem. They determined that the vibration caused by driving piles would upset the delicate press machinery in the *Chicago Herald* building next door. To avoid this, contractors dug shafts deep into the soil and filled them with concrete. Here was one of the first instances of caisson construction in America. The resulting publicity helped popularize the use of caissons throughout the country, and today many tall buildings have caisson foundations.

The perfection of the elevator, effective fireproofing, and solid foundations were all necessary requisites for tall buildings; there remained one last technological breakthrough. That was the development of the steel-skeleton frame. Tall buildings with masonry load-bearing walls were feasible: Burnham and Root's Monadnock (1891) was sixteen stories, the highest such building ever constructed. While its uncluttered design was truly beautiful, the walls had to be all of *six feet* thick at the base. While the sweeping flare of the lower walls integrated this structural peculiarity nicely into the design, thick walls diminished both the interior space and the amount of sunlight that could come through the tunnel-like windows.

It is difficult to identify who first conceived of the skyscraper. European architects had suggested it as early as the mid-nineteenth century, and L. S. Buffington of Minneapolis tried unsuccessfully to patent it in the 1880s. But it was William LeBaron Jenney who first accomplished it. In 1885 the Home Insurance Company asked him to design a new office tower, and he persuaded them to allow him to erect an iron skeleton to bear the total weight of the building. Midway through construction he was notified by the Carnegie-Phipps Steel Company that it could provide steel beams instead of iron. He seized the opportunity eagerly. Not only did the Home Insurance Building become the first true skyscraper with an interior frame that carried the structure, it was also the first tall building to employ structural steel.

The steel-skeleton building was greeted with skepticism. Jenney himself was concerned that the frame would expand and contract so much with changes in the temperature that he devised an ingenious way to hang each floor independently on the frame, thus creating expansion spaces between the stories. This, he correctly deduced, would prevent cracked plaster and burst pipes. The transition to steel framing did not take place immediately. Costs remained high, while the size of buildings such as the Auditorium posed engineering problems that were complicated enough already without introducing a new structural technology. Some buildings had partial steel frames. The Rookery, for instance, used curtain walls facing the interior light-court. Until the mid-1890s many architects regarded the new building technique as a curiosity, or at best an occasional alternative to the traditional load-bearing wall.

Nevertheless, the steel frame had many advantages. It was fireproof. Its thin exterior walls increased interior space and rental revenues sufficiently to offset the additional cost, about a third more than masonry walls. Steel was much lighter than masonry, thus easing the burden on the foundations. It was also comparatively easy to add new floors or expand the frontage. Some concerns, such as the Chicago Telephone Company, foresaw that sooner or later they would have to expand their facilities in certain parts of the city. A steel frame allowed enlarging buildings as needed.

A new building could be erected with amazing speed. Developers began advertising office space before the foundations were in the ground, and hung "For Rent" signs on unfinished frames. It required only fourteen days to complete thirteen and one-half stories of framework for the Fisher Building (D. H. Burnham & Co., 1896). Because the frame rather than the walls bore the weight, the floors could literally be finished from the top down, and the heavy stonework often used on the ground floor could be set in place after the upper walls were complete. Perhaps the most unusual building procedure involved the construction of the Reliance Building (D. H. Burnham & Co., 1895). The site had initially been occupied by the First National Bank, a five-story masonry-wall building. The bank soon moved out of the first two floors, but the leases on the floors above ran until 1894. The architects responded with great ingenuity, supporting the top floors with jacks while they replaced the bottom with a new foundation and steel frame. Carson Pirie Scott & Co. then occupied the ground level. When the tenants finally vacated the upper floors in the spring of 1894 the builders set to work finishing the rest of the modern skyscraper. They tore away the original masonry walls and by July 16 had completed the frame to the seventh floor. It reached the fourteenth floor by July 28 and was topped out at sixteen stories on August 1. By November 8 the curtain walls were in place, and the initial tenants moved in at the first of the year.

The Reliance Building was also notable for its extensive use of glass and terra cotta. While the latter had been manufactured in Chicago since 1866, it had been used primarily for minor ornamentation and to fireproof iron beams. With the steel skeleton, however, it emerged as a major building material. The Rand McNally Building (Burnham and Root, 1890) was the first to use it exclusively on the streetside facades, while the Reliance employed an enameled variety on all sides. Architects were excited about its possibilities. It could be cast in any color or shape, and its hard surface washed clean in the rain. In a city known around the world for its smoky atmosphere, this was an important consideration. Many earlier structures had turned a uniform black in the bituminous clouds of the nation's railway capital.

The Result: Practical Aesthetics

The achievements of the Chicago architects went far beyond mere technological innovation. They involved a new relationship between the structure as an engineering feat, the facade as a work of art, and a combination of both as a workplace or home. Foreign travelers and professional architecture critics alike noted that Chicago's drawing boards tended to produce a style that upgraded and edified the most mundane of activities. It was this sensitivity to everyday life—as well as the poetic pronouncements by Louis Sullivan—that made Chicago's architecture seem peculiarly democratic.

The balloon frame had been the earliest manifestation of Chicago's bent for the practical, but that approach found a most articulate advocate in William LeBaron Jenney. In one of his frequent columns advising beginners, he set down certain principles that he felt should govern the design of all buildings. "No arrangement for the health, convenience and pleasure of the occupants should be sacrificed to any ideas of symmetry or external effect," he wrote. Ornament should not be added unless it had a definite purpose or clearly reflected the activity inside. The architect must choose materials whose characteristics best fit the task at hand, and they should never be camouflaged to look like something they were not. In pungent prose Jenney belittled "stone" columns made from wood. Finally, all the various elements of a building—inside and out, back and front, cornice and foundation—must "fit together."

At the turn of the century, Montgomery Schuyler, an eastern architecture critic, wrote that "The 'business block,' strictly utilitarian in purpose and monumental only in magnitude and solidity of construction, is the true and typical embodiment in the building of the Chicago idea." This was true. The most important structures in Chicago were nearly all office buildings. Investors had considered these chancy, for the wrong location or plan could mean bankruptcy. So, the architect had been asked to come up with a structure that would attract tenants and keep them happy, while simultaneously pleasing the landlord with minimal upkeep. If those who had to work in the offices were uncomfortable, their output of work might decline.

The Chicago architects met the challenge. One of their most important innovations was the "Chicago window." This was a broad expanse of glass that featured a large fixed center-pane with movable sashes on either side. It was a direct outgrowth of the skeleton frame, merely the substitution of a piece of glass for a portion of the curtain wall. In buildings where the walls had to carry the weight, windows had been crowded and comparatively small. The steel frame, on the other hand, allowed the designer to use an almost unlimited amount of glass. The Chicago window was usually flush rather than protruding. This was partly because bay windows had become the center of a bitter controversy that began in the 1880s. Reformers complained that the bays often projected over the property-line onto sidewalks and alleys, adding floor space that was literally stolen from the public. Owners of traditional masonry-wall buildings countered that bay windows were the only way they could capture breezes and garner sufficient light for their employees to work efficiently. The new-style window was a boon in that, even though flush, it admitted sufficient light and air to compensate for the poor quality of electric lighting and the effect of the hot sun beaming down on concrete sidewalks and stone buildings. The Chicago window made work more pleasant.

The best architects also designed the hallways and other public areas of buildings to be attractive and comfortable for tenants. Corridors were no longer dark, for sunlight streamed through skylights and glass floors. Stairways were no longer steep, dimly lit, and inconveniently located. Interior offices, once the commercial equivalent of windowless tenements, looked out on light courts often lined with white terra cotta to reflect sunlight through the windows. As for elevators, these became part of the social as well as physical planning of the building. Proper location could greatly increase efficiency. The manager of Holabird and Roche's Marquette could boast that no visitor had to walk more than fifty feet in any upstairs hallway. Architects realized that their buildings would be used by so many people that the interior spaces were, in effect, public places. As such, they ought to be efficient and comfortable as well.

The Chicago office tower minimized disparities between utility and beauty. Exterior trim was frequently kept to a minimum. Burnham and Root's Monadnock was virtually devoid of ornamentation, its stark pressed-brick walls punctuated by square window openings and graceful bays. Although subject to criticism when new, the exterior met the desire of the owners for a simple facade that left no place for pigeons to roost. Some local architects were heavily influenced by the Romanesque style popularized by Boston's Henry Hobson Richardson, yet the facades were kept simple even on such buildings as the Rookery and the Auditorium. Romanesque granite buildings could effectively convey a sense of massiveness, when that was what the owners wanted. Everything had some purpose.

Local architects sometimes applied their talents to structures that eastern architects thought beneath their dignity. For instance, in 1889 Burnham and Root planned an armory for the First Regiment of the Illinois National Guard. Its Romanesque style was so beautiful that it enhanced rather than degraded the upper class neighborhood nearby. Other architects designed warehouses. Around the turn of the century changes in urban lifestyles—frequent moves or travel abroad—prompted the growth of the furniture-storage business. Moving company operators did not want to erect their multi-floor warehouses in dangerous neighborhoods; that would be bad for business. Nor did they wish to offend residents of better neighborhoods by building an eyesore. Firms like Holabird and Roche responded by designing structures that were both attractive and highly functional.

The Rookery, lobby, before 1905. Burnham and Root's light-court served as an interior "street" that linked offices and shops. This was a superb example of the attention that Chicago architects lavished on the most utilitarian parts of their buildings.

The Rookery, lobby, after 1905. The result of Frank Lloyd Wright's remodeling was a dramatic, though eclectic, blend of the original iron frills and the bold geometric shapes of the Prairie School.

The Studebaker Building, S. S. Beman, 1895. This steel-frame structure clearly shows the advantages of the Chicago window—sunlight pours in on offices, shops, and showrooms. The location was 629 S. Wabash.

The Prairie School

The skyscraper represented a logical solution to a major urban problem: the demand for space. The forces of economic growth, along with improved national and local transportation, had created the impetus for downtown centralization. The Chicago architects met this challenge by taking full advantage of the latest technologies such as elevators, fireproofing, and the steel-skeleton frame. At the same time, however, there was an opposite force at work, a centrifugal, decentralizing force. This stemmed from tradition as well as from technology, for the goal of a private lot and a single-family home had long captivated Chicagoans. European immigrants and rural migrants sought independence and privacy in home ownership, even if the home were only a small balloon-frame cottage surrounded by a picket fence. Those who wanted more room might choose a home in one of the dozens of look-alike subdivisions in the vast outlying regions the city annexed in 1889. Still others might opt for even more space in the suburbs. Local trains served a number of suburban areas, while the elevated and streetcar systems reached as far as Evanston and Oak Park. Thus, the same transportation systems that helped pull commercial growth in to the Loop also pushed residential growth out to the hinterlands.

The expansion of "Greater Chicago" created enormous opportunities for young architects. The larger the potential pool of clients, the greater the likelihood that the future householder would demand something different, some departure from the usual. It was therefore no accident that Chicagoans would be responsible for an ingenious new style of domestic architecture called the "Prairie School."

This type of building had a definite parallel to the best of the commercial buildings. There was no physical resemblance—quite the opposite—but they shared important principles. Neither was especially influenced by prevailing styles. Both emphasized the dominant axis of the building: in the skyscraper it was vertical, in the Prairie house it was horizontal. The long, low lot-hugging designs were a celebration of space that seemed to suggest the flatness of the prairie even if the house had a second story and was located in a built-up neighborhood. In places like Oak Park or River Forest, the horizontal dimension stressed the spaciousness of the suburban lot, virtually integrating the long linear windows into the landscaping. In a city the fenestration could be smaller and moved nearer the roofline, while the house sat half a story out of the ground. This kept occupants out of view of passersby, yet, when necessary, a long wall not only emphasized the horizontal dimension, but also rendered private the space between the house and the street.

Prairie houses, like Chicago skyscrapers, eschewed common practice in ornamentation. Although some of the early works of Frank Lloyd Wright embodied elaborate decoration, the more mature structures bore thin decorative lines and bands of color that reiterated the horizontal dimensions, as did the flat, elongated brick that was often used. Perhaps the most elaborately ornamented features were the windows; small panes of leaded or stained glass created a variegated pattern in the sunlight, a "living" ornament whose cheerfulness made it practical. Even the furnishings, from chairs and tables down to rugs and tapestries, followed the same themes of simplicity and geometric decoration.

The commercial and Prairie-School buildings both exhibited a concern for shared interior spaces. In the former, such elements as elevator grills and lobbies were carefully decorated to create a pleasing impression. Chicago's most creative domestic architecture, the Prairie School, achieved the same goal. Partitions, which had usually divided middle- or upper-class homes into small rooms with specialized functions, disappeared. Wright's houses had few interior doors. L-shaped spaces or rooms separated by different levels, not interior walls, delineated the areas of the house, and the result was common living spaces that seemed larger than they actually were. The fireplace was the center of attention, much as the central light-court functioned as a focal point in the Rookery Building. Homes and offices, the architects reasoned, were for use by people in groups, whether families or corporations.

The most prominent member of the Prairie School was Frank Lloyd Wright. Born in Richland Center, Wisconsin, in 1867, Wright spent a few years at the University of Wisconsin, then worked for a Madison builder and learned the rudiments of construction. He might have remained in his native state, but the opportunities in Chicago were just too attractive. In 1887 he sneaked away to the big city, where his uncle, a prominent Unitarian minister named Jenkin Lloyd Jones, helped him secure his first job. Rev. Jones had just completed a new church building, and he introduced young Frank to the architect, J. L. Silsbee. Thus began the career of a Chicagoan who fundamentally reshaped American ideas of domestic architecture.

Silsbee was a newcomer to Chicago himself, having arrived in 1883. Although he had attended Harvard University and graduated from the Boston Technological School, he had managed to remain impervious to stuffy eastern influences. Not even two years in Europe could convince him that architecture ought merely to adapt classical ideas. He designed several downtown buildings and the conservatory in Lincoln Park. Silsbee's office, in which Wright was employed as a draftsman, also designed numerous houses. Characterized by a rather casual style, these were often made of wood and had little of the classical ornamentation usually found in the homes of the middle class and the wealthy.

Wright remained with Silsbee only for a short time, then moved on to the office of Adler and Sullivan. After convincing Sullivan that he was skilled in designing intricate ornament, Wright was given a major responsibility for executing the interior of the Auditorium. He also did much of the firm's private residential work, a service it usually performed only for clients who had contracted for commercial buildings. Wright began to design houses on his own in his spare time, often using a pseudonym on the building permit so his employers would not know. This outside work eventually precipitated a break between the headstrong Wright and his employers in 1893. Only in his mid-twenties,

Frank Lloyd Wright (1867-1959), 1910. While Prairie-School houses, with their open interior spaces, were meant to bring families together, Wright himself was beset by domestic woes. In 1909 he abandoned his family to elope with the wife of a client.
Library of Congress

Walter Burley Griffin (1876-1937), c1910. Forsaking a promising career in America to migrate to Australia, Griffin became the foremost urban planner down under.
Library of Congress

Marion Mahony (1871-1962), c1910. A pioneer woman architect, Miss Mahony spent several years as Wright's assistant, designing furnishings and ornamental detail. Later, she married Walter Burley Griffin and moved to Australia.
The Art Institute of Chicago

Frank Lloyd Wright's reply to Harriet Monroe, 1907. Miss Monroe was a famous poet and architecture critic. In reply to her negative assessment of the Prairie School, Wright explained his philosophy of architecture.
University of Chicago Library

My dear Miss Monroe - and at the beginning let me say that to me "My dear Miss Monroe" for the moment is a TYPE and this rude but not ill-natured resentment is inscribed to the "type".

Architects have learned, long since, that the professional critic's commodity, ~~remarks otherwise of the "type"~~, when related to architecture at least either has to be "steered" from the inside or intelligently so prejudiced or deliberately manufactured so or it is quite apt to be of the "I-may-not-know-what -Art-is-but-I-know-what-I-like"variety, -bromidic and utterly useless.

Personally, I am ~~hungry for the honest~~ genuine criticism that searches the soul of the thing and sifts the form. Praise isn't needed especially. There is enough of that, such as it is, but we all need intelligent painstaking inquiry leading into the nature of the proposition to be characterized before with airy grace the subject is lightly touched up with House Beautiful English for the mob.

The struggle behind vital work of any kind is naturally difficult enough but it is precisely the Harriet Monroe in this sense in society that makes the struggle unnecessarily grim and temporarily thankless. Her commodity has no power to harm the inherent virtue of good work but it does serve to hamper the man and to confuse and hinder a practical issue that deserves all the help and strength that, grudgingly enough in any case, may come to it from a public in these matters diffident or indifferent. Fashion and Sham rule the day. When an independent effort to be true to a worthy ideal has the courage to lift its head it deserves something more than the capricious slap-stick of "the type", even if the slap appeals to the gallery, in other words to"our very best people".

Personally, again, I have met little more than the superficial snap-judgment insult of the "artistically informed". I am ● used to it, glad to owe it nothing in any final outcome. But, meanwhile the Cause suffers delay! That is the price the public pays for "the type" and it is the serious side of the matter.

I cannot believe you altogether insensible to fundamental qualities but what a flimsy characterization of the Ideal behind the work to which I have given my life, you have on record!— "The old orders all worked out",(starting to do a new stunt to bring down "the gallery"[o]I suppose). "Progress before precedent" perhaps? Believe me, dear Miss Monroe, it is all not one half so silly. Need I say that it is the very spirit that gave life to the old forms that this work courts? That it is the true inspiration that made of the time honored precedent in its own time a living thing that it craves? Venerable traditional forms are held by this work still too sacred to be paraded as a meretricious mask for the indecencies and iniquities of the market place!

Long ago, yes ages ago, from Nature came inspiration to the Architect and back to Nature with the principles deduced from these dead forms or formulae we will go again for inspiration. I know we shall find it for the Gods still live.

In the average of this work you saw merely a curious experiment with certain boxes, withal a "square" and a "squat" that offended your dainty love of fleshly curves and sensuous graces, a love that after all is in the last analysis rather cheap and not merely because it is common. But, is it impossible that the exquisite delicacy of the living nature that we all love may bloom more vividly where the "Architectural", which is primarily the background for this life, itself becomes a more quiet and restrained convention than has yet been practiced? Why usurp what by nature belongs to the other members of the family - Sculpture, Painting, Literature and Music? For one I decline to be obsessed as are most artists and almost all

arts by the literal or by literature. My conception of the architectural art is somewhat higher than that.

Need I remind you that the pyramid is just a pyramid - that's all?--the obelisk a huge billet of stone up-ended?- a Greek temple a rectangle with simpler excrescences -the Parthenon a box with a lid.

Perhaps it might be well to mention in this connection that one of the "Muse", formless, nameless structures of your story was a small scale plaster model for a cast concrete column for Unity Church. In the edifice the column itself stands two feet six inches by thirteen feet high. This is one of the buildings wherein imagination halts!

Concerning our perennial friend the "squat"— we happen to be living on the prairie. The prairie has a beauty of its own. A building on the prairie should recognize the features of its quiet level and accentuate them harmoniously. It should be quiet, broad, inclusive, a welcome associate of trees and flowers not a nervous, fussy interloper, and should be "married" to the ground. Hence, broad, sheltering eaves over determined masses, gentle roofs, spreading base and outreaching walls.

What is publicly set forth in this little collection could hardly be American Architecture. No- not yet- but I say that if a given type, (like the type or like it not,)be handled with the organic consistency and such individuality as is manifest in this aggregation here, then, an American Architecture is a possibility and will be a definite probability when conscientious efforts of this nature wherever they may be found, receive the encouragement on their native heath that they already have received in conservative old England or in France where these square, squat experiments with boxes have been accorded the rare virtue of originality without eccentricity. Buildings,like people,must be honest, must be sincere and withal as lovable and gracious as may be. But, unfortunately for the man who dares, we, as a people, artistically, have a deadly and painfully provincial horror of doing the "incorrect thing" which the self-conscious dangerous small-knowledge of the provincial art critic only serves to intensify, making it just so much more difficult for us as a people to come into our own.

Some day, as Mc Andrews prayed in his "Hymn", even the"first class passenger" will understand that the classic is no matter of the dead letter of former glory and will know that the old spirit which was so vital then is vital now and living in forms the newspapers pronounce eccentric. They may even proclaim that after all these forms are truly classic in the best sense of that much abused term.

But why be serious? Are not the limitations already obvious and fixed? The progress made already marked in the public prints by such shoddy fustian from the architectural rag-bag,-as"Ottenheimer's clock", such chenille as "Wilson's graceful residences"?

sincerely,
[signature]

Robie House, Frank Lloyd Wright, 1909. Often considered the classic statement of the Prairie School, this structure has a horizontal emphasis despite being three stories tall. The overhang of the roof, the planter, and the brick-work add to an illusion of flatness. The windows, though generous in size, did not permit passersby to see inside.
Richard Nickel Committee

Early rendering of Unity Temple, Frank Lloyd Wright, c1904. Created of cast concrete, the interior plan shaped the exterior contours. The total cost of the auditorium and adjacent parish house was less than $35,000.
The Art Institute of Chicago

Francisco Terrace, Frank Lloyd Wright, 1895. Although Wright is most famous for his single-family homes, he also designed a few apartment buildings. The one shown here was intended for low-income families. To enhance a sense of community, the front doors of all units faced a common courtyard.
Oak Park Public Library

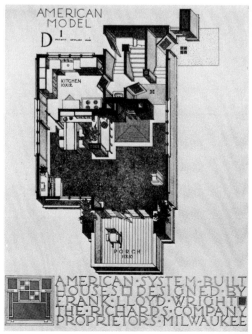

Midway Gardens promotional booklet, 1914. One of the most interesting of Wright's non-residential designs was this outdoor restaurant and cabaret, advertised as "the first permanent home in this country for outdoor summer music." Unfortunately, the place fell upon hard times shortly after opening and became a common beer garden.

Unity Temple, auditorium, Frank Lloyd Wright, 1907. The design is at once simple and ornate. Geometric shapes replace traditional church decoration, and the room is scaled-down to "human size."
Milwaukee Journal

Broadside issued by a builder of small family homes designed by Frank Lloyd Wright.
Oak Park Public Library

Wright was on his own. He moved his practice to Oak Park where he enlarged his home and studio.

Although he was the most articulate, the most flamboyant, and consequently the most famous, Wright was by no means the only Prairie-School architect. He met two others while working for Silsbee. George Grant Elmslie was a native of Scotland. Trained at M.I.T., he left Silsbee's office in 1889, after Wright had persuaded Adler and Sullivan that the young draftsman had talent. Elmslie was responsible for transforming many of Sullivan's intricate designs into ornamental ironwork and terra cotta. Another graduate of Silsbee's office was George W. Maher. Born in West Virginia, Maher had come with his impoverished family to Indiana and, later, to Chicago. He received only six years of formal schooling. At the age of thirteen he became an apprentice architect, first in the office of Bauer and Hill, who designed schoolhouses and other public buildings, and then with Silsbee. In 1888 he established his own practice.

Several Prairie-School architects (including Wright briefly) established an informal firm in the loft floor of Steinway Hall, a downtown office building, where they jointly planned buildings and traded ideas. Among them was Walter Burley Griffin. A native of Oak Park and a graduate of the University of Illinois, Griffin had started his career designing barns and coachhouses in the suburbs. In 1899 he moved his fledgling practice to Steinway Hall, but within two years he had departed for Oak Park to assist Wright. Another of the loft group also made the move to Oak Park. This was Marion Mahony, a native of Chicago who had been one of the first women to graduate from M.I.T. Initially, she handled many of Wright's drafting and design details, but, as his practice grew, she began to assume larger responsibilities; much of the interior detail, furniture, and tapestries credited to Wright were actually hers. Like everyone who worked with Wright, Mahony and Griffin both contributed and learned, but, unfortunately, the relationship lasted for only a few years. In 1905, after a quarrel over the management of the office, Griffin left. Wright himself left Oak Park in 1909, fleeing to Europe with

Madlener House, Richard Schmidt, 1902. Although central heating was in wide use by this time, the fireplace remained the focal-point of many houses constructed before World War I. Richard Schmidt, a Prairie-School designer, created this masterpiece of simplicity.
Richard Nickel Committee

Swift Hall, Northwestern University, George W. Maher, 1908-9. This is an outstanding example of the Prairie School applied to institutional architecture. Maher saw the simple, angular design as a compatible antidote to the standard "university Gothic" style. The functional Chicago windows let bright sunlight in. Formerly the location of the engineering department, the building is now part of the university's biological sciences complex.
Northwestern University Archives

Carl Schurz High School, Dwight Perkins, 1909-10. The horizontal emphasis of the Prairie School worked well in structures, such as schools, where elevators were not practical. This graceful building still stands at the corner of Milwaukee and Addison.

the wife of a client. Mahony ended up going back to Steinway Hall, and in 1911 she and Griffin married.

The Prairie-School architects shared a conceptual outlook and a philosophy built on the idea that structures ought to conform to the needs of people. The basic simplicity of the design also made it extremely adaptable to various uses. Thus, in 1906, Wright could design a Unitarian Church in Oak Park out of concrete, an inexpensive medium. In 1906 he also submitted a design for a seven-room "fireproof house for $5,000," the plans for which were published by the *Ladies Home Journal.* This reinforced concrete house was, in Wright's words, "within the reach of the average home-maker." By making all four sides alike, he reduced the basic construction cost to a minimum. The use of metal lath or hollow tiles for the walls made it fireproof, and thus assuaged one of the great fears of homeowners.

Wright's friends and followers applied Prairie-School principles to a wide variety of buildings. Two associates, Richard Schmidt of Steinway Hall and Hugh M. Garden, created the beautiful Madlener House on Burton Place, but their reputation derived principally from their commercial work. In 1902 they designed a large hop warehouse and a powerhouse for the Schoenhofen Brewing Company, and two years later the wholesale liquor firm of Chapin and Gore asked them to plan a combined warehouse, office building, and retail outlet on Adams Street. Schmidt and Garden were also responsible for the huge Montgomery Ward warehouse on the North Branch of the Chicago River. Its graceful lines and elongated window configuration made it one of the most pleasing utilitarian structures in Chicago.

Finally, another member of the group distinguished himself through the design of schoolhouses. Dwight Perkins had been born in Memphis, in 1867, but his parents brought him to Chicago at an early age. Trained at M.I.T., where he taught for a short time, Perkins returned to Chicago in 1888 and joined Burnham and Root. During the Columbian Exposition he managed the routine business of the office, but, when the effects of the Panic of 1893 finally hit post-Exposition Chicago, Perkins found himself without a job. He practiced on his own for several years, then in 1905 the Chicago School Board hired him as its official architect. In that position he designed several schools, most notably Grover Cleveland and Trumball. These bore the mark of the Prairie School—plain, unadorned windows, and linear striping in the brickwork that emphasized the perimeters of the exterior walls. His masterpiece was the Carl Schurz High School. Long and visually horizontal, it displayed the characteristic overhanging roof and sharp geometrical juxtaposition of windows and trim.

A truly American Architecture

In their commercial work and in the Prairie School, Chicagoans produced what has been recognized as America's most creative architecture. For much of the late nineteenth century architectural writers continually wondered when Americans were going to cease copying classical and European forms and create a "truly American architecture." The commercial architects came close. The new technology was later copied around the world. The exterior design was a mixture of old and new, with H. H. Richardson's influence dominant in every major office at one time or another. In some buildings, such as Sullivan's Schlesinger and Mayer store and Burnham and Root's Monadnock Building and Reliance Building, the facades were strikingly innovative and uniquely Chicagoan.

The Prairie School was unique in almost every aspect. As the new houses took shape, crowds would stand in the street and crack jokes about their strange appearance; the children and grandchildren of those gawkers would buy "ranch-style" houses which sat low to the ground, with interiors characterized by flowing spaces and "split levels." Most important of all, however, both Prairie and commercial architects designed buildings for people in groups, whether families or crowds. Comfort and convenience were the primary determinants of design and style, while the problems of the site challenged the technological imagination. This was an architecture that was truly democratic—and truly American.

Chicago Skyscrapers. While Daniel Burnham's Reliance Building of 1890-5 is dwarfed by modern skyscrapers, the extensive use of glass allows this important landmark to carry its years with grace. All contemporary skyscrapers are descendants of the skeleton-frame building invented more than ninety years ago by William LeBaron Jenney.
Richard Nickel Committee

Planning
on the Prairie

The skyscraper represented a triumph of humanity as well as technology. Human ingenuity had devised a way to adapt the city to the needs of people as well as the marketplace. The triumph of the skyscraper in making efficient use of private and semi-public spaces was matched by another triumph in the conception and design of the city's public places. Chicago's tradition of innovative city planning derived both from efforts to control future growth and to make the best use of the city as it already existed.

Plan of Chicago, bird's-eye view of the lakefront, 1909. This Jules Guerin rendering indicates Burnham's concept of the harbor as Chicago's "front door." The chain of planned recreational islands can be seen stretching southward from the harbor.

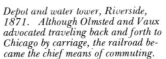

Riverside Improvement Company letterhead, 1871. The original concept of this town as a combination resort and residential suburb is clearly evident. Architect William LeBaron Jenney's importance to the project is also evident.

Depot and water tower, Riverside, 1871. Although Olmsted and Vaux advocated traveling back and forth to Chicago by carriage, the railroad became the chief means of commuting.

Frederick Law Olmsted (1822-1903). Chicagoans who use Jackson Park and Washington Park enjoy facilities Olmsted designed. His landscaping "improved upon" nature by providing for the efficient use of open space by large urban crowds.
Olmsted Associates, Inc.

Riverside: Birthplace of a Tradition

Riverside began as just one of dozens of Chicago suburbs established in the decade following the Civil War. Typically, these were started by speculators hoping to capitalize on fears of crime and disease in the city, as well as take advantage of an expanding commuter railway system. The Great Fire of 1871 dramatically disclosed the safety of dispersed housing. Most of the speculators laid out streets and lots in a grid pattern and set aside token parcels of land for parks, churches, and other public purposes. But Riverside proved to be unique. When Emery Childs and a group of eastern investors established the Riverside Improvement Company in 1868, it was clear that their suburb would be based on an aim and philosophy that transcended mere money-making.

The Childs group began by hiring one of the nation's leading landscape architects, Frederick Law Olmsted. In his forty-six years Olmsted had accomplished an amazing variety of things. Apprenticed as a civil engineer, he had become interested in experimental self-sufficient farming and had involved himself in the early campaigns to save Yosemite Valley and Niagara Falls from despoilation. He was one of the first to advocate a system of national parks. He had walked across Britain and had made a similar trek through the antebellum South. His greatest challenge had begun in 1857, when he became superintendent of Central Park in

New York City, then undeveloped. Taking on additional duties the following year as architect-in-charge, he had created a beautiful urban setting that attracted world-wide attention.

Childs gave Olmsted and his partner, Calvert Vaux, virtually complete freedom to design Riverside. Although the Riverside Improvement Company went bankrupt in the Panic of 1873, its planners managed to achieve a substantial portion of their goal. They created a small city on principles that were in many respects precisely the antithesis of Chicago. Chicago was laid out on a traditional grid pattern, efficient in commercial districts but inherently boring and monotonous in residential neighborhoods. In Riverside, Olmsted and Vaux substituted broad, gently-curving streets forming a pattern that resembled the veins in a leaf. Chicago lacked sufficient park space, even though public health experts were convinced that trees acted as a city's "lungs" and purified the air. Riverside, on the other hand, set aside 700 of its 1,600 acres as tree-lined roadways and parks. Much of Chicago's riverbank and lakefront was occupied by industry or by private estates, but all of Riverside's shoreline was reserved as parkland. Finally, much of Chicago lacked sidewalks, gas mains for streetlamps, and proper drainage. In Riverside, all of these public amenities were installed before residents moved in.

The town's architecture matched its planning. William LeBaron Jenney, who later became a world-renowned architect, supervised the landscaping and construction, and

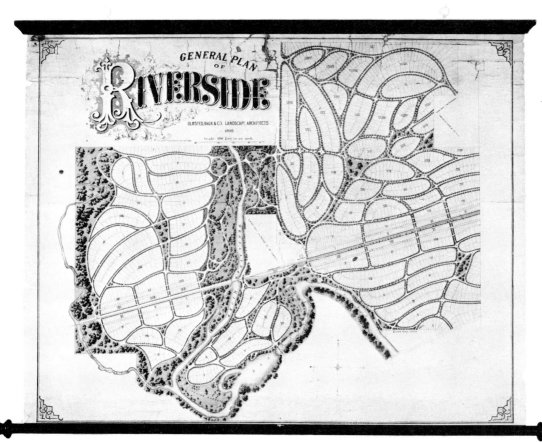

exercised a right of veto over all building plans. He designed the distinctive water tower and the comfortable Riverside Hotel. The latter was a wood-frame resort, three stories high, with a long veranda and "music pagoda." He also designed many other buildings, including his own home, for which he chose a modified Swiss style. This, he claimed, matched the overall plan: well organized, yet informal and rustic.

The model town of Riverside brought the amenities of the city to the country. But Olmsted also sought to correct what he perceived as another shortcoming of the metropolis, its lack of public space "for the purpose of easy, friendly, unceremonious greetings, for the enjoyment of a change of scene, of cheerful and exhilarating sights and sounds, and of various good cheer, to which the people of a town, of all classes, harmoniously resort on equal grounds, as to a common property." To meet this need, Olmsted planned a baseball field as well as park space, and attempted to turn every street into a recreation ground. Property owners were prohibited from building too close to the sidewalk and were required to plant trees that would shield all structures from view. A small dam across the Des Plaines River backed up water for recreational boating.

The most unusual feature of the Riverside plan was the proposal for a special nine-mile drive to Chicago. Complaining that the growing popularity of the railroad had been responsible for the deteriorating condition of ordinary roads, Olmsted envisioned a limited-access highway. The central lanes were to be reserved for carriages and horseback riders, while the outside lanes would handle freight and provide access to nearby houses. No industry, retail stores, or large institutional buildings, with what Olmsted called their "dead walls," would be allowed to front on this drive. Instead, it would be completely lined with trees planted in a natural irregular pattern. The greenery would hide "ill-proportioned, vilely-colored, shabby-genteel dwelling-houses, pushing their gables or eaveboards impertinently over the sidewalk as if for the advertising of domestic infelicity and eagerness for public sympathy." The linear forest would also have resting places with fountains, seats, and watering troughs for the horses. The commuting experience, according to Olmsted, should be simultaneously recreational.

This 1860s version of the modern turnpike was, of course, never built. The control Olmsted exercised over public land within Riverside could not be extended beyond its borders. Those who planned the modern expressway system probably did not realize that such a sophisticated scheme existed so long ago. On the other hand, the town itself has received deserved recognition as having one of the earliest comprehensive plans in America. The subject of intense study across the country, the Riverside plan inspired others who rejected the monotony of the grid pattern. The stress on beautifying public places and the skillful integration of parks and residences provided a model for the experimental "greenbelt" towns of the 1930s as well as for many suburbs of today.

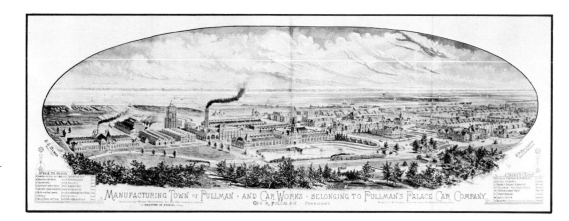

Pullman, bird's-eye view, Western Manufacturer, *1881. This view shows the machine-like order of Pullman's model town. The factory area was clearly set off from the housing, with the most comfortable homes visible from passing Illinois Central trains. Smoking chimneys were viewed as a sign of prosperity.*

Pullman's Planned Town

Riverside was eleven years old when architects and designers began to conceive another planned community several miles to the southeast. This was Pullman. It, too, was a suburb designed as a retreat from the city of Chicago. Its planners shared Olmsted's concern about the town's public areas, and its architect had control over the design of every building. Pullman, as it turned out, was a very different kind of place, whose notoriety derived more from events that happened there than from the community itself. Nonetheless, it marked a significant milestone in the history of American city planning.

George Pullman arrived in Chicago at an opportune time. The city was about to embark on one of the most ambitious civil engineering projects yet undertaken in America. For years its central business district had wallowed in mud, because the site was only a few feet above the level of Lake Michigan. Now, in the mid-1850s, City Engineer Ellis Chesbrough proposed to solve Chicago's drainage problem by constructing a sewer system laid on the existing street surface. Fill-dirt placed on top of the pipes would form the base for a new roadway at a higher elevation. The major problem, however, concerned what to do with buildings whose ground floors would be buried. While some people advocated leveling the city and starting all over, Pullman devised a scheme to raise the buildings with jacks so that their foundations could be built up underneath. This system worked so smoothly that guests at the giant Tremont House were not aware that their building had grown several feet taller in one night.

Pullman immediately invested his profits from this venture in a company that constructed rudimentary sleeping cars for railways. By the late 1870s he had taken control of the firm, changed its name, and transformed its cars into rolling palaces. Pullman drove nearly all his competitors out of business and soon found himself short on factory space. He realized that his car-building operation required one-story buildings situated on a large tract of land. This precluded a downtown site, so he purchased 3,600 acres nearly fifteen miles from the Loop. That distance, however, posed a problem: daily commutation on the Illinois Central would be too expensive for most workers. Pullman decided that the only alternative was to build them a town. Before many years passed, his creation had incidentally become synonymous with Chicago's reputation for labor strife.

The sleeping-car magnate chose two young New Yorkers to design his company town. Solon S. Beman was only twenty-seven years old and virtually unknown as an architect. He had met Pullman through a mutual friend, a landscape architect named Nathan F. Barrett, who had helped redesign an estate Pullman owned in New Jersey. Pullman hired Beman to supervise remodeling the interior of his Prairie Avenue home. He was so pleased with the work of both young men that he commissioned them to plan his town. Beman was assigned the task of creating the structures, while Barrett assisted by working the factory buildings and 1,800 housing units into a rational plan. The team established offices in Pullman's building in the Loop and submitted their proposal late in 1879. Pullman approved and construction began immediately.

Its isolation from Chicago forced the town of Pullman to become a model of efficiency even during construction. The banks of nearby Lake Calumet yielded clay for the bricks that were turned out at a rate exceeding a million a year. The initial factory buildings housed woodworking shops that turned out window sash and doors. Building supplies were purchased in huge quantities for houses put up in assembly line fashion, a hundred at a time. These were solidly built of brick, with wood used only sparingly on the exteriors. The rowhouse pattern, which employed common walls, made construction simpler, conserved space, and minimized heat loss in the cold prairie winds.

Beman and Barrett followed a traditional grid pattern, but they modified it to please Pullman. They were conscious of the health hazards in urban slums, where industry and housing were indiscriminately mixed; industrial waste and fumes are conducive to respiratory ailments and epidemics. Since workers could seldom afford carfare, they had to live near their employment, no matter how unpleasant. This problem was virtually eliminated in Pullman by placing most of the carshops to the north end of town, separating them from the residential section by Florence Boulevard (now 111th Street). In addition, the planners provided front and rear yards for nearly all the houses, and installed paved alleys. A scavenger, whose fee was included in the rent, picked up the garbage. The company, which owned all the housing, planted and maintained trees that gave the streets a park-like atmosphere.

In most cities the worst housing fronted the railroad tracks, noisy and smoky, but in Pullman the opposite was true. Beman situated his most ornate buildings in full view of the Illinois Central; passengers stared in amazement. One of these buildings, the Florence Hotel, was an elaborate Queen Anne structure with one hundred sumptuous guestrooms. Pullman himself used a suite there when he did not feel like traveling to his Prairie Avenue home. The Greenstone Church stood at one corner of Arcade Park, while the impressive Arcade Building embodied an indoor street with a bank, post office, theater, library, and numerous small shops. Beman wanted to centralize shopping in two areas, the Arcade and Market Square. The latter was a two-story structure that stood at the intersection of two residential streets. On the upper level was a large meeting hall, while the lower floor had stalls for the sale of meat and produce.

The town of Pullman was self-sufficient. It had its own utilities. Sewage was pumped to a 160-acre farm and used as fertilizer; the produce grown there was in turn sold in the Market Building. The stores had everything anybody could want. Some called it a utopia. Oscar DeWolf, Chicago's Commissioner of Health, believed that the physical environment, so clean and orderly, improved the personal habits of the working-class residents:

> There are no special requirements to induce change in the habits of people taking up residence in Pullman, but it is a matter of common observation that unsanitary habits . . . soon vanish under the silent but powerful influence of public opinion as shown in the habits of neighbors. Families with dirty, broken furniture soon find it convenient to obtain furniture more in accord with their surroundings. Men who are accustomed to lounge on their front stoops, smoking pipes, and in dirty shirt sleeves, soon dress and act more in accordance with the requirements of society. All of this is accomplished by the silent educational influence of their surroundings.

Critics, however, said Pullman, the town, was oppressive. Jane Addams labeled Pullman, the man, "A Modern King Lear." He owned everything in town and took a substantial portion of each worker's wages for rent. The library charged a three-dollar fee to use its facilities. Pullman claimed this would insure serious patronage, but critics pointed out that only 200 of the town's 8,500 people used the library at all, and that the few working men who did use it were shunted away from the opulent reading rooms to an undecorated back room. Tensions mounted during the depression of 1894 when Pullman lowered wages but not rents. The ensuing strike was one of the most bitter in American history. Four years later the courts forced Pullman's company to sell the town, and, while it remained physically, the social experiment was over.

S. S. Beman blueprint for Pullman row houses, early 1880s. Row houses were easier to plan and less expensive than detached dwellings. Each house cost $1,200.
The Art Institute of Chicago

The Pullman Library, Arcade Building. Pullman was interested in uplifting his workers and donated many of his own books to stock a library for their use.

The Pullman Strike, 1894. One of the most bitter labor controversies in American history brought a call for federal troops, some of whom are shown here in front of the Arcade Building.

Pullman was one of the first fully planned industrial towns in America and it set a new standard of order and beauty for the development of manufacturing centers. More important, however, was the way it sustained a population density almost as great as the average for Chicago and yet appeared almost like a tranquil park. A capability for handling crowds was much admired in a city that grew as fast as Chicago. This was especially important in 1893, when the population was temporarily inflated by millions of visitors attending the World's Columbian Exposition.

The Exposition was important to Chicago in several respects. From the standpoint of information exchange, it constituted one of the most significant events in the entire nineteenth century. Important figures in the arts, sciences, and social studies gathered to trade ideas in a series of congresses. The Exposition brought together great works of art from all over the world for millions to view. Visitors got a preview of the future, as a seemingly endless array of inventions went on display. While the main grounds were an enormous museum, the Midway was one of the largest and most complex entertainment districts in the world.

The most controversial aspect of the Exposition was its architecture. Some felt it was out of place in a new city like Chicago. Others laughed at the "White City" and its pretentious classical buildings with exterior surfaces composed of a mixture of plaster and straw. Boosters had bragged about the place so much that it gained the nickname "Windy City." A few commentators such as the architecture critic Barr Ferree were more sympathetic. "What manufacturer of soap and pills," he noted, "would not bankrupt himself if in the end his wares would be as much talked of as Chicago is now and as she will be—shall I say it?—for all time to come?"

How strange that Chicago, a city known for its innovative architecture, would stage an exposition in such retrogressive buildings. Some blamed it on Daniel Burnham, the chief architect. His partner, John Wellborn Root, had died

Columbian Exposition stock certificate, 1892. Although the city provided many essential services, the Columbian Exposition was actually a private venture, funded by donations and stock sales.

Bust of the "I Will" woman, 1893. Civic leaders sponsored a contest to find a suitable symbol for Chicago as the site of the Columbian Exposition. The winner, "I will," represented Chicago's rebirth after the Fire and its determination to host the fair.

World's Columbian Exposition grounds, 1893. Because the Exposition was often open far into the night, its designers installed thousands of electric lamps.

Columbian Exposition site clearance, October 22, 1891. Hundreds of workers transformed a lakeshore swamp into a beautifully landscaped park. This view looks north from the site of the Art Palace.

Columbian Exposition statues, 1892. The fair was so enormous that artists literally mass-produced its decorative art-work.

Columbian Exposition, Horticultural Hall under construction, February 1892. Although most buildings were made of a plaster compound, they had a solid framework of steel underneath.

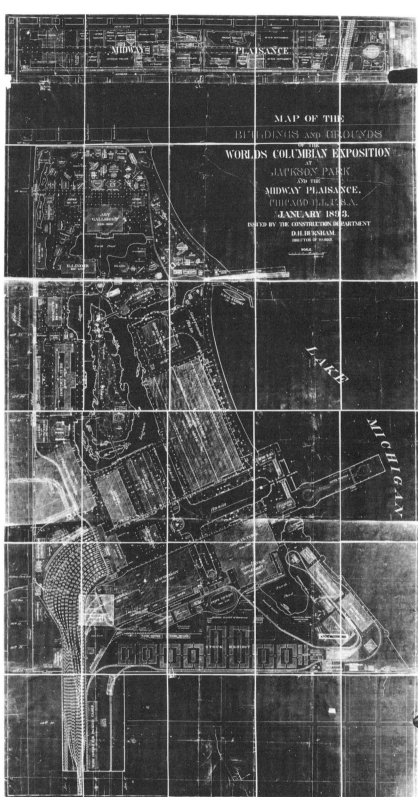

The World's Columbian Exposition, original blueprint of grounds. An architectural marvel, the fair was also a study in planning and crowd control. The designers, led by Daniel Burnham, grouped similar exhibits together and provided for the comfort of millions of visitors. The Wooded Island, center, was a pastoral contrast to the man-made spectacle surrounding it.

in 1891, and Burnham's detractors claimed that, with the true genius of the team gone, the survivor had allowed eastern architects to dominate the style of the fair. Meanwhile, some upper-class Chicagoans liked the fair's architecture because they thought it presented an image of maturity and sophistication to the world.

As recent scholars have pointed out, however, that view is grossly oversimplified. It is true that Chicagoans went to great pains to attract the fair by offering development money, promising to alter public and private facilities to handle the crowds, and incessantly boasting about the city's honest government and ideal climate. But Chicagoans appeared to be more dominant on boards of directors than was actually the case. The Exposition was a national event, not a local one. It was far too large for Chicago architects alone to design, and furthermore many of their truly innovative plans were for skyscrapers rather than for the horizontally spacious Exposition buildings. Yet the classical style was so universally familiar that a number of architects working independently created buildings that did not clash. This visual unity was important, for it supplemented another physical harmony, the plan of the site.

The design of the fairgrounds itself was one of the marvels of the event. The directors chose Frederick Law Olmsted to supervise the work. Olmsted was known not only for Riverside, but also for his recommendations for the development of Jackson Park, which became the site of the fair. His first task was to fill in hundreds of acres of swampland. This was accomplished early in 1891. Olmsted and the architects agreed that the main buildings should face a large basin and canal. Other structures were grouped according to their type. Horticultural Hall appropriately faced Wooded Island and the lagoon. The buildings housing the technological wonders of transportation, electricity, and mining composed another complex, while to the south of the Grand Basin were the substantial agricultural exhibits. The fine arts occupied a spacious building, 320 by 500 feet, with two large annexes, surrounded by state exhibits which also stressed folk and popular arts. Finally, there was the Midway with entertainments and replicas of foreign villages.

This logical plan left a deep impression on many visitors. The sidewalks and entrances seemed scientifically designed to handle large crowds, which, in turn, became an organism rather than an aggregation. Magazine writers commented that the architecture was beautiful rather than monotonous. The sense of physical order appeared to promote an ideal social order. One observer went so far as to contrast the miniature utopia of plaster with the modern industrial city, which he called the singular failure of civilization. The Exposition security guards earned their jobs on the basis of abilities, not politics. Visitors could walk about with a sense of absolute safety; outside the grounds, however, bands of "carfriskers," or pickpockets, operated on the streetcar routes downtown. On the grounds there were no open saloons; drinkers had to sit down at a table, and water was available gratis. The most buoyant optimists claimed that the White City had solved nearly every problem found in the real city outside. What had started out as merely a desolate swamp had become a model metropolis within a metropolis.

Columbian Exposition, 1893. The fair's classical style was quite conservative compared to the skyscrapers in the Loop. Some critics even thought that this architecture was pretentious in a town that had been a tiny village only sixty years ago. This view was taken looking south across the west end of the Basin.

Columbian Exposition, the Midway, 1893. The new University of Chicago appears in the background.

Columbian Exposition, moving sidewalk, 1893. Due to pressure from chair-pushing concessionaires, this interesting means of moving crowds never had a chance to demonstrate its true potential.

Columbian Exposition, Chicago Day, 1893. Tens of thousands of people could attend the fair at the same time and still move about freely.

Burnham and the Public City

Meanwhile, the city outside the fairgrounds seemed to deteriorate with each passing year. Citizens complained about the smoke that poured from furnaces and locomotives. Thousands of trains converged on the city from all directions every day. The din of street vendors, streetcar bells, industrial machinery, and rowdy citizens drew an endless stream of complaints. Itinerant salesmen filled the sidewalks, pushing pedestrians from the curbstone. Signboards completely covered some buildings, and advertising awnings hung so low that the careless nighttime stroller was apt to lose an eye. Streetcar accidents became daily events, as cars derailed or ran people down. With each passing decade after the Civil War, an increasing number of self-appointed seers predicted the imminent demise of urban civilization.

The major causes of these problems were obvious. One was congestion: too many people and too little efficiency in the use of space. Chicago had solved its shortage of private or semi-public space by constructing skyscrapers and new department stores and theaters. But the crowds that these structures generated filled the streets and sidewalks to capacity. The roadways could not be widened. The skyscrapers were criticized for creating "canyons" in some streets. Those whose property fell in the shadows complained about falling property values, while public health experts warned that streets that failed to receive sufficient sunlight would harbor epidemics. Self-proclaimed reformers managed to get the City Council to pass ordinances limiting the height of buildings, but their real aim soon became evident: properly placed bribes would yield "amended" laws or "exceptions" to the rules. It was clear that skyscrapers, huge stores, and theaters were a permanent part of the urban landscape.

Another problem was the ill-defined distinction between what was public property and what was private. This issue was at the center of one of the major debates in Chicago at the turn of the century, the debate over who owned the streets. The streetcar companies thought they did, and their franchises allowed them to operate with few restrictions. The street vendors assumed that peddling was a right, and attempts to ban them from the sidewalks failed. Vendors divided up the Loop and residential streets into territories, and the din they made as they shouted their wares often drowned out business transactions conducted indoors. Store owners and residents regularly used the streets as a dump, sweeping trash into the thick coating of mud and manure that covered the pavement. Contractors who erected new office buildings piled materials on the sidewalk, while utility companies tore up pavement without warning. One astute newspaper columnist compared commuting into the Loop to running the barricades of Paris in 1848.

Gradually, civic-minded citizens began to resist. Their letters to the newspapers bristled with indignation. The Citizens' Association feared that many visitors to the Columbian Exposition had left with a negative impression of their raw metropolis. This, it warned, was bad for business. What out-of-towner would want to come back to such a squalid city? Municipal officials appeared to be corrupt and lethargic, prompting citizens to take certain matters into their own hands. In neighborhoods all over the city irate householders banded together to repair sidewalks and pavements, clean alleys, and see to landscaping and other public improvements. In 1904 two business associations, the Commercial Club and the Merchants Club, jointly assumed responsibility for sweeping the Loop's streets. They hired a sanitation expert, Richard T. Fox of Boston, and assembled their own force of "whitewings," so named because of their snappy uniforms.

The two associations also collaborated on another project, forming a committee to explore the possibility of drawing up a master plan for the city. In 1906, they merged under the name of the Commercial Club, and at the same time resolved to sponsor a major planning project. The group chose Daniel Burnham to head the project. Because his leadership in designing the Columbian Exposition had made him a civic celebrity, his association with the plan would establish its credibility. After the Exposition he had become fascinated with the idea of applying the lessons learned in 1893 to whole cities. In 1901 he had undertaken a project to update L'Enfant's Plan of Washington. This was followed in quick succession by comprehensive plans for Cleveland, San Francisco, and Bagnio and Manila in the Philippines. By 1907 Burnham and his young assistant, an English-trained architect named Edward Bennett, were at work on the Plan of Chicago. Two years later they were finished.

The unveiling of the Plan was a major event that received national news coverage. Chicago was the largest city in America to have undergone such an examination, and the fact that it had been done without charge by Daniel Burnham aroused considerable interest. Two friends, Jules Guerin and Jules Janin, did sketches, the one in color, the other in black and white. Charles Moore, another friend and former member of the World's Fair Fine Arts Commission, edited the text, while Walter L. Fisher, legal counsel for the Commercial Club, added a scholarly appendix on the precedents and anticipated difficulties involved in implementing it. Handsome though it was, the Plan of Chicago was little more than wise advice from people who had no official power. In accepting a copy, Mayor Fred Busse was careful to note that its proposals were not "hard and fast" and would not result in any immediate changes. The unofficial nature of the venture inspired Charles Eliot, the retired president of Harvard, to write:

> *That a club of business men should have engaged in such an undertaking, and have brought it successfully to its present stage, affords a favorable illustration of the working of the American democracy. The democracy is not going to be dependent on the rare appearance of a Pericles, an Augustus, a Colbert, or a Christopher Wren. It will be able to work toward the best ideals through the agency of groups of intelligent and public spirited citizens who know how to employ experts to advantage.*

The Committee on the Plan of Chicago, dining in Daniel Burnham's office, surrounded by renderings of their concept. Edward B. Butler, Chairman, is at the far left; next to him is Burnham. Edward H. Bennett, Burnham's assistant, is sixth from the left. Charles H. Wacker, who later became Chairman of the Chicago Plan Commission, is at the far right.

Plan of Chicago, model for lakefront park. Efforts to inform the public about the Burnham Plan included the construction of a number of models like this one. The Plan called for construction of a library and museum in what is now Grant Park, but a series of court cases instigated by Montgomery Ward, kept the park free of structures.

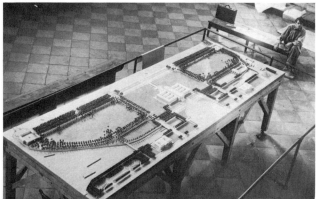

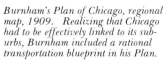

Burnham's Plan of Chicago, regional map, 1909. Realizing that Chicago had to be effectively linked to its suburbs, Burnham included a rational transportation blueprint in his Plan.

Draft of Daniel Burnham's Chicago Plan, c1908. An architect turned planner, Burnham wrote much of the text of the Plan himself, including an articulate explanation of its principle and argument for its implementation.
The Art Institute of Chicago

The Plan had several important features. It was regional in scope, perhaps the first that did not merely add a brim of countryside around the edges of an urban plan. Rather, it took into account the growing interconnection between city and countryside, especially with regard to the role the automobile would play. Electric interurban and steam commuter railroads already existed, but the highway system remained largely undeveloped. The Plan called for four suburban highways encircling the city at varying distances, the outermost stretching in a broad arc from Kenosha, Wisconsin, to Michigan City, Indiana. The Plan went on to note, "It needs no argument to show that direct highways leading from the outlying towns to Chicago as the center are a necessity for both; and it is also apparent that suburban towns should be connected with one another in the best manner." Highways were best, and, while the Plan was only a general scheme, it warned that "bad kinks and sharp turns" should be avoided, and surfaces should be of asphalt or cement, because automobiles had "introduced on the roads a new sort of wear and tear."

Burnham's blueprint sought to alleviate many of the daily inconveniences that beset people on the streets. Chicagoans had long been concerned with the hazard of falling power and telegraph wires, which were also a nuisance to firemen; the Plan wanted to bury wires wherever feasible. Slow-moving wagons held up traffic; Burnham wanted to ban them from certain streets. Michigan Avenue, the proposed link between the North and South Side, was to be divided into lanes for through traffic and for vehicles making local stops, much in the same manner as Olmsted's projected road between Riverside and Chicago. Major streets were to be widened, and new diagonal thoroughfares built to funnel traffic to and from the loop. Viaducts and bridges would eliminate another major hazard and cause of traffic problems, the grade-level railway crossing. Even though the Plan was grandiose, the proposed alleviation of these common dangers and inconveniences was very attractive to the average citizen.

Chicago traffic congestion, Clark and Adams, c1910-14. As massive traffic jams such as this became commonplace in the Loop, businessmen feared that unless something were done, the downtown would decline.

John T. McCutcheon on Chicago City Planning. An influential Tribune *cartoonist, McCutcheon supported the Burnham Plan. This cartoon expresses his frustration about delays in construction of the Plan's Michigan Avenue bridge.*

Opening of the Michigan Avenue Bridge, 1920. The Michigan Avenue Bridge opened up the North Side to downtown shopping traffic and created the "Magnificent Mile."

The Plan also sought to solve the problem of railway congestion. While the steam locomotive had been largely responsible for Chicago's spectacular growth, during the late nineteenth century the railroads seemed about to destroy it. Locomotives belched heavy smoke and made incessant noise; stations and yards blocked the southward expansion of the Loop. Depots were scattered around the perimeter of the downtown area, a serious inconvenience for travelers trying to make connections between trains. The proposal included the creation of a Union Station to the west of the Loop, another to the south, and the abandonment of trackage north of Twelfth Street. Only the Illinois Central was to be allowed to run its suburban line on the lakefront. All freight traffic was to be shunted around the downtown area. This proposed arrangement would not only remove depot-related street traffic from the Loop, but vacated yards would also provide room for downtown expansion.

Burnham dreamed on a grand scale. Public buildings were not simply functional, they were monuments. He proposed to take advantage of his new avenues and boulevards to revive the Near West Side. Congress Street was to be turned into a broad boulevard leading to an impressive Civic Center resembling the grandiose Administration Building of the Columbian Exposition. The new City Hall sat in the center of a pentagonal public square that was surrounded on four sides by governmental buildings. This new center, located just southwest of the Loop, was designed to instill life into a dying neighborhood as well as to remove a major cause of downtown congestion. The crowds that transacted business at City Hall would not need to travel into the center of the shopping district.

Parks were a special feature of the Plan. Burnham recommended the acquisition of forested tracts surrounding the metropolitan area. Eventually these could form a green

Referendum rally, Garrick Theater, 1919. Each Chicago Plan project required citizen approval of a bond proposal. This one was successful and resulted in the construction of Wacker Drive and the Michigan Avenue Bridge.

belt to which city dwellers might escape. The large Lakefront (now Grant) Park was to contain the Field Museum and the John Crerar Library, but the most spectacular feature was a series of roadways, beaches, and lagoons that would stretch most of the length of the lakefront from Wilmette to South Chicago. This string of pleasure islands was to be created from cinders and refuse. The lagoon that separated it from the shore was designed to provide still water for safe boating and, when frozen, an enormous skating surface.

Burnham included numerous small parks as well. He was aware that the poor depended on such public areas for recreation. Green spots were their only escape from a crowded, dreary existence in tenements. Where possible, trees were to replace obsolete utility poles. The improved transportation plan would make the larger parks more accessible to neighborhoods that had been isolated by rail yards and poor public transportation. The Plan made little further mention of the problems of the slum resident, but not because it favored the business elite over the poor. Burnham realized that he and Bennett were planning public space rather than private. It was relatively easy to fill in the lakeshore or to condemn private real estate and clear it to create a new street or widen an existing one.

Government was able to do anything it wanted with public land, or it could take private property for a common use. But the regulation of tenements was another matter. Regulations were difficult to enforce, and the courts frequently struck down reform legislation. Burnham knew that civic reform groups were already battling the tenement curse. Finally, other contemporary city plans likewise omitted

proposals to eradicate bad housing on an individual basis. Instead, the common practice was to make public areas attractive and efficient; the hope was that private property would follow suit.

One of the most remarkable things about the Burnham Plan was the manner in which it was presented to the public. Shortly after it was unveiled, Mayor Fred Busse established the Chicago Plan Commission. Its 328 members were to help promote the Plan and give advice on how to execute its details. Although educators, politicians, architects, and social workers appeared on its rolls, most of its members were businessmen. A prominent brewer, Charles H. Wacker, served as its first chairman. The Commission went to work immediately, turning out reams of press releases and magazine articles that appeared all over the country. Its chief publicist, Walter D. Moody, wrote an eighth-grade summary of the Plan, naming it the Wacker Manual after the hard-working chairman. The Chicago Board of Education bought 15,000 copies, making it, in the words of the Commission, "the first to adopt for any school system in American cities" a textbook on "Right Citizenship and City Planning." School children learned the advantages of planning as a matter of rote memorization. Meanwhile, the Commission turned out thousands of copies of pamphlets with titles like "Chicago's Greatest Issue," "An S-O-S to the Public Spirited Citizens of Chicago," and "The War and the Chicago Plan." Lecturers appeared before dozens of civic groups and neighborhood associations, and the Commission even made its own film. Nickelodeon customers who expected to see more lusty films were startled to get "A Tale of One City" and lessons about the advantages of city planning.

City Club Residential Planning Competition, 1913. Frank Lloyd Wright's noncompetitive entry entwined green spaces throughout the district, making no home more than two blocks from open space. This plan was an early version of Broadacre City, Wright's blueprint for a decentralized utopian city.

City Club Residential Planning Competition, 1913. This first-prize entry shows clearly the concept of specialized districts within a self-contained neighborhood. Wilhelm Bernhard was a Prairie-School architect.

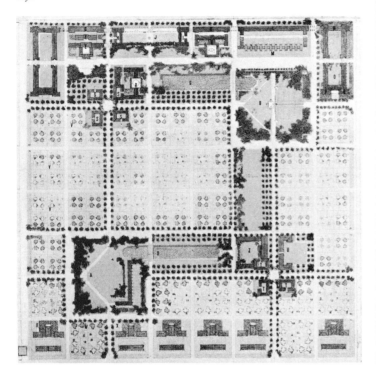

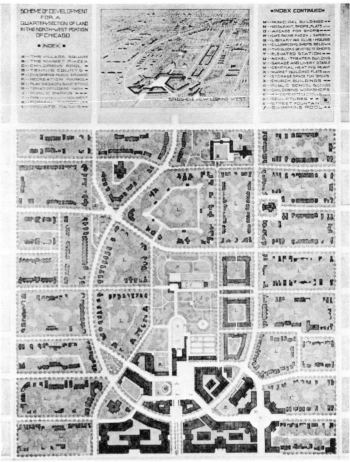

Filling in the Plan

The adoption of the Chicago Plan was an important milestone in the city's physical development. It fixed in the public mind the idea that the lakefront must be preserved for public use. Today, most of the shoreline consists of public beach. A number of streets, including Twelfth Street (now Roosevelt Road), South Water Street (now double-decked Wacker Drive), Ogden Avenue, LaSalle Street, and Michigan Avenue, were all widened into boulevards. The latter became a major artery, opening the Near North Side as a shopping district. Wacker Drive, completed in 1926, provided a badly needed route around the perimeter of the Loop, while the construction of the Outer Drive on landfill had the added benefit of opening miles of free public beaches. The new Union Station (1924) partially centralized rail passenger traffic, while in 1927 the city's public works department went one step beyond the Plan when it began straightening a portion of the South Branch of the Chicago River.

One significant omission in the 1909 plan was any kind of general blueprint for the development of new neighborhoods. Chicago had annexed large areas of land since 1889, most of which was vacant. Contractors had subsequently purchased tracts and erected rows of identical houses. Much to the distress of architects and planners, the

City Council had failed to regulate this. Block after block of tract housing filled in the monotonous grid pattern of streets. Businesses and light industry appeared where economically convenient, regardless of the impact on the surrounding neighborhood. Even the system of naming and numbering streets broke down. Every street already had its own address sequence, and kept it after annexation. In suburbs, contractors named new streets themselves, frequently resulting in confusing duplication. Finally, in 1908 the City Council decided to start renumbering the whole city and change hundreds of repetitive street names. This took care of one contemporary problem, but what about future growth?

A few architects had already begun to explore the possibilities of neighborhood planning. In 1901 Frank Lloyd Wright had published, in the *Ladies' Home Journal*, plans for "A Home in a Prairie Town." The plans entailed connecting four of his Prairie-School houses together to enclose a small plot. Wright's former associate, Walter Burley Griffin, took this idea a step further. He designed whole developments in Montana, in Iowa, and in Decatur, Illinois. In 1910 he drew up plans for Trier Center in suburban Winnetka. This compact nine-acre community called for thirty houses, all in Griffin's version of the Prairie style. The street pattern was grid, but the paired houses faced common garden plots. Griffin and his wife, Marion Mahony, left Chicago for Australia in 1913 and so never saw the Trier project through to completion. Griffin later gained fame

Mary McDowell letter to the City Plan Commission, 1910. Upset because the Burnham Plan failed to provide relief for congested slum neighborhoods, Mary McDowell protested.

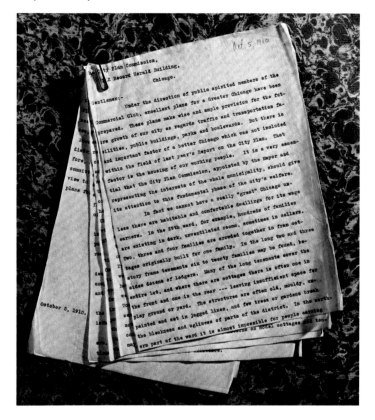

City Planning: An Ideal

The City Club competition was a fitting climax to the most creative era in the development of Chicago urban planning. It had started with Frederick Law Olmsted's beautiful Riverside. This idyllic suburb proved that the public areas of a city could be attractive and in harmony with nature and with residential development. Solon S. Beman's Pullman was proof that the principles of machine-like efficiency could be applied to a densely settled area. This red-brick town was, in theory, like a single building with its various functions scattered about the site. Riverside was a splendid example of planning; Pullman was an achievement in architecture. The World's Columbian Exposition was an attempt to combine excellence in both realms. Although its classical style was controversial—Louis Sullivan claimed that it set American architecture back a half century—there is little doubt that the ground plan of the fair was a creation of genius.

Burnham's master blueprint for the city drew heavily on earlier experiences, yet it was different. Olmsted, Beman, and the Exposition planners had benefitted from their position as benevolent dictators over small plots of prairie. Because they had started with undeveloped land they were able to mold both public and private spaces to suit themselves. By the time Burnham and Bennett began their work on Chicago, however, it was already growing out of control. Population had increased by one million people since 1893 and the city limits had extended several miles further into the countryside. The skyscraper idea had become so popular that it was destroying its own advantages of convenience by creating the worse inconvenience of congestion in the streets. Ironically, Burnham himself had contributed to the very problem that he was now trying to solve. Furthermore, the city was not nearly as malleable as an undeveloped tract. It was an accumulation of decades of building, economic ties, and human habits. Thousands of citizens owned private land. Neither Burnham nor any public official could do anything with this short of outright condemnation and seizure.

Burnham and Bennett settled for designing beautiful public places, hoping these would inspire private landowners to beautify their holdings. That attitude also dominated the City Club competition. Since most Chicagoans were hostile to the idea of public housing, this competition was primarily for the benefit of private contractors who might be able to attract potential buyers to small suburban subdivisions. The compact size; a quarter-section, made this seem like a realistic goal. Although a complete project of this type was never attempted within the city limits of Chicago, some of the best features of the City Club plans were integrated into suburbs such as Park Forest.

In any event, the 1913 competition, like all similar efforts previously, was aimed at adapting the city more efficiently to the needs of its citizens. But the Chicago of the drawing board and the aerial photograph never looks quite the same from the street, and so city planning has remained an ideal never fully achieved.

when he drafted a Burnham-type plan for the city of Canberra in his adopted country.

By 1913 the City Club of Chicago, a reform group, had become interested in neighborhood planning. About to hold a major exhibition on urban housing, the club decided to sponsor a competition. Entrants were instructed to prepare plans for a quarter-section of undeveloped land eight miles from the center of Chicago. Each section was square, a half-mile on each side; two sides had streetcar lines. Twenty-five competitors submitted plans, including William E. Drummond, a Prairie-School architect. Griffin supervised an entry by his young associate, Edgar Lawrence. The winner was Wilhelm Bernhard of Chicago, but most notable was a non-competitive entry by Frank Lloyd Wright.

The most successful plans had several features in common. In the tradition of Riverside, there were few, if any, through streets. Most abandoned the grid pattern altogether in favor of gently-curving free-form streets or geometrically balanced star patterns. They carefully segregated business and residential land and provided for large amounts of public parkland. They called for some low-rise apartments and duplexes, but the emphasis was on single-family dwellings. Each plan also included a civic center that contained churches, schools, community recreation facilities, and a hospital. All entrants concentrated on planning for domestic life, keeping the size and number of commercial establishments to a minimum.

Reforming Urban Society

Chicago's rapid growth assured that its tragedies as well as its triumphs would assume grand proportions. The Loop presented an impressive image to visitors in 1893, and the Columbian Exposition itself was a model of organization. But not far away one could find some of the worst slums in the world. To the northwest was Goose Island, a tough weave of tenements and factories that reputedly spawned a majority of the city's most notorious criminals. A mile south of Goose Island, along Halsted Street, was the Near West Side. Never a very splendid neighborhood, it had been ruined by the Fire of 1871—not by the flames, but by the thousands who took refuge in its already jammed buildings. Years of overcrowding had bred a slum whose population density rivaled the squalor of Calcutta. A visitor who traveled a few more miles south came upon Bridgeport, Canaryville, and Back-of-the-Yards, collectively known as Packingtown. Its slums ringed the Union stockyards. Most towns had moved their meatpacking industry out into the country; Chicago built a city around its.

Tumble-down housing and filthy streets were only the most obvious problems of the poor. They were also beset by unemployment and low wages. Industrial accidents were commonplace, and health conditions in some areas were so bad that a child had less than an even chance to reach the age of five. Juvenile delinquents—often the product of broken homes—prowled the streets. Alcoholism drove men and women to waste their precious dollars. But even while the problems seemed nearly hopeless, Chicago was giving rise to social movements that would substantially alleviate the plight of the poor. During the city's most troubled time, its citizens made some of their finest contributions.

Hull-House, c1910. The settlement, located at Halsted and Polk Streets, became a complex of specialized activities designed to meet the special needs of the neighborhood residents.

Moody and the street urchins. Dwight L. Moody's first evangelistic project was to save the souls of Chicago's street urchins. He is shown here with John V. Farwell, a merchant philanthropist, and their first Sunday School class.

Moral Reform in Transition

The earliest efforts at social reform tended to focus attention on individual moral adjustment to society rather than on society itself. Reformers regarded the individual as basically in control of his or her own fate. Social problems, drunkenness, vice, crime, and poverty were not seen as anonymous and unconquerable forces; instead, they were rooted in individual sinfulness, a matter that the drunkard, criminal, or poor person could only solve himself. The aim of these reformers was to persuade sinners to mend their ways. Then, they reasoned, social problems would simply disappear.

This view of society shaped the lifelong crusade of the most famous evangelist of the nineteenth century, Dwight L. Moody. Born in 1837 in Northfield, Massachusetts, Moody had left school at an early age to work in his uncle's Boston shoeshop. He became active in the Boston YMCA, and in the mid-1850s he experienced a religious conversion. Still determined to become a successful businessman, however, he moved to Chicago to seek his fortune. After a few years as a boot and shoe salesman, young Moody decided that he ought to dedicate his life to bringing religion into the everyday life of the masses.

Moody began his religious work at the North Market Mission, located in a small corner of a market hall on Wells Street. He soon expanded the mission's activities to include a school for street urchins. He also made a special appeal to the elderly poor, a group virtually ignored by established congregations. Fire destroyed the original mission in 1859. After spending a few years in temporary quarters, Moody applied his sales experience to raising funds for a new build-

ing. By the time he opened his Illinois Street Church in 1863, Moody was already well known in Chicago.

He believed that religion could be "sold" to people. Success at this required an appeal that was both broad and dynamic. He applied this technique not only in his own church, but also at the Chicago YMCA. Having once been a lonely young man in the city himself, he was aware of its many sinful temptations. He also knew that people easily got bored. To keep them coming to the YMCA he perfected ways to enliven his sermons. First, they had to be kept short, so he had an assistant ring a bell after three minutes were up. He surrounded himself with interesting drawings and large pictures. A piano player, Ira D. Sankey, accompanied him. Moody thought that the YMCA should be more than a noon-hour church and reading room. So, once again drawing on his fund-raising abilities, he built a new YMCA building in the Loop. This structure, opened in 1867, had exercise rooms and a residence hall; indeed, it was, in the words of one historian, "the first fully-equipped Y.M.C.A. building in the United States." Throughout the rest of his career, Moody continued to promote the YMCA as a means of saving the souls of young people.

By the 1870s Moody's evangelism had reached across the nation. He had been familiar with evangelistic crusades as a boy, but now he brought the mass revival right into the city, sometimes using a public auditorium, sometimes a tent. With Sankey at his side, Moody would deliver a fundamentalist message, make an appeal, and issue a warning about damnation. Moody and Sankey ultimately traveled all over the world saving souls. Moody also founded several academies for training evangelistic workers, the most important of which was the Moody Bible Institute in Chicago, his home base. Since 1887 this institution has carried out his philosophy of bringing religion to the masses.

Prayer-meeting broadside, 1868. The first YMCA Building, Farwell Hall, burned in 1868, but Moody simply announced that noon prayer meeting would be held elsewhere.

A Moody gospel tent. Moody often used a portable tent—an idea he borrowed from the circus—for his gospel meetings.
Moody Bible Institute

Dwight L. Moody's sermons, 1893-5. To avoid giving the same sermon twice to the same audience, Moody kept an envelope for each, jotting down where and when he had delivered it.
Moody Bible Institute

A share in the North Market Hall Sabbath School Association. Moody held religious classes in a room over a market. John T. Dale, a teacher there, noted that "It was a large, dingy, dilapidated-looking brick building on the outside, while the inside was a great grimy hall with blackened walls and ceiling, and as bare and uninviting as can be imagined." Moody sold stock to build a new structure, the Illinois Street Church.
Moody Bible Institute

The Woman's Temple, 1906.
Burnham and Root designed this
"feminized" structure in 1892 for the
Woman's Christian Temperance
Union, which rented most of the
ground level to banks. The building
was razed in 1926.

Frances Willard (1839-98). As an
educator, lecturer, and WCTU organizer, Miss Willard had gained international fame. She represents Illinois in Statuary Hall of the United
States Capitol.

Frances Willard's traveling tea set. In
an attempt to speak about the WCTU
in every American city with a population of more than 10,000, Miss Willard and her secretary, Anna Adams
Gordon, traveled over 30,000 miles in
just two years. They founded chapters
in every state and territory. This tea-
making outfit was always part of their
luggage.
Woman's Christian Temperance
Union

Like urban evangelism, the temperance movement also expected individuals to help themselves. The Washingtonian
temperance crusade of the mid-nineteenth century relied
heavily on the "pledge," a public promise never to take
another drink. Again, the burden of reform was on the
individual. This attitude also prevailed initially within the
Woman's Christian Temperance Union. A direct descen-
dant of the tent revival, the WCTU was founded in 1874 in a
presbyterian church in Hillsboro, Ohio. It quickly became
a national movement, establishing headquarters in Chicago
in the 1880s and in 1900 moving to Evanston, a Chicago
suburb that had always been dry. Its first national president, Mrs. Annie Wittenmyer of Philadelphia, lent the
young organization considerable prestige, for she had
helped organize the United States Sanitary Commission
during the Civil War, and was one of the most famous
women of her day.

It soon became clear, however, that the real driving force
behind the movement was its corresponding secretary,
Frances E. Willard. Born in upstate New York in 1839,
Miss Willard had been raised in rural Wisconsin. Unlike
most women during that period, she was able to continue
her education, graduating from the Evanston Female College in 1859. Later, when this institution was merged with
Northwestern University, she became Dean of Women.
But temperance was her true calling, and, when the opportunity appeared, she resigned to be a professional temperance worker. She became president of the WCTU in 1879
and during the next nineteen years she commanded its far-
flung attack on sin.

Although the "pledge" continued to play a central role in the
crusade, Miss Willard and her co-workers relied on reason-
ing as well as moralizing to enlist recruits. They stressed the
deleterious physiological effects of liquor and persuaded
most states to pass "Scientific Temperance" laws requiring
local school boards to see that their health classes promoted
abstinence. The idea was to save children from the ravages
of alcohol when they became adults. The WCTU also expanded its attempts to obtain pledges from railway workers
and others often thought to be beyond redemption. It established coffee houses that competed directly with saloons.
It organized junior temperance leagues and massive "White
Ribbon" parades, and it distributed temperance leaflets by
the thousands. Miss Willard called this a "Do-Everything
Policy."

The expanding activities of the WCTU were indicative of a
movement in transition, a transition marking a major shift
in the philosophy of American reform movements. This
involved moving away from the notion that the individual
caused his own problems and thus could cure them too, toward a belief that society as a whole shared responsibility for
both cause and cure. Inequality, crime, disease, and poverty were everyone's burden. Reforming society and its institutions thus became as important as regenerating individuals. This new attitude was best illustrated in the work
of Jane Addams's Hull-House.

The Settlement House: Helping the Neighborhood

Chicago's most important contribution to American reform was the popularization of the settlement house. This constituted a significant new philosophical departure. Old-fashioned charity work had operated under severe limitations. Charity workers lacked an intimate contact with life in the slums. After a few hours visiting the poor, they returned to the pleasant comfort of their own middle-class homes. Often they did not really understand the cultural values of the slum neighborhood. Nor were charity workers trained to ascertain the causes of poverty. Instead, the idea was to sort out the "worthy" poor from the "unworthy." Those who were deemed deserving received a small amount of food, or the opportunity to work for it. All of this was carried out in an atmosphere of condescending moralism. "Moral uplift" was seen as the key to social regeneration.

The settlement house was different. Staff members were called "residents" because they lived in the settlement house itself, right in the midst of the slums. The settlement was a tangible building, a permanent physical place open to all. While residents might inquire about the background of someone who came there, they made no negative presumptions about the causes of family misfortune. No tests of worthiness were administered; everyone was treated alike.

Actually, the settlement house movement started in England, not Chicago. In 1884 a group of Oxford students established Toynbee Hall in the Whitechapel slums of London. Here they lived and provided the poor with educational programs and recreational activities. In the late 1880s, several Americans visited Toynbee Hall, including Stanton Coit who established the first American settlement, Neighborhood Guild (later University Settlement) in New York City. Another American who witnessed the work in Whitechapel was a 28 year-old woman from Cedarville, Illinois, Jane Addams. A graduate of Rockford Seminary, Addams had enrolled at the Woman's Medical College of Pennsylvania, but poor health subsequently forced her to withdraw. After several years of intermittent illness, she visited London with Ellen Gates Starr, an old friend from college. There they both discovered their life's work.

In 1889 the two women moved to Chicago. They found an old mansion on the Near West Side, one of the city's most congested slums. The building, once the residence of Charles J. Hull, had subsequently been used as an asylum for alcoholic women and as a warehouse. Addams and Starr first established apartments for themselves and then opened up the remainder of the building to the community. They began a kindergarten in the old drawing-room, and established clubs to draw children in off the street. Hull-House also offered classes in sewing, cooking, art, and various crafts. Eventually, with the help of Allen Pond and his brother Irving, who contributed their architectural talents, Hull-House became a complex of thirteen buildings—a department store of humanitarianism in the midst of one of Chicago's most squalid slums.

Hull-House, 1912. The nation's most famous settlement house began in 1889 in an old Near West Side mansion that had become a warehouse. By 1907, the settlement's thirteen buildings covered an entire block. Hull-House continued operations until 1963, when the buildings were razed to make way for the new Chicago campus of the University of Illinois. Only a rebuilt mansion and the residents' dining hall remain as a museum.

Hull-House street cleaning brigade, c1900. When city authorities failed to do the job, Jane Addams enlisted volunteers to clean up the neighborhood.

Jane Addams (1860-1935), 1890. America's most famous social worker, Miss Addams applied an English idea, the settlement, to American tenement conditions. In 1931 she received the Nobel Peace Prize.
Jane Addams Memorial Collection, University of Illinois at Chicago Circle.

Ellen Gates Starr (1860-1940), on the witness stand, 1914. The co-founder of Hull-House, Miss Starr was a strong labor activist. She had been arrested when she joined a picket-line of waitresses striking against the Henrici Restaurant.

Florence Kelley (1859-1932). An expert on labor problems, Miss Kelley was the first head of the Illinois Bureau of Factory Inspection.
Tribune Company Archives

Julia Lathrop (1858-1932). A long time Hull-House resident, Miss Lathrop became the first head of the United States Children's Bureau in 1912.
Jane Addams Memorial Collection, University of Illinois at Chicago Circle

Ellen Gates Starr (left), one of her bookbinding pupils, and Jane Addams having tea in a corner of the Hull-House Labor Museum, c1910.
Jane Addams Memorial Collection, University of Illinois at Chicago Circle.

HULL-HOUSE BULLETIN

PUBLISHED AT 335 SOUTH HALSTED STREET, CHICAGO, ILL. TELEPHONE MONROE 70.

Vol. VI.   MID-WINTER, 1903-4   No. 1

OBJECT OF HULL-HOUSE (as stated in its Charter): To provide a center for a higher civic and social life; to institute and maintain educational and philanthropic enterprises, and to investigate and improve the conditions in the industrial districts of Chicago.

ENTERTAINMENTS IN THE AUDITORIUM.

SUNDAY EVENING LECTURES.

Illustrated by stereopticon. 8 p. m. at the Hull-House Auditorium, Admission free.

Nov. 1—**India.** Mr. Fleming.
Nov. 8—**Italy.** Miss Hamilton.
Nov. 15—**The English Lake Country.** Miss Myra Reynolds.
Nov. 22—**American Sculpture.** Mr. Lorado Taft.
Nov. 29—**Beautiful Japan.** Dr. Toyokichi Iyenaga, University of Chicago.
Dec. 6—**The Alcestes of Euripides** (recital). Prof. R. G. Moulton, University of Chicago.
Dec. 13—**The Antigone of Sophocles** (recital). Prof. S. H. Clark, University of Chicago.
Dec. 20—**The People of the Slavic World.** Prof. E. A. Steiner, University of Chicago.
Dec. 27—**The Messiah,** by the Evanston Choral Society.
Jan 3—**The Holy Land.** Prof. Shailer Matthews.

The following course of six illustrated lectures on Economic Geography, by Prof. Goode, University of Chicago:

Jan. 10—**The Iron Industry.**
Jan. 17—**The Lumber Industry.**
Jan. 24—**Our Largest Cereal Crop—Corn.**
Jan. 31—**The Economic Significance of the Great Plains.**
Feb. 7—**Cotton as a Social Factor.**
Feb. 14—**The Reclamation of the Arid Lands.**

The following course of six lectures on the Capitals of Europe, by Prof. Raymond, University of Chicago:

Feb. 21—**Madrid**
Feb. 28—**Brussels.**
March 6—**Rome.**
March 13—**Copenhagen.**
March 20—**Berne.**
March 27—**Athens.**

AUDITORIUM ENTERTAINMENTS.

Oct. 14—8 p. m.—**Neighborhood Party,** given by Hull-House Woman's Club, Admission by invitation.
Oct. 16—**Reception and Dance,** Men's Club Foot Ball Team.
Oct. 17—**Reception and Dance,** Washington Irving Club.
Oct. 19—**Reception,** given by Industrial Committee of Hull-House Woman's Club to Union Label League.
Oct. 23—**Dancing Party,** Ida Wright Club.
Oct. 24—**Dancing Party,** Gernon Club.
Oct. 25, 4 p. m.—**Concert.**
Oct. 30—**Dance,** Lincoln Social Club.
Oct. 31—**Dance,** Hull-House Men's Club.
Nov. 1, 4 p. m.—**Concert.**
Nov. 4—**Reunion and Dance,** Henry Learned Club.
Nov. 6—**Dancing Party,** Athos Club.
Nov. 13—**Dancing Party,** Fleur de Lis Club.
Nov. 14—**Dance,** Men's Club Foot Ball Team.
Nov. 16—**Lecture,** by Judge Dunne, on "Municipal Ownership," under auspices of Nineteenth Ward Improvement Association.
Nov. 20—**Neighborhood Party,** given by Hull-House Woman's Club. Admission by invitation.
Nov. 21—**Buddhism and Buddhist Art,** Prof. Paul Caros, under the auspices of Ethical Culture Society.
Nov. 23, 8 p. m.—**Hull-House Woman's Club Harvest Home Party,** for benefit of Woman's Club Chorus. Admission, 15 cents.
Nov. 26—**Greek Reception,** followed by stereopticon lecture on "Greece," by Miss Harriet A. Boyd.
Nov. 28—**Afternoon,** meeting of Smith College Alumnæ.
8 p. m.—**Dance,** Hull-House Men's Club.
Nov. 29, 4 p. m.—**Concert.**
Nov. 30, 8 p. m.—**Play, "School,"** by Hull-House Dramatic Association. Admission, 25 cents.

The Hull-House Bulletin. By the turn of the century activities at Hull-House had become so multiplex that it was necessary to publish a schedule of events. The Bulletin also publicized the settlement idea in the metropolitan community and was used to respond to questions and criticisms.

Working People's Social Science Club, Hull-House, 1892. The settlement created this organization as an educational forum and discussion group for neighborhood people.
Jane Addams Memorial Collection, University of Illinois at Chicago Circle

1892.

Working People's Social Science Club, Hull House, 335 So. Halsted St. meets Tuesdays at 8 O'clock P.M.
A speech of 45 minutes is followed by a discussion.

PROGRAM.

Feb. 2, "Child Labor" Mrs. Florence Kelley.
Feb. 9, "Our Jury System" Sigmund Zeisler.
Feb. 16, "The Chicago Police" Major R.W. McClaughry.
Feb. 23, "The Cook County House of Correction" Mr. Mark Crawford.
Mar. 1, "Competition" Col. Aldace F. Walker.
Mar. 8, "The Cook Co. Courts" Judge M. F. Tuley.
Mar. 15, "The Municipal Control of Heat, Light, and Transportation" Col. Augustus Jacobson.

THE JANE CLUB,

A Boarding Club for Working Girls, on the Co-operative Plan.

—AT—

249 and 253 EWING STREET, (West Side),

Half a Block from Blue Island Ave. and Halsted St. Cars.

TERMS FOR ROOM AND BOARD, - - $3.00 A WEEK.

APPLICANTS may call during the day at Hull-House, 335 South Halsted St., or during the evening at the Club Rooms.

The Jane Club ad, Hull-House, 1893. Many social reformers were concerned about the fate of young women who came to Chicago seeking jobs. Hull-House offered them room and board at what became known as The Jane Club.
Jane Addams Memorial Collection, University of Illinois at Chicago Circle

Hull-House dance, 1916. Settlement workers attempted to combat the influence of saloons, nickelodeons, and dance halls by providing wholesome substitutes.

THE CHICAGO BAND
WILLIAM WEIL, CONDUCTOR
HULL HOUSE
AUG. 26   SATURDAY—8 P. M. NINETEEN HUNDRED SIXTEEN

CONCERT ON GROUNDS
MARY CRANE NURSERY
HALSTED STREET AND GILPIN PLACE

Illinois Industrial School for Girls exhibit, 1911. This was part of the Child Welfare Exhibit sponsored by the social work department of the University of Chicago to acquaint Chicagoans with the many different institutions that aimed to improve the lives of children.

Child Welfare Exhibit ribbon, 1911.

Mary Crane Nursery, Hull-House. Informal day care facilities at Hull-House gradually evolved into the Mary Crane Nursery, a large pre-school that was operated with the aid of the National College of Education, the Infant Welfare Society, and the United Charities of Chicago.

The settlement idea might easily have failed. The residents of Hull-House were primarily well-educated, middle-class people who had grown up in small towns; those who lived in the surrounding slum were poor and uneducated. But the residents managed to establish a working relationship and the movement prospered. The number of settlements in Chicago grew almost yearly, and by 1920 there were sixty-eight. Several others besides Hull-House gained international fame. At Augusta and Noble streets, on the Near Northwest Side, stood the Northwestern University Settlement. Founded in 1891 in a neighborhood of Polish immigrants, it became a portal into the slums, where college students and teachers learned first-hand about urban pathologies. In 1894 Graham Taylor, a Congregationalist minister from New York, established Chicago Commons. From small beginnings there eventually grew an important settlement whose activities were based on thorough and extensive door-to-door surveys of local conditions. Finally, also in 1894, Mary McDowell moved from Evanston to the "Back-of-the-Yards" district and established the University of Chicago Settlement. Dozens more of these institutions appeared in later years, but always their purpose remained: "How can we help?"

Expansion of the settlement movement was primarily due to the democratic nature of these institutions. While the poor did not sit on boards of directors or establish policy in an official way, they could, in effect, "vote with their feet." Settlements succeeded because their residents knew the real needs of the neighborhood. They were able to assess this by careful observation and extensive surveys. Many settlement activities simply compensated for whatever was lacking in crowded slums. Tenements, for instance, lacked bathing facilities and play space for children; Hull-House badgered city officials into building the first municipally-owned bathhouse. There was a playground nearby. If a tenement mother had to work, she could leave her children in any one of several settlement day-nurseries. If a confused immigrant did not know English, he or she could learn it in a settlement classroom.

Jane Addams was more than just a competent organizer and fund raiser, she was also a skilled publicist who contributed greatly to the rapid dissemination of the settlement idea. She made countless speeches and was interviewed hundreds of times. She could write books that warranted serious scholarly discussion, or talk to a group of immigrants who could barely understand English.

Simultaneously, another Chicago settlement leader was making a similar contribution. In 1903 Graham Taylor began a series of lectures on social work at the University of Chicago. Within four years these early efforts had become the Chicago School of Civics and Philanthrophy. Although not the first on the subject, Taylor's classes on "helping" were perhaps the most thorough. Prospective settlement residents from all parts of the country came to study about how slums developed, why families disintegrated, how industrial conditions impaired health, why children became delinquents, and much else. The curriculum often sounded like an unpleasant litany of social ills, but those who graduated carried the valuable lessons they had learned in Chicago to all parts of the land.

Dedication of Chicago Commons Clock, 1901. Public timepieces were important in tenement neighborhoods where personal clocks and watches were a luxury.

A map of the Social Influences in the Chicago Commons neighborhood, 1912. The Chicago Commons staff developed maps like this one which shows the positive and negative conditions in their Near Northwest Side slum ward. Note the number of saloons scattered throughout the ward, as many as seven in one small block.

Graham Taylor (1851-1938), 1910. In 1894 Taylor established the Chicago Commons settlement. Many seminary students served as residents.

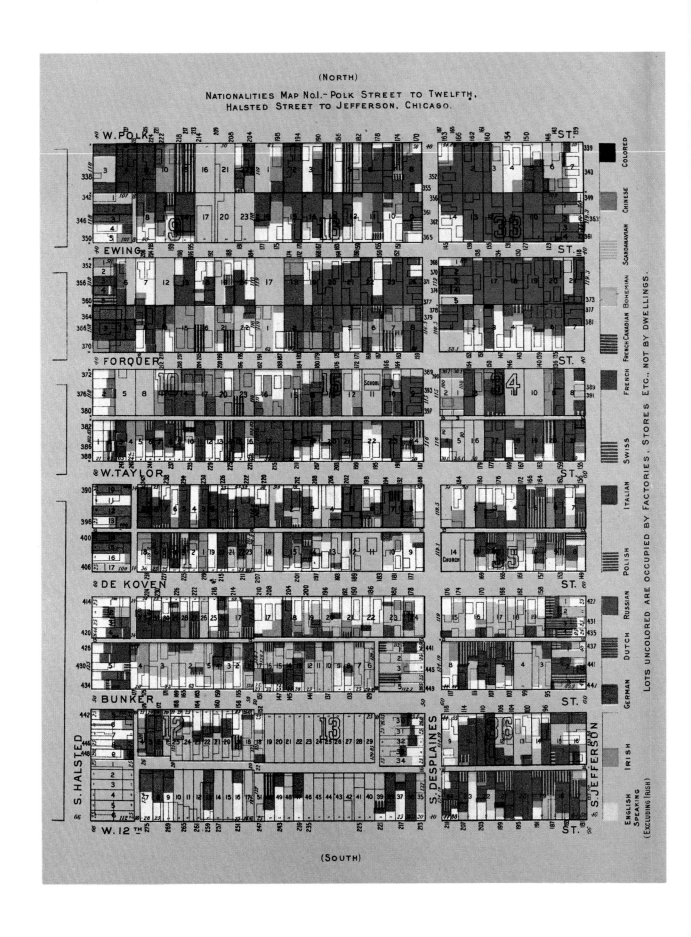

(NORTH)

NATIONALITIES MAP NO.1.- POLK STREET TO TWELFTH,
HALSTED STREET TO JEFFERSON, CHICAGO.

(SOUTH)

66

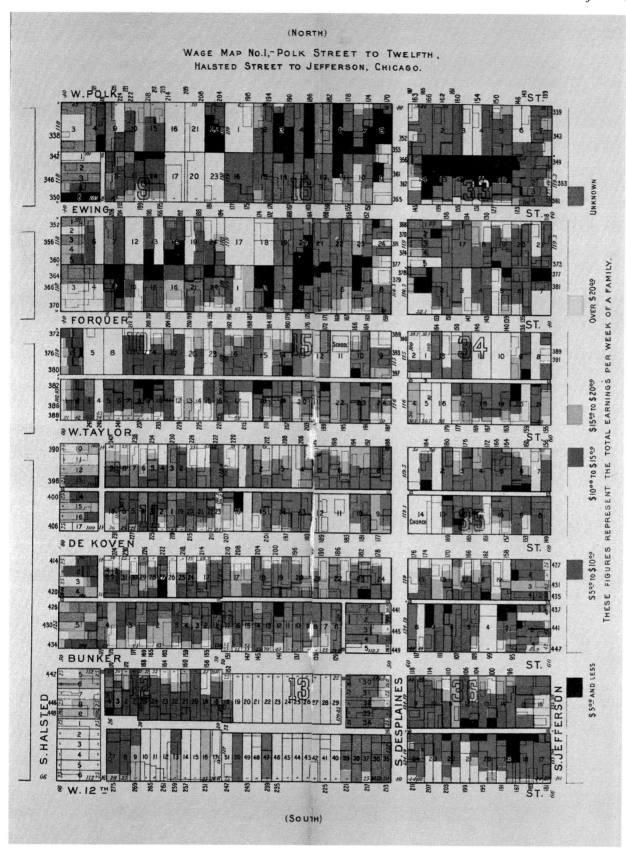

(NORTH)

WAGE MAP NO.1,—POLK STREET TO TWELFTH,
HALSTED STREET TO JEFFERSON, CHICAGO.

(SOUTH)

*Hull-House maps, 1895. The settle-
ment house staff cooperated with the
U.S. Department of Labor to produce
these maps of typical blocks in the West
Side slums.*

Visiting Nurse Association ad,
Chicago Post, *May 1921.*

Society ladies raising funds for settlement milk stations, 1917.

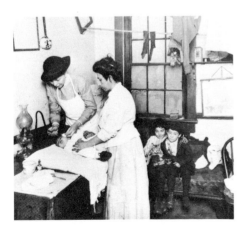

Infant Welfare Society nurse, c1910. When tenement dwellers could not go to a doctor, a visiting nurse came to them.

Infant Welfare Society nurse, c1907. The Infant Welfare Society sponsored a visiting nurse program to care for slum children. Here a nurse shows a recently arrived mother the proper way to bathe her baby.

Chicago Tuberculosis Institute exhibition, Chicago Public Library, 1906. Local physicians and the Visiting Nurse Association formed the Chicago Tuberculosis Institute to disseminate information and lobby for public health legislation.

Reaching Out: Health and the Judicial System

Settlement work was obviously not confined just within institutional walls. Each initial inquiry into the roots of a problem led to a more extensive survey which usually pointed to deeper causes. The residents became involved in municipal and state government. They conducted investigations of narcotics problems, slum housing, truancy, unemployment, and many other indices of social disorganization. Settlement residents also assumed leading roles in other movements aimed at reforming society's ills.

In tenements, one of the most pressing problems was disease. Crowded conditions and lack of sanitation spread epidemics. Sewers backed up. Primitive privy vaults remained uncleaned. Garbage and horse manure turned to knee-deep mud in the rain, or to eye-stinging dust clouds during drought. Windowless tenements nurtured tuberculosis. The general situation seemed almost hopeless. Settlement residents and their allies in the medical field decided to attack one component, the most poignant: infant welfare. Nearly all of the larger settlements had a staff physician or at least a room set aside as an emergency infirmary. The day nurseries also saw to it that each child left in their care received a medical examination.

Public health was one of the most important community activities of the settlement house. Upset with the poor performance of her ward's garbage inspector, Jane Addams took over the position herself and forced the private scavengers to do their job. Settlements also operated their own "milk stations." Companies that transported milk in from the country often left it unrefrigerated or stored it in germ-laden containers. They also watered it and added chalk or even bluing to give it a bright, wholesome appearance. Therefore, settlements took responsibility for distributing fresh, undiluted milk, bottled under sanitary conditions, and sold at a reasonable price. To spread the word about

their milk stations, the settlements printed handbills, in several languages; the Italian mother knew immediately the meaning of "Latte Puro pei Bambini."

In 1890 a group of women incorporated the Visiting Nurse Association, which employed dozens of trained nurses to care for sick indigents in the tenements. Using settlement houses and local apothecary shops as headquarters, the nurses, with their broad-brimmed hats and black bags, became a familiar sight in Chicago's slums. When not helping a doctor deliver a baby or taking someone's temperature, they instructed the poor on the need for cleanliness and good nutrition, and even helped with household chores. Through their work, the broad influence of the settlement house reached directly into the tenement.

Reformers were also concerned about the problem of idle youth in the city. Chicago's streets provided an unending series of temptations: everything from nickelodeons to fakirs who sold worthless gadgets. Brazen saloonkeepers sold liquor to minors and harbored members of juvenile street gangs. Moreover, Illinois lacked an effective mandatory school attendance law. This worried settlement workers who saw the delinquency that often resulted. Furthermore, juveniles who got into trouble were mishandled by the courts. They were treated as adults, given severe sentences, and incarcerated indiscriminately among hardened criminals.

As early as 1883, the Chicago Woman's Club had begun to agitate for reform, though it was nearly a decade before the issue attracted significant attention. In 1891 a member of the Chicago Bar Association helped draft a reform law, but it failed to pass the General Assembly. Four years later the Woman's Club presented its own bill, but subsequently decided to withdraw it in the face of certain defeat. In desperation, reformers sent Mrs. Lucy Flower east to study various court systems. After she returned, she helped Julia Lathrop of Hull-House present a comprehensive reform measure to the legislators. Finally, on April 21, 1899, Gov-

The Juvenile Court Record, 1905. Published by the Visitation and Aid Society of Chicago, The Juvenile Court Record ran news of the nationwide juvenile court movement.

Louise deKoven Bowen (1859-1953). A wealthy society matron, Louise deKoven Bowen became the city's leading advocate of juvenile reform.

Juvenile Detention Home, 1919. This Juvenile Detention Home provided shelter and educational programs for children who were wards of the court.

ernor John Tanner signed a law establishing the first juvenile court in the United States.

The new law attempted to deal with every aspect of the delinquency problem. It gave the courts authority to take a child from the custody of parents judged unworthy. Judges had the power to define delinquency and to place an offender on probation, or in a foster home, or in an institution. Children were never exposed to adult criminals. The new law was a milestone, but there was neither money nor personnel to administer it beyond the courtroom itself. Settlement houses and the Woman's Club once again came to the rescue. The court was located near Hull-House, which also happened to be in one of the districts of highest delinquency. Reformers provided the court with a detention center for children awaiting hearings, and also established and operated the probation system.

After a few years these efforts became the basis for a new organization, the Juvenile Court Committee. Later renamed the Juvenile Protection Association, it became one of America's leading organizations for reform in matters relating to urban youth. The J.P.A. studied the causes of delinquency, especially unsavory street activities. Chicagoans were shocked when it published statistics and narrative details about the city's seamy dance halls. It investigated the evils of nickelodeons and tried to explain why poorly-paid shopgirls ended up in brothels. Its leader, Louise deKoven Bowen, had lobbied in Springfield and in the City Council for new laws that removed some of these temptations. Although the Victorian morality that colored its exposes now seems dated, the investigative techniques and passionate propaganda of the J.P.A. served as a model often copied throughout the United States.

The instant success of the juvenile court aroused the hopes of Chicago's reformers, who advocated overhauling the whole system. All but the most serious cases were handled by justices of the peace, often untrained, who operated what the press called "justice shops" in their home or place of business. Their fees came from the fines they levied. The decentralized nature of this system meant that payoffs were common. Since the court system had failed to keep pace with urban development, however, there seemed little that anyone could do.

In 1905 the Chicago Bar Association finally pushed a court reform bill through the General Assembly. It required an amendment to the constitution, and that process took a year. But the new system that went into operation became a model that was adopted by more than forty major American cities. The bill created a single court to adjudicate all cases, criminal or civil. A chief judge presided over the whole system. Because judges were not assigned to any specific branch, the system had the flexibility to meet temporary overloads or changing needs. Faced with an increasing number of divorce cases, for example, the court opened a Domestic Relations Branch. Soon after, it added an Automobile Branch, and in 1913 a Morals Branch. In each instance, Chicago was either first to adopt these special branches, or else was responsible for popularizing the idea. Finally, in 1914 the court established a Psychopathic Lab to study the "criminal mind." This was the nation's pioneer effort in that important field.

Swearing-in of Chicago Municipal Judges, 1906. About to inaugurate Chicago's new court system, the jurists shown here are gathered in Jackson Park to receive their commissions.

Night Court, 1915. Chief Judge Harry Olson, a leading advocate of court reform, presides over a session of the Night Court. Olson was Chief Judge from 1906 until 1920.

Sweatshop, 1903. In many small garment factories, poor lighting, lack of ventilation, and unsanitary conditions posed a hazard to workers. Here, representatives from the Illinois Bureau of Factory Inspection examine sweatshop conditions.

The 1910-11 Garment Workers' strike. Much of the conflict during this bitter strike was about the right to picket and parade.

The Rights of Labor

Settlement reformers quickly learned the power of publicity and the importance of organization, both especially important to the labor movement. Hull-House had been open less than two years when Jane Addams came out in support of shirtmakers who had gone on strike because of a wage cut. Almost continuously thereafter at least one of the settlements was involved in some kind of local strike. Most of these walkouts were relatively small, although Addams did attempt to negotiate an early end to the great Pullman Strike of 1894. Their efforts on behalf of labor drew social workers more deeply into the community, where they witnessed working conditions at first-hand. In 1891, Hull-House tried to alleviate the unemployment problem by establishing an employment bureau, an idea later copied by the state of Illinois and by state governments in other heavily industrialized parts of the nation. Florence Kelley, an associate of Jane Addams, lobbied so hard for a factory inspection act that Governor John Peter Altgeld appointed her as Factory Inspector in 1893. Kelley fought capitalists who employed underaged children, worked women and older children more than eight hours a day, or failed to maintain decent working conditions.

Hull-House and other settlements were also involved in the growth of the woman's labor movement, which attempted to combat long hours, low pay, and hazardous industrial conditions. Early efforts to organize female workers failed, largely because women workers tended to regard their jobs as only temporary and were simply not interested in unionization. Around the turn of the century, however, the movement began to take hold. Newspaper exposes and investigations by state labor bureaus spotlighted working conditions that aroused public sympathy. Settlement houses helped provide a new generation of leadership, and those in Chicago proved instrumental in extending the benefits of unionization to women.

The turning point came in 1903 when the National Women's Trade Union League was organized in New York. Jane Addams became a vice president. The Chicago chapter, founded the next year, was headed by Mary McDowell, a director of the national group. Margaret Dreier had been a leader of the New York chapter when she met Raymond Robins, a Chicago social worker and head of the Municipal Lodging House. The couple married and moved to Chicago, where she became head of the local chapter in 1907. During her directorship, it worked on behalf of the eight-hour day, a minimum wage, full political rights for women, and equal pay for equal work. It also helped working women obtain decent housing and health care, and sponsored social activities and Americanization classes.

Efforts to publicize the union movement received a great boost in 1907, when several settlement houses, unions, and civic reform groups jointly organized the Chicago Industrial Exhibit at Brooke's Casino. This was aimed at calling public attention to the problems of children and women in the labor force, an idea initially proposed by the Chicago Woman's Club. Photos and charts dramatized miseries and hazards as they existed, while exhibits of machinery equipped with adequate safeguards and methods of assuring proper sanitation showed conditions as they could be. Ten thousand visitors viewed the exhibits in one week; they took home books and souvenirs that served as continuous reminders that inhumane industrial conditions bred epidemics and crime. One settlement worker, Graham Romelyn Taylor, commented that, "For the first time on a comprehensive scale . . . . People were made to realize the extent to which the interests and welfare of wage-earners are coincident with the interests and welfare of the whole people."

A few years after the Chicago Industrial Exhibit, settlement reformers involved themselves in a memorable labor confrontation. By 1910 the city had become one of the nation's largest centers for clothing manufacture, employing about 34,000 workers, mostly women, in nearly seven hundred plants. The work was long and tedious, whether in small sweatshops or in enormous factories. Hart, Schaffner and Marx, the city's largest clothing maker, employed some 7,500 people. While the owners were said to be friendly and generous towards their workers, their department "bosses" definitely were not. The bosses, who had authority to adjust wages according to the workload, were infamous for their vicious attitude. For several months the United Garment Workers had been attempting to organize the plant, and tensions were mounting. Then, on September 22, 1910, one of the bosses cut the pay of pants-seamers by a penny an hour. The seamers walked off the job and within a few days the whole plant had closed down.

The strikers rapidly gained support. The Women's Trade Union League and the Chicago Federation of Labor helped organize picket lines, and provided food and fuel for the strikers. Settlements and women's clubs staged dances and parades on behalf of the strikers, while ministers preached sermons about their cause. Even Mayor Fred Busse and the City Council threw their support behind the union. Finally, at the beginning of 1911, the two sides began to show a greater willingness to negotiate, and on January 14 they reached an agreement. The company recognized the union and began improving wages and working conditions; the bosses lost much of their power.

This strike was significant for several reasons. It brought unionism to one of the largest and toughest bastions of industrialism in the country. The victory in Chicago made it easier for unions to organize in smaller towns. A generation of women workers learned the techniques and strategy of organizing. But the most significant development came later. During the course of the strike it had become obvious that the leadership of the United Garment Workers, mostly German-born or native, had great difficulty communicating with the majority of the membership, which was primarily Polish, Jewish, or Bohemian. Even though the U.G.W. won the strike, in 1914 the majority of workers joined a secessionist movement led by Sidney and Bessie Hillman. The new Amalgamated Clothing Workers of America emerged as representing the interests of the recent immigrant laborers and soon became one of the nation's most important unions.

National Women's Trade Union League convention, 1917. Chicago labor leaders joined their sisters from across the nation for this Kansas City gathering.
Library of Congress

Garment Workers' strike, 1910. Chicago Police unceremoniously arrest a striker.

Glove Makers Union ribbon. Begun in 1901 as the Glove Workers Union, this group changed its name to the Glove Makers Union in 1902 when it obtained a charter from the American Federation of Labor.

Stockyards strike, 1904. Settlement workers involved themselves in the labor movement by providing meeting places, food, and encouragement for striking Packingtown butchers.

Seal of the National Women's Trade
Union League, 1903. The Chicago
chapter of this organization remained
active until 1950, expanding its concerns to Social Security and Federal
aid to education.

Mary McDowell, (1854-1936). A
former resident of Hull-House, Miss
McDowell established the University of
Chicago Settlement in 1894.

Agnes Nestor (1880-1948), 1928.
From 1913 to 1948 Miss Nestor
headed the Chicago Women's Trade
Union League.

Raymond and Margaret Robins,
1914. Raymond and Margaret
Robins both were active leaders in
Chicago reform, she as leader of the
Women's Trade Union League, he
with the Chicago Commons and
Northwestern University settlements.

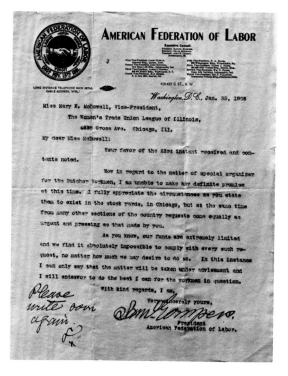

Garment Workers' strike, 1915. Four
years after a union victory at Hart,
Schaffner and Marx, the new Amalgamated Clothing Workers organized a
strike against the garment industry.
Here, the union's president, Sidney
Hillman, leads the workers back to
their jobs.

Organizational efforts in
Packingtown, 1908. In this letter
Mary McDowell asked Samuel Gom-
pers of the American Federation of
Labor to find a replacement for
Michael Donnelly, an organizer who
had left Chicago after failing to
unionize its packinghouse workers in
1904.

The significant events in the history of education in Chicago were shaped by a desire to present innovative ideas to large numbers of people. Chicago's development as a stronghold of "progressive education" began in 1883 when Col. Francis W. Parker arrived to head the Cook County Normal School. Parker had already compiled a distinguished record as head of the school system in Quincy, Massachusetts. During his early years as a teacher he had become concerned about the lack of creative expression among children. They could read, but did not seem to understand much. Their powers of imagination had apparently been stunted by rote learning. At Quincy, Parker opened up the curriculum to include art, and encouraged students to creative endeavors. The daily reading assignments included the newspaper, and geography classes included field trips. Mathematics teachers taught theory as well as tables and other matters of rote. Parker sought both to adjust education to the interests of young people and to tie it into the real world outside the classroom.

During the sixteen years that "The Colonel" ran the Cook County Normal School, Chicago teachers were exposed to some of the most progressive ideas current in America. As Parker was nearing retirement, he noted with satisfaction the rise of another educator and another institution that were concerned with adapting education to fit the needs of people rather than to the demands of tradition. This was John Dewey, who taught at the new University of Chicago. During the decade after 1894 Dewey gained a national reputation, while the university implemented several revolutionary innovations in higher education.

Francis Parker (1837-1902). A Chicagoan from Quincy, Massachusetts, Parker revolutionized teacher training in progressive cities across the country.

Graduating class, Cook County Normal School, 1890. Under Francis Parker's direction this school was open to everyone.

John Dewey's The School and Society, *1899. One of the most influential books on education ever written,* The School and Society *convinced thousands of principals and teachers that education should be a process of discovery, not rote-learning.*
University of Chicago Library

John Dewey (1859-1952). Known as the father of progressive education, Dewey introduced many of his famous ideas while on the faculty of the University of Chicago from 1894 to 1904.
Jane Addams Memorial Collection, University of Illinois at Chicago Circle

William Rainey Harper (1856-1906). Before becoming the first president of the University of Chicago, Harper had been a distinguished biblical scholar at Yale.

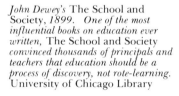

The University of Chicago Extension lecture notice, Chicago Tribune, *January 1894. These lectures were made available to everyone in the Midwest by the University of Chicago Extension.*

Laboratory School classroom. According to John Dewey, education had been centered for too long "in the teacher, the text-book, anywhere and everywhere you please except in the immediate instincts and activities of the child himself." Laboratory School projects ranged from growing gardens and firing pottery to field trips throughout Chicago.
University of Chicago Library

Actually, the new University of Chicago was the reincarnation of an earlier institution that had gone bankrupt in 1886. The following year a group of local businessmen approached the Baptist group that had operated the defunct institution with a proposal they had worked out in concert with John D. Rockefeller. The oil baron would donate $600,000, provided that $400,000 could be raised locally. By the spring of 1890 the opening of the new university was assured. Chicago would not suffer the embarrassment of hosting the Columbian Exposition while lacking a major academic institution. For the presidency, the trustees chose William Rainey Harper, a Yale professor who had some unusual ideas about higher education.

Harper felt that the university should emphasize graduate and advanced undergraduate studies; other midwestern colleges would send their very best students to the Midway. This seemed terribly elitist, but another Harper proposal provided a suitable counterbalance. A pioneer University Extension was established to bring the faculty and facilities into closer contact with the community at large. A wide selection of evening courses was offered at reasonable cost. Harper also broadened the literal meaning of the term extension: a farmer in Iowa or a housewife in Indiana could join the university community through its correspondence courses. The University of Chicago Press, one of the first in the United States, provided an outlet for faculty scholarship. Harper also encouraged direct involvement in community problems. In response, faculty members joined civic reform groups and offered their expertise for the benefit of the general public. The University's sociology department created a new field, urban sociology, and *The American Journal of Sociology*, edited and published on campus, frequently focused its attention on Chicago.

Harper wanted to make his university a truly meaningful part of the community, much as John Dewey wanted to make the child a part of the larger world. In 1896 Dewey established the Laboratory School at the University. As its name implied, this was a place where faculty tested new ideas about teaching. The principal aim of this experimentation was clearly defined: to integrate the school and the community. At each grade-level the student's perspective was to be widened. At the beginning, this involved the home and the schoolroom. Later, the neighborhood, the city, the nation, and finally the whole world became part of the curriculum. Field trips took students outside the classroom, while such subjects as industrial arts brought the expectations of the larger world into the school.

Dewey, who remained at Chicago until 1904, was not the only educational innovator who wanted to see his graduates better equipped for life. Another unique educational experiment was the Armour Institute of Technology. Its story dated back to 1874 and the founding of the Plymouth Mission. This was an early version of an "institutional church," a congregation which opened its facilities to the neighborhood and provided recreational and educational amenities for the underprivileged. Joseph Armour, of the meat-packing family, had taken a philanthropic interest in the mission, and when he died in 1881 he left it $100,000. A few years later its name was changed to the Armour Mission, and in 1886 it moved to a spacious new building de-

signed by Daniel Burnham and John Wellborn Root. That was only the start. Joseph Armour's brother, Philip, also took an active interest in the endeavor and helped expand its activities. A dynamic minister named Frank Gunsaulus persuaded the family to finance a kindergarten and classes in dressmaking, clay modeling, and cooking for residents of the poor South Side neighborhood. The Armour Flats, a "model tenement," provided 194 apartments.

The most important activity, however, turned out to be the trade school. Gunsaulus had traveled the country in search of ideas. The Armour Mission already held craft classes on weekends, and it would have been easy to extend these to a full-time basis. Several eastern cities already had trade schools that taught craft skills to slum children. But, as plans for an Armour Institute firmed up after 1890, Gunsaulus and Armour decided to make it a technological institute instead, including classes in advanced theory and design. The new institute opened in the fall of 1892 and quickly gained worldwide recognition for its experiments in electricity. Eventually such important engineers as Lee DeForest, "the father of radio," joined its faculty. The school added a department of domestic science and classes in library science—the "only school in the West" to offer this. In 1893, the Armour Institute and the Art Institute jointly opened a new architecture department. The former contributed its faculty expertise to structural techniques; the latter taught the aesthetic side of the subject. For some years there was actually a "Chicago School of Architecture" as an operating academic department!

Although the institute and the mission were separate institutions, they shared the same philanthropic spirit. In an 1894 article, the *Chicago Inter-Ocean* commented, "It is the boast of the school that no one has been turned away because of inability to pay tuition, and hundreds of young men and women are earning their board and clothes while taking courses of instruction." The following year the school's own *Circular of Information* noted:

> It is hoped that its benefits may reach all classes. It is not intended for the poor or rich, as sections of society, but for any and all who are earnestly seeking practical education. Its aim is broadly philanthropic. . . . Armour Institute is not a free school; but its charges for instruction are in harmony with the spirit which animates alike the founder, the trustees, and the faculty; namely, the desire to help those who wish to help themselves.

To accommodate working students, the institute established night classes, and after 1903 a student could obtain a degree in any field it offered by attending the evening school.

Students at the Chicago School of Architecture, 1894. These future architects received training that was an exciting experiment in institutional cooperation.

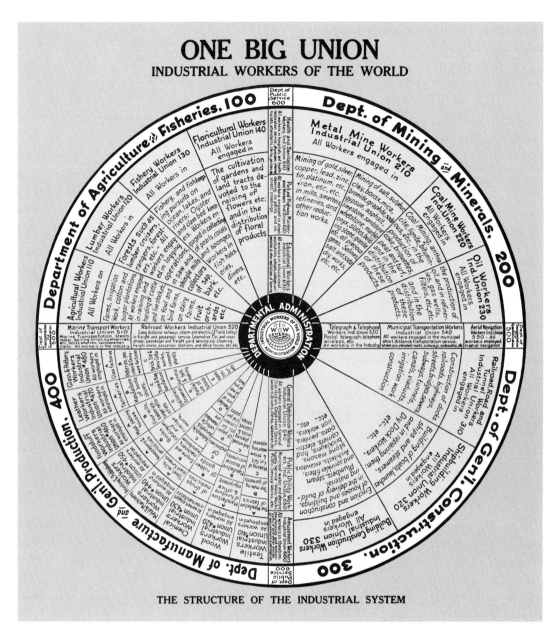

One Big Union, *1924. The I.W.W. published the* One Big Union *as a means of expounding its ideological viewpoint.*

Industrial Workers of the World poster, c1909. This chart illustrates the I.W.W.'s goal, to consolidate representation of every industrial trade in "One Big Union."

Dispersing Reform Ideas to America

Just as Jane Addams became a leader in popularizing the settlement movement, so Chicago became a leader in dispersing social reform movements throughout the Midwest and throughout the country. Chicago's location at the heart of the national railway network made it a place where reform ideas as well as economic goods were exchanged. It was for this reason that Chicago became the home of the Industrial Workers of the World. This organization, founded in June 1905, began as a protest against the "craft unionism" of the American Federation of Labor. The A.F.L. was primarily concerned with organizing workers skilled in the techniques of specific crafts. William D. "Big Bill" Haywood, Eugene Debs, and the other radicals who formed the I.W.W. regarded the A.F.L. as too conservative and too uncritical of the capitalist system. Most important, the radicals wanted to form "One Big Union" to extend the benefits of organization to *all* workers, even those who performed the most menial of tasks.

Although the influence of the I.W.W. was limited and short-lived because of public reaction to its radical rhetoric, it did accomplish something. It popularized the notion that every worker in a given industry, skilled or unskilled, ought to belong to the same union. Many years later this became the basis for the industrial unionism of John L. Lewis's C.I.O.

Ida B. Wells-Barnett (1862-1931). Born a slave in Mississippi, Ida B. Wells-Barnett became a leading advocate of equal rights for blacks and women.
University of Chicago Library

The Reason Why, 1893. Ida B. Wells used pamphlets such as this one (with an introduction in French, German, and English) to inform foreign visitors to the Exposition of racial discrimination in America.
Alfreda M. Barnett Duster

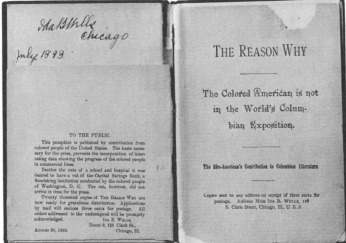

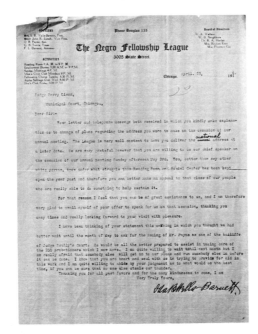

Two reformers correspond, 1914. In this letter Ida B. Wells-Barnett thanked Judge Harry Olson for agreeing to speak before her social group, the Negro Fellowship League. She was the first woman probation officer appointed by Judge Olson.

The labor unions were not alone in discovering the advantages of Chicago's location. For example, Chicago played an important role in the early development of a national civil rights movement. During the Columbian Exposition a group of blacks became concerned about the absence of exhibits indicating the contributions of non-whites to American development. Their leader was Ida B. Wells, a former Memphis teacher who had migrated to Chicago a few years earlier. Along with her future husband, newspaper publisher Ferdinand Barnett, and others, she launched a nationwide campaign to correct this shortcoming. As a result, blacks were granted a special "Colored Americans Day." They were also assured that there would be no discrimination in the use of public facilities.

Though scarcely a major victory, this did suggest that a protest launched in Chicago could readily become national in scope. That, indeed, was the key to the success of a young black man who arrived in Chicago in 1897, Robert S. Abbott. Born on an island off the coast of Georgia, the son of ex-slaves, Abbott had spent most of his childhood in Savannah and had attended Hampton Institute, where he mastered the printer's trade. He became one of the pioneers in what would later become a massive black migration to northern cities. In Chicago he attended Kent College of Law, graduating in 1899. Friends convinced him, however, that his skin was too dark for him to succeed as an attorney, so he went to work in a printing plant.

Early in 1905 Abbott decided to go into business for himself. With a total capital of twenty-five cents, he founded a newspaper called the *Defender.* It seemed rather certain to fail. There were already three black newspapers in Chicago, which had, at that time, only 40,000 black residents. The young publisher wisely realized, however, that the railroads linking Chicago with all parts of the South provided an excellent overnight delivery service. Moreover, he and his assistant contacted black ministers throughout the country to learn the names of reliable sales representatives. As a result, national circulation increased dramatically, reaching 230,000 by 1920. Since there were no substantial black magazines at that time, the *Defender* became one of the few means by which black businessmen could reach out to national markets.

Abbott's publication had a forceful editorial policy. He applauded achievements by blacks and lauded "race heroes" such as Dr. Daniel Hale Williams, who had performed the first open-heart surgery. Abbott also demanded an end to discrimination, representation on urban police forces, jobs in public transit, equal access to trade unions, and a black in the President's cabinet. He described life in the North in glowing terms, and urged blacks to migrate to freedom. People all over the South read or heard about the opportunities in Chicago. Carl Sandburg, then working for the *Chicago Daily News,* said that Abbott's *Defender* was responsible for guiding a large proportion of the World War I migration toward Chicago. "A colored man," the poet wrote, "caught with a copy in his possession was suspected of 'Northern Fever' and other so-called disloyalties."

Chicago and Reform

Robert S. Abbott (1870-1940). The son of ex-slaves, Abbott founded one of America's leading newspapers. His editorials attacked the accommodationist pleas of Booker T. Washington.
Chicago Defender

Roscoe Conkling Simmons (1878-1951). A famed Republican orator, Simmons became the Defender's *best-known writer, and made many publicity trips throughout the United States to boost circulation.*
Tribune Company Archives

During the last years of the nineteenth century Chicago was a curiosity among the world's cities. In little more than a generation it had developed from a mudhole to a metropolis. It had produced America's most innovative architecture, the dazzling Columbian Exposition, and an extensive commercial-industrial base. Yet Chicago had also produced corrupt politics, crime, and squalor as bad as in any other city in the country. It was out of this atmosphere of contrast that reform emerged. In part, this was a matter of accident. Jane Addams, Francis Parker, and Louise deKoven Bowen might have gone to New York instead of Chicago. Yet it was also the response to an obvious need. Reform in Chicago had to overcome many fundamental obstacles. A city with so many diverse cultures in its slums required an effort that was both ingenious and Herculean.

The reforms begun or nurtured in Chicago influenced the whole nation. The spectacular growth of the city, and the Exposition, attracted visitors from everywhere. When they sought out the good people among the bad, they found Jane Addams and a great many others. Chicago's national influence was also helped along by the willingness of people such as Addams, Bowen, Parker, and Harper to write, to travel, and to lecture about their work. In the meantime, the city's situation as the railway hub of the nation facilitated disseminating the ideas of quiet, unassuming people like Robert Abbott, or unpopular causes like the I.W.W. An extraordinary capability for bringing new ideas to large audiences was the essence of creative Chicago.

The Chicago Defender, 1905. Though by no means the first black newspaper in Chicago, Robert S. Abbott's Defender *became the most influential.*

Chicago tenement-dwellers, c1912.

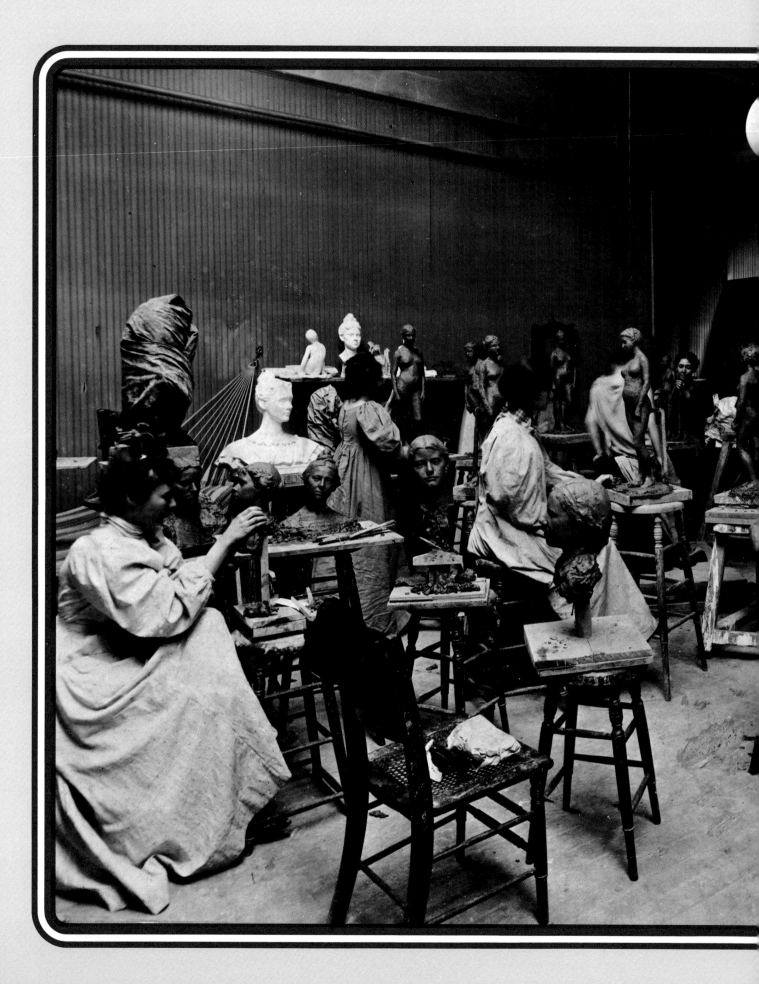

Culture: Expanding the Audience

The term *city* has many definitions. It is an area within specific boundaries, a governmental unit, and an assemblage of economic activities. It may simply be an agglomeration of population that has reached a certain size. It may be a self-defined unit, such as an incorporated area, or it may be defined by outsiders such as the Census Bureau. A city may be all of these things, but it is also a state of mind, an intellectual and cultural congress, and an interchange of ideas. In this role a city both preserves traditions and destroys them.

The story of the arts in Chicago illustrates an important principle underlying the cultural role of cities. This is the way in which a minority of its population interested in the fine arts joined together to create something that could be enjoyed by the majority. In the nineteenth century, connoisseurs of art and music were nearly helpless when scattered about the countryside. They might purchase reproductions of famous paintings and some recorded music, but could not enjoy these things first-hand. Brought together by a common experience known as Chicago, they created art museums and a fine orchestra. In typical Chicago fashion these institutions were designed to reach out to all the city's people. Art in Chicago was a matter of cultural involvement, an almost evangelistic zeal to make creativity a part of everyday life.

Art Institute sculpturing class, c1918. Art Institute classes were taught by such notables as George Bellows.

The Art Institute of Chicago, logotype,
c1890. From its inception the Art
Institute has preserved great works,
taught and evaluated contemporary
art, and provided studios for artists.

Bringing Art to the People

Chicago was not a major art center during the mid-nineteenth century, far from it. It did not have one professional artist until G.P.A. Healy, a portrait painter, arrived in 1855, or an art dealer until 1856. Its first resident sculptor, Leonard Volk, arrived in 1857. By the late 1850s the city had attracted enough people with sufficient wealth and leisure time to excite some interest in the arts. In 1859 Chicagoans hosted their first major exhibition of paintings from abroad. During the next few years many aspiring young portrait and landscape artists moved into the prairie town. By 1866 they had created their first association, the Chicago Academy of Design, and later that same year they staged their first exhibition.

Many of these artists painted portraits of the city's wealthy business elite, and, by so doing, they attracted considerable financial support for their fledgling association. Soon the Academy was able to afford a substantial marble-front building on Adams Street and begin publishing the *Chicago Art Journal*, the first of its kind in the Midwest. The directors wanted classes and lectures opened to a large audience, and membership made available inexpensively. This established a pattern in the history of Chicago's art institutions: success was measured as much by the size of membership rolls and attendance as by the quality of the actual collection.

The Academy, however, did not survive the Great Fire and the depression of the 1870s that shattered so many Chicago fortunes. It was not until 1879 that a replacement appeared. During the interval, the Interstate Exposition (an optimistic display to the world that Chicago would rebuild)

functioned as the city's major art center. When the new Chicago Academy of Fine Arts did appear, it was, as the first one had been, heavily supported by wealthy patrons who held strong views favoring a broad membership. In 1882 the trustees changed the name to the Art Institute of Chicago. By then it was already developing a distinctive identity and a national reputation.

During its early years the Institute faced several crucial decisions. One was the matter of location. Many civic leaders thought it ought to relocate in Jackson Park, near the fashionable suburb of Hyde Park. But the trustees felt that it should remain centrally located and therefore accessible to a larger number of Chicagoans. Then there was the matter of membership fees and privileges. The trustees chose to have a large membership paying low fees rather than a small membership paying high fees. Governing members paid $25 a year; regular members paid only $10. While even this was far beyond the means of the tenement-dweller, the Institute did attract many middle-class members. The general exhibits were, of course, open to all, but the advantages of membership were several. Members could use a growing art library and attend special lectures and openings. These affairs were not just small gatherings of Chicago's elite; the art reporter for the *Tribune* captured the spirit of one opening:

> Over 1,500 persons last night showed that they were more interested in good pictures, or at any rate of some sort, than in preserving their health; the way they showed it was by crowding the rooms of the institute as no one has ever seen them crowded before. . . . It wasn't a society gathering; people came dressed just as their independence and the bad weather and whose good sense suggested. . . . It was pleasant to see a young man whose hair made the young man look as if he had left the shop before the barber was through, who had mud on his boots and wore no cuffs, glaring at a Hobbema landscape.

Chicago's cultural center, Michigan Avenue, 1890. The buildings left to right are: the Auditorium, the Studebaker Wagon Company which became the Fine Arts Building, the Chicago Musical College, and the Art Institute. The Auditorium and Fine Arts Building still stand.

Democratic policies also governed the Institute's school. Its predecessor, the Academy of Design, had established one of the first museum-based art schools in America, but now the Art Institute invited the general public to attend classes. The trustees added evening classes and more instructors to handle a growing daytime enrollment. As art critic Lucy Monroe described it, "Drawn from all classes, the pupils spread about them an interest in art which leavens the lump of materialism." In addition, free Saturday classes for children made it possible for teachers to discover talented youngsters and encourage them to enroll in the school as regular students. Indeed, the Institute adopted a policy of cultivating talent wherever found. In November 1895 the director, W.M.R. French, received a letter which read: "Respected Sir: I hereby inform you that we have a carving club called the Michael Angelo Club. A number of people have seen our work and think it good. We would like to consider that it would go to the Art Institute, Respectfully yours, Fred Aulich, pres." French was so impressed that he gave the club exhibition space. The *Inter-Ocean* suggested that this was not quite the work of a salon. It reported that "the Michael Angelo Club of five Jewish boys is giving an exhibition at the Art Institute. . . . It consists of carvings in hard plaster. . . . The boys are from twelve to thirteen years old and have never had a teacher. They are ragged little urchins who meet in a small dark kitchen four or five nights a week."

The Institute school was popular not only for the quality of its instructors, but also for the practical appeal of its curriculum. Trade-school subjects such as lithography, wood-carving, and stained-glass work were mixed with classes in sculpture and painting. A writer for *Harper's Weekly* noted that, "The Art Institute school breaks ground in classes for instruction in the art of illustrating magazines, newspapers, books, and advertising, in pen and ink and wash. I confess this shocked my sense of dignity of such a school. . . . Maybe no harm will come." The Institute also established a cooperative program with the Armour Institute of Technology, the "Chicago School of Architecture."

The school attracted large numbers of students, in part because it was willing to cooperate with other institutions in bringing art to young children. In 1894 a group of settlement house workers and school reformers founded the Public School Art Society. Its purpose was to "obtain and to place works of art in and about the schools of the city and to assist in the education and development in art of the children of the Schools." The society bought cheap reproductions by the hundreds and distributed them throughout the city. The Art Institute collaborated in this venture by helping obtain the pictures and by providing a model school room.

The purpose of all this was to familiarize the people of Chicago with art, and to enliven their interest in the Institute. The plan succeeded beyond all expectations. Soon the new downtown building, initially erected for the Columbian Exposition, was filled to capacity. The Institute quickly became one of the most popular institutions of its kind in the country, a popularity that continues today. Membership and attendance ran only slightly behind that of the Metropolitan Museum in New York. In Chicago, the success of an institution was measured by its utility to the general public. By this standard, the Art Institute was a resounding success. That success fostered a search for even more inventive ways to make the arts an important and useful part of everyday life.

The Municipal Art League was founded at a meeting in the studio of Ralph Clarkson in 1899, and officially chartered the following year. It was a confederation of nearly sixty local art clubs, plus numerous individuals; within a few years it had over 15,000 members. The board of directors included painters, sculptors, architects, laymen, and representatives of the city's three divisional park districts. Its membership included businessmen, settlement house residents, and writers, as well as architects and artists.

Soon after its founding the League merged with the Art Association of Chicago, and initiated an annual exhibition of local artists, using the profits to purchase outstanding paintings and sculpture. This collection, known as the Municipal Art Gallery, at one time or another was displayed at the Art Institute, the City Club, the University of Chicago library, and a community service building in Eckhart Park. The League also took the Gallery to the Municipal (now Navy) Pier for summer exhibitions. As one annual report noted, Chicago was "the first city in this country to hang a collection of valuable paintings in a great public recreation center such as this."

The initial and principal purpose of the Art Association, however, had been to beautify the public environment of Chicago. Only a few weeks after its formal organization it was asked to advise the city on the design of bridges. Under the direction of Franklin McVeagh, a wealthy wholesale grocer and civic reformer, the League began a program to rid Chicago's air of smoke. Back in 1874 Chicago had be-

Benjamin F. Ferguson (1839-1905). A prosperous Chicago lumberman, Ferguson bequeathed one million dollars to commission monumental art for Chicago's public spaces.

Eugene Field Memorial by Edward McCartan, 1922. This Ferguson Fund statue still stands in Lincoln Park. Well known for his barbed humor, Field also wrote children's poetry including "Wynken, Blynken and Nod" and "Little Boy Blue."
Staples & Charles

Sculptured plaque, Marquette Building, 1894. This relief by Herman A. MacNeil depicts the arrival of Marquette and Joliet in 1673.

come the first American city to enact an anti-smoke law, but this ordinance had since fallen into disuse. A wave of concern about the city's appearance that preceded the Columbian Exposition aroused some interest in smoke abatement, but during the depression of the 1890s Chicagoans preferred the smoking chimney of prosperity to a clean sky. During the anthracite strike of 1901-2, which forced everyone to burn bituminous coal, Chicago's sky sometimes became so dark that the streetlights were turned on at noon. That crisis drew the new Municipal Art League directly into the reform efforts. In 1903 it joined with other groups and persuaded the City Council to establish a boiler inspection department. Finally, in 1907, the Council did set up a Department of Smoke Abatement, appointing engineers as inspectors.

The League's purpose, "to promote in every practical way the beautifying of the Streets, Public Buildings, and places of Chicago," also entailed a vigorous attack against billboards. Although legally placed on private property, these were a visual pollutant, always situated so as to attract the attention of the largest number of people. A local paper even ran a cartoon depicting the "Billboard Man's Dream," an enormous sign that spanned the roofs of the Auditorium, the Academy of Fine Arts, and the Chicago Club. A rube stood gazing skyward at its message. In 1907 the League's relentless publicity campaign finally shamed the Council into enacting an ordinance that restricted the size of billboards and stipulated that they be made of non-combustible material. A more restrictive law enacted four years later was successfully defended before the U.S. Supreme Court. In 1923, a sixteen-year crusade for zoning legislation finally achieved its goal. Principally, this aimed at beautifying the city's public places by confining signboards and ugly factories within certain restricted districts.

The League saw its role as more than that of a policeman. Many of its members had traveled widely in Europe and sought to imbue Chicagoans with the continental notion of public areas as places of grandeur. It established a "Lake Front Committee" to promote formal plantings and monuments along the shoreline. It also helped establish a Municipal Museum in the Public Library building. Models and dioramas showed how other cities had approached municipal improvements, and League members presented lectures on beautification. The League also cooperated with the city's numerous neighborhood improvement associations in promoting parks, fountains, and boulevards.

At about the same time the League began its work, Chicagoans started to realize that their city had few statues in its public parks. Indeed, foreign visitors to the Columbian Exposition had commented on the relative plainness of the city's public places, and the Municipal Art League had begun a campaign to erect more monuments. Then, in 1906, Chicagoans received a unique gift from Benjamin F. Ferguson, who had been prominent in the lumber trade, once one of the city's most important industries. When he died, Ferguson left an estate in excess of $3,000,000, a third of which he willed as a special fund to be administered by the trustees of the Art Institute. The interest, about $30,000 a year, was to be used to erect monumental statuary, public art for the enjoyment and edification of the masses.

Lorado Taft and Public Art

Chicago's leading proponent of municipal art, Lorado Taft, was most influential in determining how the Ferguson Fund was spent. Born in suburban Elmwood Park in 1860, Taft had grown up near the campus of the University of Illinois in Urbana, where his father was a professor and where he himself graduated in 1880. He subsequently went to Paris to attend the École des Beaux Arts, along with many other American artists of the day. When he returned a few years later, he became an instructor at the Art Institute, where he continued to teach until 1907. His first major design project was "The Sleep of the Flowers" and "The Awakening of the Flowers," a pair of giant statues that flanked the entrance to Horticultural Hall at the Columbian Exposition. At about this time he assumed a lectureship in the extension division of the new University of Chicago, a job he kept for ten years, until 1902. His lectures included American art history. During this period he was writing his *History of American Sculpture,* which was published in 1903 and remained the standard book on the subject for many years.

Over the years Taft had several studios. One was at "Eagle's Nest," a summertime artists' colony at a camp on a high bluff overlooking the Rock River at Oregon, Illinois. A second was at Edison Park, likewise a small artists' colony, while yet a third studio was located in the Fine Arts Building. Finally, there was the Midway Studio at the University of Chicago. Here, he assembled a group of bright young students who assisted him while learning the craft themselves.

Taft produced many important works including "The Blind" (1908), his first statue completed with support from the Ferguson Fund. His largest project, however, was to be for the Midway Plaissance. This narrow strip of land, slightly less than a mile long, served as the Midway for the Columbian Exposition and also linked Jackson Park with Washington Park. Soon after the tawdry attractions of 1893 were dismantled, it was deeded to the University of Chicago. The original post-Fair plans, drawn up by Frederick Law Olmsted, called for a small lagoon extending for part of its length, but the South Park Commissioners subsequently hired Taft to devise a new plan. His proposal called for one of the most ambitious public art projects ever undertaken in Chicago. It included a boat canal running the full length of the strip. Along parallel boulevards there would be as many as forty bronze statues of important figures in world civilization. At either end of the Midway would be a giant sculptured marble fountain over half a block long. One, the "Fountain of Creation," depicted the evolution of mankind, using thirty-six giant figures. It was to stand at the east end, near the Illinois Central Railroad embankment. The other, the "Fountain of Time," depicted the cycle of human life by means of a progression of figures passing in review before Father Time.

Aside from producing great works of his own, Taft was noted for discovering and training talented sculptors. He found one pupil, Charles Mulligan, toiling in a suburban lapidary works. Another, Leonard Crunelle, was a French-born coal miner living in Decatur whose hobby was

Just a word of praise from a worse artist.

Your Solitude of Soul. Beautiful. The simplicity — art. I keep coming back to it.

Best wishes

Chas. Chaplin

Charlie Chaplin compliments Lorado Taft, 1925. Chaplin was so fascinated by Taft's "The Solitude of the Soul" that he asked a friend to pass on this note.

carving chunks of coal into statues. He purchased Crunelle's "Squirrel Boy" for the Municipal Art Gallery. Crunelle, who later became famous as a sculptor of children, belonged to what one art journal dubbed "The Western School of Sculptors." This school also included Nellie Walker and Miss Clyde Chandler of Dallas. These sculptors were distinguished by their realistic depiction of everyday people facing the common problems of life, something that seemed uniquely fresh and "Western."

Taft set high standards, and was not reticent about criticizing the work of others. He believed that Louis Rebisso's equestrian statue of Grant was a work characterized by "complete absence of artistic distinction." Other works he thought were poorly situated. In a descriptive article on the statues of Lincoln Park he asked:

> Why are they here? The one spot on the North Side where one hopes to find a glimpse of nature, the joy of flowers and trees, is encumbered with metal coats and trousers. Every eligible site and vista culminates in something which you do not wish to see. The impulse to erect memorials is worthy and indeed irrepressible, but why not put the formal bronzes in formal places, along avenues and against buildings—anywhere but here where greensward and sky-line are so infinitely precious?

More than anything else Taft wanted to bring art to the people. In 1894 he and novelist Hamlin Garland formed the Central Art Association. Many small Midwestern communities had tried to form art appreciation associations, but these efforts had generally failed for want of art expertise and access to great works. The Central Art Association tried to help this situation by providing Chautauqua-like lectures and traveling exhibitions. Often these had to be held in rather unsuitable places: an empty hotel or an abandoned storefront. Nevertheless, any town that had an art club with a least thirty members was eligible to rent a traveling exhibit, along with a speaker for one evening. In addition, the Association maintained a "bureau of criticism" to help aspiring artists evaluate their own work. The bureau selected superior works for display in Chicago or on tour, thus giving newcomers valuable exposure and at least a regional reputation.

Lorado Taft and Fountain of Creation model, 1910. Taft envisioned this fountain standing at the east end of the Midway.

Theodore Thomas (1835-1905). Often called "America's Musical Missionary," Thomas toured the country promoting the idea of municipal symphony orchestras.

Theodore Thomas and the Chicago Symphony, Auditorium Theater, c1899. Despite the near-perfect acoustics of the Auditorium, Thomas disliked the place and continuously tinkered with the sound of his orchestra, changing seating arrangements and employing various kinds of resonant stage backgrounds.
Chicago Symphony Orchestra

The Orchestra and the People

Chicago's sculptors and painters were not the only artists who used their talents to reach out to the people. A similar tradition developed in the city's musical heritage. This story also begins in the mid-nineteenth century. Chicago's classical musicians faced a difficult problem: the public mainly enjoyed beer-garden music, and, as a result, orchestral work was usually poorly received. Yet, Chicagoans who appreciated serious music still had hope. In an attempt to uplift the public taste they invited a bright young conductor named Theodore Thomas to conduct a series of concerts.

Thomas had been born in Germany in 1835. He came to America with his family when he was ten. His father was a music teacher, and Thomas quickly became his most talented pupil. After establishing a reputation in New York, he elected to form a traveling orchestra and become what he called a "musical missionary," bringing music to the masses. He and his musicians covered thousands of miles, playing dozens of small cities. In 1869 the Chicago music critic George P. Upton, having heard of Thomas's achievements as a violin virtuoso and his New York chamber music concerts, induced him to bring his orchestra to perform in Chicago.

Thomas played in Chicago for the next nineteen years. There were several special engagements, often with the Apollo Music Club, a large mixed chorus. The most popu-lar of these was a series of "Summer-Night" concerts in an auditorium inside the Interstate Exposition Building, a series started in 1877 and continued for several years. By the late 1880s the *Tribune* was expressing hope that funds could be found so that Thomas might lead a permanent orchestra in Chicago. But none were forthcoming, so, to make a living, Thomas continued his road tours. The outlook seemed bleak, when, one day in 1891, Thomas encountered Chicagoan Charles N. Fay on a New York street. The conductor revealed that he was nearly bankrupt and that the traveling concerts were ruining his health. Fay, a utilities magnate, returned to Chicago and approached several of the city's leading businessmen. He reminded them that the Columbian Exposition would open in less than two years, and that Chicagoans would be embarrassed if it were revealed to the world that they had no permanent orchestra. Finally, George Pullman, Marshall Field, Philip D. Armour, Cyrus Hall McCormick, and others provided the financial backing that was needed and the Orchestral Association was born with Thomas as its conductor.

The Association had many problems at first. Thomas was a hard taskmaster and demanded complete control of the orchestra. He was criticized by the local press because so many of his musicians were imported from New York, but he explained that the lack of a classical music tradition in Chicago had stunted the growth of local talent. Finally, there was the problem of the Auditorium. Although Dankmar Adler's design had made it acoustically perfect, it was too large for a fledgling orchestra. The ample seating meant that few people bothered to purchase season tickets,

The Chicago Symphony Orchestra

FREDERICK STOCK, Conductor
ERIC DeLAMARTER, Assistant Conductor

90 Musicians   WILL GIVE   **90** Musicians

FIVE
POPULAR CONCERTS

——AT——

International Amphitheater
FORTY-THIRD and HALSTED STREETS
UNION STOCK YARDS
——AT A——

Popular Price **50c**

THE DATES
MONDAY EVENINGS at 8:15
NOVEMBER 16—December 28—
January 18—February 15—March 15

HEAR CHICAGO'S GREAT ORCHESTRA IN YOUR OWN NEIGHBORHOOD AND AMID UNUSUAL SURROUNDINGS.

For thirty-four years the Chicago Symphony Orchestra has been known the world over as one without a peer. Its conductor, Frederick Stock, is famed in musical circles everywhere as one of the greatest conductors time has known, and as a musician of unexcelled knowledge and understanding and ability. To come under his spell at the Popular Concerts is to experience a joy in music seldom attained. Northwestern University, the University of Michigan and the University of Chicago have each given public recognition of their regard for his talents by conferring upon him the degree of Doctor of Music; and on October 16th of this year the Government of France honored his genius by bestowing upon him the grand cross of the Legion of Honor.

Program for the First Concert
Monday Evening, November 16, at 8:15

Overture, "Carnival," . . . . DVOŘÁK

Andante from Symphony No. 5, ... BEETHOVEN

Suite, "Peer Gynt," No. 1, ... GRIEG
    Morning.
    Aase's Death.
    Anitra's Dance.
    The Hall of the Mountain King.

Hungarian Rhapsody No. 2, ... LISZT

INTERMISSION

Selections from Ballet Suite "Feramors," . . RUBINSTEIN
    Dance of the Bayaderes.
    Torch Dance of the Brides of Kashmire.
    Wedding Procession.

Scène Religieuse, ... MASSENET
    (Violoncello obbligato by Alfred Wallenstein)

The Year 1812, ... TSCHAIKOWSKY

TICKETS NOW ON SALE AT
Stock Yards National Bank......4150 S. Halsted St.
Becker Ryan & Co.........6245 S. Halsted St., cor. 63d.
Chicago Daily Drovers Journal....836 Exchange Av.
Chas. E. Ross' Drug Store........800 E. 63d St., cor. Cottage Grove Av.
Park Pharmacy.........6901 Wentworth Av.
A. C. Williams' Drug Store........1603 W. 63d St.
J. F. Thome's Drug Store........6301 S. Western Av.
B. J. Glidewell's Drug Store........3183 W. 63d St., cor. Kedzie Av.
Rutzon's Pharmacy.........5900 Wentworth Av.
Paul M. Kepner's Drug Store......500 W. 59th St., cor. Normal Blvd.
Herman A. Yates' Drug Store......5859 S. Ashland Av., cor 59th St.
Geo. C. Goeppner's Drug Store......5901 S. Kedzie Av.
Kidder and Lewis' Drug Store......5058 Cottage Grove Av., cor. 51st St.
Tischart and Fortier's Drug Store 5058 S. Halsted St., cor. 51st St.
Mrazek Bros.' Drug Store......5058 S. Ashland Ave., cor. 51st St.
John A. Roska's Drug Store......5058 S. Western Av., cor. 51st St.
Ortenstein's Drug Store......4701 Cottage Grove Av.
Gans Bros.' Drug Store......4658 S. Ashland Ave., cor. 47th St.
Lawrence Blahnik's Drug Store....4701 S. Robey St.
Aldona Drug Store.........4700 S. Western Av.
Wm. F. Stulpin's Drug Store......3459 S. Halsted St., cor. 35th St.
Jos. J. Shine's Drug Store......3501 S. Western Av.
Jas. P. Crowley's Drug Store......800 W. 31st St., cor. Halsted St.

Tickets 50c

For the convenience of those who *know* the Popular Concerts, and will want to assure themselves of admission to all five performances, season tickets are offered. Price, $2.50. The boxes (seating six) are reserved. They may be purchased at the Stock Yards National Bank. Price $6.00 per concert, or $30.00 for the season. No tax.

PRESS OF FAULKNER-RYAN CO.   (OVER)

since they could virtually be assured of a seat at any given concert. This placed the orchestra at the mercy of the weather and prevented long-range planning. It did, however, reinforce one of Thomas's strongest beliefs: that the orchestra would have to develop a broad appeal in order to survive.

The energetic conductor continued to think of himself as a musical missionary. As music director for the World's Columbian Exposition, he had the opportunity to perform a wide variety of innovative music, much of which he added to his local programs. Although the Chicago press sometimes complained that his music was "too foreign," he gradually educated his audiences to accept the works of unfamiliar composers. It was Thomas who had introduced Americans to the works of Wagner and Strauss and who first brought the brilliant Polish pianist Ignace Paderewski to perform in this country. He was careful, however, to remain in touch with his audiences. He played occasional request concerts and talked frequently with members of the Orchestral Association to determine how far his listeners' taste had progressed toward a full appreciation of classical music.

Thomas was aware that few slum-dwellers had any opportunity to enjoy fine music. And so, in January 1893, he inaugurated a series of "Workingmen's" or "People's Concerts." Admission ranged from a dime to a quarter for the best seats in the house. Over 4,000 citizens, most from very humble backgrounds, packed the Auditorium. Louis Sullivan's dream had been to fill the place with as many seats as possible, thereby bringing the performing arts to large crowds; these concerts fulfilled that dream. The *Tribune* noted that:

> The audience last night left not a vacant place in boxes, parquet and balcony. A more appreciative audience company of listeners the great Conductor and his men may have had, but certainly none that ever followed their work more closely or evinced a keener desire to understand and appreciate their work.

Thomas, sadly, lived through only thirteen seasons; he never saw the completion of the new hall he had so wanted. The Symphony played its inaugural concert in Orchestra Hall while it was still under construction. Paint fumes and the damp coldness of wet plaster hung heavily in the air on opening night, December 14, 1904. Thomas, already exhausted by the preparations, came down with pneumonia and died the following January 4. His successor for the next thirty-seven years, Frederick Stock, continued some of Thomas's policies. In 1914 another group, the Civic Music Association, enlarged the popular audience. With the aid of the Chicago Woman's Club, the Association staged dozens of popular concerts. In all parts of the city, including the worst tenement districts, music filled the air. The Symphony played in parks, field houses, schools, and almost any place that could accommodate a crowd. This helped perpetuate an important Chicago cultural tradition: bringing music to the people.

Chicago Symphony Orchestra handbill, 1925. Theodore Thomas's idea of workingmen's concerts survived for decades. This handbill advertises concerts for Packingtown.

Selig Polyscope Company studios, 1911. Although Chicago producers helped perfect artificial lighting, sunlight was still important to moviemaking. In this photo, Selig's first studio, built in 1907, is on the left; a 1911 addition is on the right. Academy of Motion Picture Arts and Sciences

"Bronco Billy" Anderson in an early Western, c1907. Spoor's partner at Essanay, Anderson was also a cowboy actor. This scene was being shot indoors under floodlamps.

Chicago and the Movies

While the Symphony appealed to a growing audience of music-lovers, Chicagoans were helping another cultural medium out of its infancy. The invention of the motion picture was an almost unheralded event of the 1880s. In 1885 George Eastman and a New Jersey minister named Hannibal Goodwin discovered that a photographic emulsion could be affixed to a flexible celluloid film. Other inventors had discovered that the rapid movement of still images through a lighted lens would produce a moving picture. It took the genius of Thomas Edison, however, to produce a workable machine. In 1889, he developed a Kinetoscope. This was a peep-show cabinet employing a continuous fifty-foot film that passed in front of the viewer as it wound through a complicated series of loops and pulleys. In 1893 Edison proudly displayed it to the world at the Columbian Exposition.

The Kinetoscope inspired a pair of young Chicagoans to begin their own experiments. George K. Spoor was a native of Highland Park. After finishing grammar school he began selling newspapers and eventually purchased his own newsstand and restaurant in the old Northwestern Station on Wells Street. After marrying in 1892 he needed additional income, so he took over the managership of the Waukegan Opera House. The next year he accidently happened upon an Edison Kinetoscope in a Loop amusement parlor. This device fascinated him so much that he pur-

chased one himself and began making plans to improve and mass-produce it. Spoor realized that the major problem with the Kinetoscope was that only one person could view it at a time. He decided that the obvious solution was to project the images on a screen. By 1894 Spoor had discovered that a calcium lamp threw enough light through a lens to illuminate an image on the wall. Almost simultaneously a Frenchman named Lumière worked out the same process. Spoor immediately began selling his "Kinodrome" machines to vaudeville theaters throughout the country, and started his own company, the National Film Renting Company, to supply them with pictures.

Spoor was not the only Chicagoan to discover the possibilities of the moving picture projector. William N. Selig had been born in the city in 1864, and after grade school had moved to California for his health. At the age of thirty he had become a magician, going on the road with a minstrel show. Selig saw his first Kinetoscope in 1895. He thought he could improve its design by applying his knowledge of the "magic lantern" to create projected motion pictures. Returning to Chicago, he opened a photographic studio to support himself, and began experimenting. He found drawings of the Lumière projector, and after some modification of the plans, he began producing projectors himself. He ascertained that a reversed version of the projection mechanism was a camera. By the end of 1896 he was selling not only the "Selig Standard Camera" and the projector, the "Selig Polyscope," but he had gone a step further, making commercial films himself and distributing them to vaudeville houses.

Essanay News

Published in the interest of Exhibitors and all Newspapers which use News of Photoplays and Players. Permission to reprint any Story or Photograph appearing herein is granted. By Publicity Department, 1333 Argyle Street, Chicago, Illinois.

Trademark Reg. U. S. Pat. 1907

Vol. VI. "FIRST TO STANDARDIZE PHOTOPLAYS" CHICAGO, JANUARY 2, 1915 "FIRST TO STANDARDIZE PHOTOPLAYS" No. 1

CHARLES CHAPLIN JOINS ESSANAY

EXHIBITORS CALL FOR BUSHMAN IN DRAMA

Essanay Player's Popularity in 'Dear Old Girl' Brings Demand for Reissue of College Play

'Surgeon Warren's Ward' Contains a Thrilling Plot of Love and Intrigue in Army Life

"DEAR OLD GIRL"
(In two acts)
CAST OF CHARACTERS

Ted Warren	FRANCIS X. BUSHMAN
Dora Allen	Beverly Bayne
John Allen	Frank Dayton
Mrs. Allen	Helen Dunbar

The Essanay photoplay, "Dear Old Girl," is a touching romance of college life with its setting at Cornell University. This drama is being reissued by Essanay because of the immense popularity it gained on its first appearance and because of the great demand from exhibitors for its reappearance on the screen.

The great success scored by Francis X. Bushman in this play brought hundreds of requests from exhibitors to have it reissued. Photoplay house managers by the scores wrote that Mr. Bushman's acting in this play was unexcelled and that the demand of their patrons was so great to see Mr. Bushman in this drama that they urged its reissuance.

The plot centers about Ted Warren, a student, who has planned to marry Dora Allen at his fraternity house, on the day of his graduation. While Warren is passing through the campus, on his wedding day, to meet his fiancee at the station, the university chimes ring out the melody of "Dear Old Girl." A few minutes later Warren receives a telegram that the train on which his sweetheart was to have arrived was wrecked and she was killed.

His mind is unbalanced by the shock and each day when the chimes ring he insists on going to the station to meet his sweetheart. When day after day she fails to arrive his spirit is broken and he is ordered to bed. There he is cared for by a faithful old servant.

One day, however, he eludes the servant and rushes to the railroad station and then up the tracks to meet the train. The servant arouses Ted's friends and they go in search of him. They find him in a ditch beside the tracks where he has been hurled by the train. He is carried to the fraternity house, dying. As his life ebbs away the spirit of his bride comes to him in a vision to welcome him to another life.

Released Friday, January 15.

"SURGEON WARREN'S WARD"
By JAMES OPPENHEIM
(In two acts)
CAST OF CHARACTERS

Alice Barth	Ruth Stonehouse
Army Surgeon Warren	Richard C. Travers
Captain Gordon	Bryant Washburn

"Surgeon Warren's Ward" is an Essanay photoplay of army life, with scenes at a military post and in the forests of the great Northwest. Army Surgeon Warren is in love with his ward, Alice Barth, but has a rival in Captain Gordon. The captain proposes to her but is refused. She loves Warren, and when he asks her to become his wife, accepts.

Their betrothal is announced at a military ball. Gordon is jealous of his successful rival and bribes a girl of the underworld to go to the ball and charge Warren with betraying her. Despite Warren's denial, the girl's story is believed. He is court-martialed and dismissed from the service. He goes to a lumber camp in the Northwest.

Gordon woos and finally weds Alice. But the sweetheart of the girl of the underworld is jealous of Gordon. He accuses her of perfidy. She repents of her action and the two go to the army headquarters where the girl confesses. An investigation is started. Gordon, fearing disgrace, deserts, taking his wife with him. He tells her he has a leave of absence and they are going on their honeymoon.

They wander from place to place, Gordon seeking to escape arrest as a deserter, until their money is gone. Finally they reach the forests where Warren is working. Gordon, facing starvation, steals from the lumber camp. He is caught, and shot and wounded. Warren then saves the captain from the wrath of the lumbermen. He asks about Miss Barth and Gordon tells him she is dead.

Warren is suspicious and trails Gordon to the shack where he finds Alice nearly dead from starvation and the hardships she had undergone. A messenger from the army post arrives and tells of Gordon's perfidy and Warren's reinstatement. Gordon sees he is trapped and ends his life. Alice never really had ceased to love Warren and gladly goes back to the post with him.

Released Friday, January 8.

"BRONCHO BILLY'S MOTHER," released by Essanay, is an exceptionally well constructed play in that the picture is vivid and completely self-explanatory without a single sub-title in the entire reel.

ANDERSON IN NEW MYSTERY PLAY

'WHEN LOVE AND HONOR CALLED'

FRONTIER LIFE IS PORTRAYED

MR. G. M. ANDERSON and MISS MARGUERITE CLAYTON, in a scene from "When Love and Honor Called."

Thrilling Drama Is Produced In Conjunction With The Ladies' World

"When Love and Honor Called" is a thrilling drama of frontier life, full of dramatic action and with a beautiful underlying love plot.

It is the fifth Essanay complete prize mystery play, produced in conjunction with The Ladies' World. The complete story will appear in the February issue of the magazine with the exception of one paragraph. Large prizes are being offered by the magazine for the best written lost paragraph. The 5,000,000 readers will look for the Essanay play, the only place the missing part of the story can be found, to solve the mystery.

This is one of G. M. Anderson's best productions. As Broncho Billy, he goes on a secret mission to a small Arizona town, where he meets a beautiful girl, Elizabeth Barton, the fiancee of Juan Martin, of the Bar-O ranch. Broncho is given a job by the foreman, George Chisholm.

At a dance Martin and another cowpuncher quarrel. Martin draws his revolver but Broncho takes it away from him.

Martin plots with other members of the outfit to poison Broncho and the foreman and steal the cattle. Broncho wakes up from a drugged sleep to find the foreman dead and the cattle stolen. He borrows a horse and rides after the thieves. In a battle with the fugitives he is overpowered. While Martin and two others bind him and take him back to town the others hurry toward Mexico with the cattle.

Miss Barton hears the cattle thieves plotting to throw the blame for the murder and theft on Broncho. She telephones the sheriff. When the trio arrive with their prisoner, he pretends to believe them so he can catch the thieves. Broncho is put in jail.

Cattlemen, who have heard the story, attempt to lynch Broncho. Miss Barton, however, makes the deputy sheriff swear herself and Broncho in as deputies. They arm themselves and fight a desperate battle with the mob, holding them at bay until the sheriff returns and tells the true story.

Broncho then turns to the girl he loves and who has saved his life. She denounces Martin and throws herself into Broncho Billy's arms.

A Few Film Facts and Fancies

G. M. ANDERSON dressed a typical western doll, which was sold at a Chicago Christmas pageant for the poor. It was dressed in regulation cowboy costume. There was lively bidding to get it, and it brought a big price.

HARRY TODD is nursing a Cyrano de Bergerac nose as the result of a battle with potatoes with "Slippery Slim" in the Essanay play, "The Battle of Snakeville." Both pelted each other fiercely with the vegetables until they were bruised from head to foot. Todd got an especially vicious blow on the proboscis that made it swell up like a small balloon.

HELEN DUNBAR'S little Japanese baby, which the Essanay actress adopted several weeks ago, saw its first Christmas tree a few days ago. Miss Dunbar decorated the tree with the usual candles and gewgaws, with many presents. The child was delighted and lisped that it was even more beautiful than a cherry tree in bloom.

JOHN H. COSSAR has been quite won over to the cause of labor. In the Essanay play, "The Lieutenant Governor," he takes the part of a Portuguese laborer. He says that the stunts he was put through has made him a sympathizer with the working man forever.

TRUE BOARDMAN, who plays the roles of sheriff and bad man in the Western Essanay dramas, gave two highwaymen the scare of their lives the other night, when they held him up in his machine, when returning to Niles, Cal., from San Francisco. When they yelled "Hands up" he pulled out two colts that looked like gattling guns and began a fusillade that quickly drove the robbers into the woods.

LILLIAN DREW nearly disrupted the scene taking in the Essanay play, "The Gallantry of Jimmy Rogers," when someone tried to play a joke on her at a dinner party by putting real wine in her champagne glass. She refuses to touch liquor and takes ginger ale. When she took one taste she suspected the glass had been tampered with and refused to go on with the scene until she got her ginger ale.

LEO WHITE, of the Essanay Company, proved himself some sharpshooter at the Evanston shooting club where a scene was taken in the Essanay comedy by George Ade, "The Fable of the Syndicate Lover." White takes the part of a dub suitor for the hand of a girl whose entire family is athletic. They take delight in showing him up and the "Old Man" makes him look like a "boob" at the shooting club, where he is unable to hit a single pigeon. After the scene White picked up the rifle and made some fancy shots, puncturing nine out of ten flying clay pigeons.

THOMAS COMMERFORD'S erect, military bearing lent a realistic atmosphere to the part he takes in George Barr McCutcheon's "Graustark," which is being filmed by Essanay, which it would be scarcely possible for another actor to create. As the fierce old warrior count of Graustark, the uncle of the Princess Yvonne, he is the most exact characterization that it could be possible to imagine.

Van Pelt Doesn't Care How High Eggs Soar

Ernest Van Pelt says he don't care how high the price of eggs soar. He never wants to buy another or even see one. In the Essanay comedy, "When Slippery Slim Went for the Eggs," he tried to foist some on Slim's hen to make Slim think she was laying. Slim caught him at it and forced him to eat so many of the eggs—age not guaranteed—that he says he has lost his taste for them entirely.

Margaret Joslin Proves Prize Cook

Outside of being a first class comedienne Margaret Joslin has won a wide reputation as a cook. Her specialty is doughnuts. She cooked two dozen of them, which were used in the Western Essanay comedy, 'Snakeville's Rising Sons." Two small boys rob her doughnut jar in the play. They were not supposed to eat them all, but the boys said they tasted so good they took advantage of their opportunity and cleaned up the last crum. And neither boy had to call a doctor.

Miss Clayton in Play Despite Sprained Ankle

Despite a sprained ankle, pretty Miss Marguerite Clayton, the Western Essanay's leading woman, succeeded in persuading Mr. G. M. Anderson to allow her to work in a production before she cast aside her crutch. Few will realize while watching her in "Broncho Billy and the Sisters," that she was scarcely able to walk, so cleverly did she work.

BUSHMAN MAKES HIT IN "BATTLE OF LOVE"

Exhibitors Tell of Great Success of Essanay Player in Photoplay of Mrs. Wilson Woodrow

G. M. Anderson Continues to Draw Great Crowds in Western Drama 'Tell-Tale Hand'

Mr. Francis X. Bushman, leading man with the Eastern Essanay stock company, has scored a great success in "The Battle of Love," the fourth Essanay complete prize mystery play produced in conjunction with The Ladies' World. Although this photoplay has been released but two weeks, exhibitors from all parts of the nation have been writing to Essanay telling of the wonderful hit it has made with spectators.

Especial emphasis was placed on the clever acting of Mr. Bushman. Exhibitors declared that their audiences were wild with enthusiasm over his part and that the play was so well constructed that the interest was sustained to the very end.

The story was written by Mrs. Wilson Woodrow, one of America's leading short story and fiction writers. It is one of exceptional merit.

Mr. Bushman also continues to draw great crowds in the first two prize mystery plays, "The Plum Tree" and "In the Glare of the Lights."

Mr. G. M. Anderson's success in "The Tell-Tale Hand" has not abated in the slightest. The drama continues to be a great drawing power in all theaters. Critics pronounce it one of the greatest western dramas yet produced, and predict that its attraction will increase.

Bushman is Seen in Quadruple Exposure

Unusual Feature in Photoplay "The Battle of Love"

A quadruple masked exposure marks an unusual feature in the Essanay prize mystery play, "The Battle of Love," recently released. In this scene Francis X. Bushman is seen in his office at the

MR. FRANCIS X. BUSHMAN, the man voted the world's most popular photoplayer.

telephone, on one side, and Miss Ruth Stonehouse, his sweetheart, at the phone on the other side. In the center is a picture of a street with the telephone wires. From these wires flash out the telephone message letter by letter. This requires a fourth exposure to work the letters into the central picture.

EXHIBITOR CALLS ESSANAY RELEASES BEST IN FILM WORLD

WE USE every Essanay film release. Francis X. Bushman, Bryant Washburn, Thomas Commerford, Ruth Stonehouse and Beverly Bayne are really wonderful favorites at this house. Personally I think the Essanay releases are just what you claim for them, the aristocrats of the film world. J. F. GORDON, Manager Goldreyer Amusement Co., Inc., 2226 Seventh Avenue, New York City.

CHARLES CHAPLIN, the funniest comedian in motion pictures, now with Essanay.

Essanay Comedian Plays Dramatic Role

Wallace Beery, the inimitable "Sweedie" of Essanay's photoplay comedy company, made a lightning jump into the leading part in a dramatic production on the speaking stage. In just one hour and fifteen minutes after he had been asked to take the leading part in "The Trail of the Lonesome Pine," at the Imperial Theater, Chicago, he had familiarized himself enough with the seventy-six pages of manuscript covering his part, to go through with the play.

Beery received a telephone message from his brother, Noah Beery, who is in the company, telling him the leading man, Wells Knibloe had a paralytic stroke and asking him to play the character of Jack Hale.

Beery mastered his first part and rushed on the stage. After that it was one mad rush from the stage to the wings to catch another glimpse of the manuscript every time he was out of the scene for a moment.

Washburn Plays Hero as Well as Villain

Bryant Washburn varies his usual role of a desperate villain in the Essanay photoplay, "The Misjudged Mr. Hartley." In this play he takes the part of a hero and enacts the role with a success that shows his versatility on the screen. Even in this drama, however, his supposed villainy crops up, as he is suspected of theft while a guest. But this suspicion proves unfounded, the circumstances are explained and he wins the beautiful maiden who had become infatuated with the much wronged hero.

Willard Uses Owl for Insomnia Cure

Lee Willard has a new pet. It is a little screech owl which he captured near the Essanay village at Niles, Cal. Lee has been troubled with insomnia. He says that when the owl screeches it puts him to sleep, as it sounds so much like a baby crying from pain he thinks he should get up and walk the floor with it. His disinclination for this pastime puts him in dreamland at once, he declares. "It's just as you always feel sleepiest when the alarm clock goes off in the morning," he explained. The other actors are looking for the owl for quite another reason.

Stock Deals Revealed

"The Place, the Time and the Man," released by Essanay, gives an excellent portrayal of the methods of "wild-cat" speculators in the financial world. It reveals the system of how unscrupulous operators manipulate the market by booming or depressing stocks artificially in order to crush competitors.

Potel Says He Drank a Barrel of Water

Victor Potel got an icy bath that he will remember for some time in taking a scene in the Essanay photoplay, "Sentimental Sophie." Potel as "Slippery Slim" steals Mustang Pete's girl. Mustang and his gang chase Slim and to escape them he jumps into a cold mountain stream. As Slim is considerably over six feet tall he did not expect to get over his head. But he stubbed his toe as he was taking the jump and landed on his face. The swift current rolled him over and over and he was unable to gain his feet. He says he swallowed a full barrel of water before he was fished out, strangled and half frozen.

Miss Bayne Rides Horse of Countess Gizycka

The mount ridden by Miss Beverly Bayne in the scenes of Essanay's photoplay, "The Crimson Wing," formerly belonged to the Countess Gizycka. It was her favorite mount and was named for her when she sold it. Miss Bayne, while an expert horsewoman, had never ridden side saddle before. The horse is an unusually spirited one and a gentler animal was urged. Miss Bayne insisted on the original mount, however, and handled it with ease. Experts declared she rode as well as though she had been using a side saddle all her life.

'Broncho Billy' Makes Injured Boy Brave

The wonderful stimulus of Essanay's "Broncho Billy" photoplays to bravery and patience, is told in a letter from William Flanders, a frontiersman near Billings, Mont. Flanders' son, Billy, goes to see the "Broncho Billy" plays every time he goes to town, the father said. He was stirred by G. M. Anderson's deeds of valor in the plays and longed to do something brave, "like 'Broncho Billy.'" His chance came, and Billy made good.

Billy and his sister were returning to their farm in a wagon when the horses ran away. He clung bravely to the lines until the wagon was overturned at a turn in the road. The little girl was unhurt, but Billy had a broken leg and an injured spine.

Billy was taken to a hospital, where he fought back the tears, although he suffered great pain. An operation was necessary, which might mean death. When the doctors asked Billy if he was afraid, he said:

"'Broncho Billy' wouldn't be afraid, and I ain't going to be, either."

In the weeks of suffering before Billy recovered, the doctors declared they had never seen a braver or more patient lad.

GREATEST PHOTOPLAY COMEDIAN WORKS ON NEW FILMS

Essanay Soon to Present New Series of Comedies Unrivaled in the Motion Picture World

Mastery of Facial Expression and Original Capers Make Him a Peer of All Players

Charles Chaplin, conceded by the entire photoplay world to be the greatest comedian in motion pictures, has joined Essanay. Mr. Chaplin already has taken up his work and shortly will be seen in his inimitable comedies on the Essanay screen.

Essanay already has received scores of congratulations from exhibitors on engaging Mr. Chaplin.

"Mr. Chaplin is a box office magnet," writes one exhibitor, which letter is typical of others. "No one in the motion picture world can draw as great crowds for comedy as Mr. Chaplin. He never fails to keep the house convulsed with laughter. We want all his comedies released."

"The comedies of Mr. Chaplin are original and unique," writes another exhibitor. "He plays in a way peculiar to himself and in a style which defies all imitators. There is none his equal."

Mr. Chaplin came to this country from England several years ago and quickly rose to a star in motion picture comedy. Before going on the silent stage he had been playing important roles in vaudeville and on the English pantomime stage.

His possibilities as a motion picture actor were quickly recognized and he made a hit from the very first. He is a master of the art of facial expression and this, together with his unique capers before the camera make him a peer of motion picture comedians.

"I have a new line of comedies that differs from anything I have ever produced," said Mr. Chaplin. "They far surpass the old comedies as fun producers. If the others were considered good, these will be a scream."

Every exhibitor who has ever used the Chaplin films book him regularly, for they know the potentialities of Mr. Chaplin as a drawing card. The Chaplin comedies never fail to fill theaters or to please the spectators.

These comedies will be released through the General Film company in the near future.

Miss Ruth Stonehouse Dresses Dolls for Poor

George Ade's Slim Princess was one of the dolls in a Chicago doll pageant to swell the Christmas fund for the needy. The doll was donated by Miss Ruth Stonehouse, the pretty Essanay actress, who takes the part of the Slim Princess in George Ade's photoplay of the same name, which has been filmed by Essanay.

The doll is beautifully dressed in silk, from a piece of Miss Stonehouse's own dress, which she wore in the photoplay scenes. The costume, that of a princess in a Turkish harem, was made by Miss Stonehouse in her dressing room. The miniature slim princess also wears a brilliant diamond ring.

Another doll dressed by Miss Stonehouse for a pageant is the Honorable Agatha, which is dressed as the character by that name in the photoplay, "The Real Agatha," written by Edith Huntington Mason and filmed by Essanay. Miss Stonehouse also plays this part in the play.

Calvert Well Adapted to Military Role

E. H. Calvert is especially adapted by training for the leading role which he plays in "The Crimson Wing," the Essanay six-reel photoplay from the novel of H. C. Chatfield-Taylor. He takes the part of the Count Ludwig von Leun-Walram, a military officer, who is actively engaged in the field. Calvert is a graduate of West Point and was a captain in the U. S. army for years, which accounts for the exactness with which he interprets the part.

Totten Shows Skill in Playing Subtle Role

Joseph Byron Totten displays great skill in the way he portrays the leading role in "An Amateur Prodigal," an Essanay photoplay taken from the story of Albert Payson Terhune. He brings out the pathos, which the part of John Andrews calls for, in a way that touches the heart, without going to the other extreme of making it too melodramatic, which fault a less skilled player might easily fall into. It is a subtle part and enacted with unusual cleverness.

◁ *Essanay hires Chaplin,* Essanay News, *1915. Charlie Chaplin was already famous when Essanay lured him away from Keystone with an offer of $1,250 a week. A year later Mutual lured him away from Essanay with an offer of $10,000 a week plus a $150,000 bonus.*

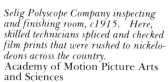

Selig Polyscope Company inspecting and finishing room, c1915. Here, skilled technicians spliced and checked film prints that were rushed to nickelodeons across the country.
Academy of Motion Picture Arts and Sciences

Gloria Swanson and George Spoor. Gloria Swanson, to the left of the camera, began her career as an Essanay extra. She and her husband, Wallace Beery, left Essanay for Keystone in 1916. George Spoor, to the right-front of the camera, closed Essanay the next year.

Selig Polyscope Company camera room, c1911. Chicago movie makers cranked out dozens of films a year, and technical crews had to keep equipment in top condition.
Academy of Motion Picture Arts and Sciences

Essanay, print drying room. Chicago film makers distributed prints to nickelodeons across the nation. Here, Essanay technicians dry processed film.

Sears, Roebuck and Co. motion picture ads, 1908. Sears sold everything needed to set up a nickelodeon: screens, projectors, films, posters, and detailed instructions.

Ebony Film Corporation ad, 1918. Chicago was the home of a pioneer black film producer, Luther Pollard, for whom comedians such as Sam Jacus and Sam Williams made a new slapstick caper every week.

Poster, "The Bandit of Point Loma," c1913.
Library of Congress

Rothacker Film Company crew, 1915. Chicago was the home of many industrial film makers whose movies were used to train salesmen, promote trade, inform stockholders, and provide information about commerce and industry.
Bill Birch

Selig's show-business experience was useful, but his most important break came quite by accident. Soon after he formed his company, he decided to shoot some industrial scenes in the city. On a trip to the Armour packing plant he had whitewashed the walls in order to produce more reflection from the limited amount of light that came through the windows. This made the plant look cleaner than it actually was, and was precisely the evidence that Armour and Company needed nearly a decade later to support certain claims about cleanliness. In 1906, when Upton Sinclair's muckraking novel, *The Jungle*, appeared, the meatpacker purchased several prints of the film and thankfully poured money into Selig's company. It cranked out dozens of short films, and gradually started producing features. Selig proved to be quite adroit at persuading noted novelists to sell the screen rights to their works. What started out as a small studio on Peck Court in the Levee district soon had become a rapidly expanding plant located on the outskirts of the city, at Irving Park Road and Western Avenue. By 1910 Selig had established a California branch and hired a company of stock actors.

In the meantime, George Spoor had also expanded his company from distribution into production. In 1907 one of the Edison company's leading actors, G. M. Anderson, proposed that he and Spoor form a partnership. The Peerless Film Manufacturing Company emerged that year, but the name soon was changed to Essanay, an acronym. Spoor supervised the production, while Anderson, who had starred in Edison's classic, *The Great Train Robbery*, capitalized on his popularity to promote Essanay films nationwide. Some of their productions were industrial advertising films. In 1911, for instance, they made *Back to the Old Farm* for International Harvester. But the staple item was the short drama. Eventually actors and actresses the likes of Beverly Bayne, Francis X. Bushman, Wallace Beery, Gloria Swanson, Ben Turpin, and Charlie Chaplin made Essanay into a major film studio.

Film production prospered in Chicago. Besides Essanay and Selig there were several other smaller companies. In 1910 Allan Dwan, a young Essanay employee who had invented a powerful studio light, joined with others to form the American Film Manufacturing Company. This short-lived concern made movie history by offering fantastic payment for sensational scripts. This started a bidding war among studios that ultimately attracted some of the best American writers to the industry in the 1920s. The Ebony Film Corporation was another Chicago producer. Started a few years after Essanay, it was probably the first black-owned and operated film studio in America. Its founder was Luther Pollard, an advertising man who believed that whites as well as blacks would pay to watch black actors in slapstick comedy.

Chicago was the logical location for the young film industry. Investment capital was available to finance new ventures. The city's industrial base was large enough to support companies that produced technical and advertising films exclusively. Since many films told realistic stories about urban life, the city became the set. Fires, crowds, streetcars, and stores provided a living backdrop for any plot. Finally, Chicago's transportation advantages meant that studios could ship prints of their films to almost any part of the country within three days.

The city attracted ambitious young people like Carl Laemmle, formerly the manager of an Oshkosh clothing store. In 1906 Laemmle arrived in Chicago and remodeled a Milwaukee Avenue clothing store into the White Front Theater. During slack periods he rented films he had on hand to other nickelodeons. In 1909 he formed his own distribution company, Independent Motion Pictures. Three years later, with the help of Irving Thalberg, he reorganized it as Universal Pictures. Although Universal soon moved to California, it, too, was created by Chicagoans.

The city's massive mail-order network also contributed to the movie industry's growth. As early as 1902, Sears, Roebuck and Co. had begun a "Department of Moving Picture Outfits." After warning readers not to confuse the Edison Kinetoscope with Magic Lanterns or Stereopticons and claiming that, "We have always been at the forefront of dealers in handling this type of equipment," a Sears catalog ad went on to state that the Edison device was simple, portable, and could project an image on any size screen. Since Edison had already initiated a series of lawsuits charging infringement of his patents by Spoor, Selig, and others, the ad reminded readers that only the Edison projector was definitely legal. Sears also offered a complete line of lights and a large stock of Edison films.

By 1908 the company was publishing a separate 160-page catalog of motion picture machines. Sears ads promised to send information to churches and clubs about how to use the outfits for fund-raising, and to businesses about how to project advertising pictures on the side of their building. Everything that one needed to open a "Five-Cent Theater" could be purchased through the Sears catalog. Sears' ad made establishing a nickelodeon look easy. It proclaimed, "Almost any vacant store room can be made into a five-cent theater by removing the glass front and replacing it with a regular theater front. . . . A show of about twenty minutes is given, and the low price of admission is an inducement which many people cannot resist."

It is impossible to say how many nickelodeon outfits Sears sold in its home city, but their number increased rapidly. City directories recorded only one in 1902, and only 29 in 1906. Two years later there were 320 and by 1913 Chicago had 606 nickelodeons. Most were converted storefronts, featuring movies designed to appeal to a broad audience. Along with the usual newsreels, Westerns, and dramatic features, there were many films that strayed a bit from popular standards of morality. Suggestive posters contributed to the problem. To many concerned citizens the new entertainment glorified immorality and crime and therefore posed a direct threat to youth. They were well aware of the attraction of moving pictures and demanded some sort of control. Jane Addams and Louise deKoven Bowen led an effort that resulted in America's first movie censorship law. In 1906 the City Council prohibited movies that imbued crime with a favorable image, and the following year an amendment made it necessary for theaters to obtain a police permit before showing any movie at all. This established the Chicago Police Department as America's first censorship bureau.

Although the motion picture industry was most distressed by the new laws, their passage actually had little to do with the unfortunate demise of film-making in Chicago. This was partly due to the climate, which compared unfavorably with that of sunny California. Both Essanay and Selig had discovered that, despite improvements in lighting, the best studios were those that let sunshine in through open roofs. Audiences preferred outdoor films because they seemed to enhance dramatic realism. Chicago's cold winters shortened the shooting season. Also, a number of the Chicago producers had joined together to form the Motion Picture Patents Company, a combine which pooled patents in an attempt to break the potential stranglehold that Thomas Edison held over the industry. The Supreme Court, however, ruled against the Patents Company, and even though Edison never again gained complete control over his invention, the resulting confusion disrupted film distribution. Some firms, including the Ebony Film Corporation, folded. Essanay and Selig both failed during World War I, although their founders continued to influence the industry. George Spoor, for instance, invented "Natural Vision," the forerunner of present-day wide-screen movies.

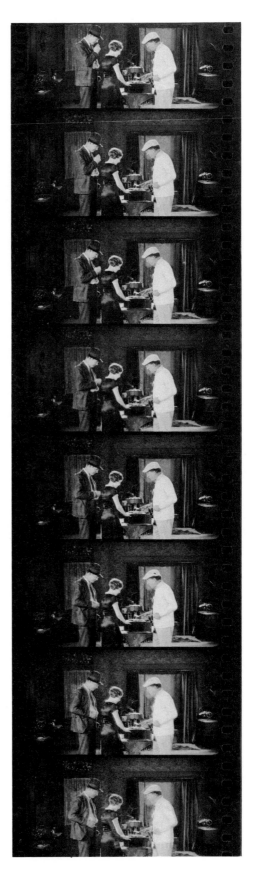

Essanay Natural Vision film strip. Natural Vision, the forerunner of widescreen movies, added what George Spoor called "the vital touch—reality and life" to moving pictures.

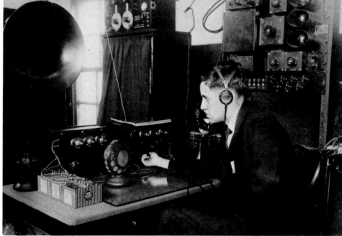

Clarence Darrow at the Scopes Trial, 1925. WGN's private telephone lines brought the trial, live, to Chicago listeners.
WGN Continental Broadcasting Company

WMAQ wireless room, 1922. The Fair Store in the Loop operated its own radio station. The Chicago Daily News, *which provided it with a news service, eventually took over the station.*

Popular Culture for the Masses

The movie industry had all but disappeared from Chicago by the time another infant communications medium came along. The story of radio began in Chicago during the Columbian Exposition. Several great European electrical experts, including Helmholtz and Marconi, journeyed to the Electrical Congress at the fair to present papers. In the audience was a young Alabaman who worked as a chair-pusher, but whose major interest was experimenting with radio waves. Lee DeForest soon left Chicago to attend Yale University where he earned a Ph.D. in engineering. Late in the 1890s he returned as a research scientist for the Western Electric division of the Bell Telephone Company. He conducted experiments for the next few years, stringing antenna wires across South Side rooftops and improving upon basic principles of transmission. Although DeForest eventually was bold enough to form his own radio company in New York, radio transmission remained primitive. The federal government assumed control of the air waves during World War I, and it was not until 1920 that America's first commercial station, KDKA in Pittsburgh, went on the air.

One of the first Chicago stations was begun by two wealthy young wireless fans, Elliot Jenkins and Thorne Donnelley. Their "9CT," with its transmitter in the new Wrigley Building, went on the air in the spring of 1921. A year later its call letters were changed to WDAP and the station moved to the Drake Hotel. The Chicago Board of Trade then purchased the station and used it to broadcast grain receipts. The small station had a number of competitors, however, and by October 1924 there were a dozen Chicago stations and even a few in the suburbs. Several of the newcomers were owned by electrical corporations. Westinghouse established KYW, and the Chicago Radio Laboratory built WSAX and WJAZ. Zenith Radio Corporation's co-

founding of WEBH represented another sort of economic interest in the new medium. Its partner, the Edgewater Beach Hotel, was anxious to use live broadcasts to advertise its ballrooms. The Rainbo Gardens (WQJ) and the Webster Hotel (WTL) had the same idea. A few non-profit institutions saw radio as a means of getting their message to the public. WDBY was owned by the North Shore Congregational Church, while WJJD, which went on the air in March 1925, was owned by the Loyal Order of Moose.

While there were only 1,200 radio receivers in Chicago when 9CT went on the air, within eighteen months that number had reached 20,000. This instant popularity naturally worried the newspapers. The *Chicago Tribune* sold its interest in the Edgewater Beach station and purchased WDAP in 1923. It changed the call letters to WGN, after its motto, "World's Greatest Newspaper." The *Daily News* soon followed suit by establishing WMAZ, and the *Herald and Examiner* followed with WRH. Even the neighborhood press got into radio; the *Southtown Economist* established WBCN late in 1924. Clearly, the local newspapers recognized the advantages of broadcasting as a means of instant news delivery. In 1924 KYW boasted about how quickly it had broadcast news of the verdict in the Leopold-Loeb trial. As the *Radio Digest* described it: "It was 9:42½ when the verdict was announced and it lacked a few seconds of being 9:43 when the news went out on the air." The fifteen-minute broadcast brought 5,000 letters from listeners. The following year WGN made history when it paid $1,000 a day to lease a telephone line to broadcast the famous Scopes trial live to Chicagoans.

Early in the 1920s Chicago investors realized that radio could reach far beyond the city limits. Both Wards and Sears sold receivers, and by 1925 both issued large special catalogs of equipment. Early sets were easily adaptable to the farm—where electricity was nonexistent—since they operated from storage batteries. By the mid-1920s transmitters had become powerful enough to reach hundreds of

Mary Garden (1877-1967), 1921.
In December 1920 Mary Garden became the general director of the faltering Chicago Opera Association. Though the association eventually went bankrupt, her radio broadcasts greatly stirred public interest in opera.

WCFL Radio Magazine, 1928.
The Chicago Federation of Labor's WCFL was the world's first labor station. Its transmitter was located at the east end of Municipal (now Navy) Pier.
Chicago Federation of Labor and Industrial Union Council

WLS ad, 1924. Aimed at rural listeners, Sears, Roebuck and Co.'s WLS started broadcasting in April 1924 and was sold to the Prairie Farmer Magazine in 1928.

Freeman Gosden and Charles Correll, 1927. As "Amos 'n' Andy" they delighted millions of Americans. Adapted to television, the series remained on the air until 1960.

miles in all directions. This fact interested Sears because of the enormous advertising potential. In 1924 it established WLS, named after its motto, "World's Largest Store." It broadcast frequent market and weather reports and also began offering music and educational features designed to appeal to the farm family. Sears failed to make much money on the venture, however, and in 1927 began hunting for a buyer. Rejecting the offer of utilities magnate Samuel Insull, it sold the station to the *Prairie Farmer Magazine*. For nearly three decades "The *Prairie Farmer* Station" carried programming more closely tailored to the interest of rural families than Chicagoans. "The WLS Barndance" was probably the most popular country music program in America, and, along with other programs, it focused the attention of thousands of Midwestern farm families on Chicago.

The hoedown, however, was not the predominant form of radio entertainment. Daily schedules actually included a considerable amount of time devoted to the fine arts. WGN set aside Sunday afternoons and a few hours each evening for classical music. In 1924 WLS and the Sears Roebuck Agricultural Foundation established the Radio Theater. Its director, Henry Saddler, declared that he was "rebuilding plays to fit the ear." "Great actors know how to draw out the human emotions," Saddler noted, "to bring tears or laughter by the turn of a hand, the dropping of an eyelid . . . . By Radio they must touch the same emotions; but by sound alone." His actors were required to develop a "Radio Stage vocabulary," and he added organ music for establishing the proper mood. He was determined to "eliminate sticky sentimentality and rid the stage of cheap vulgarity" by offering Shakespeare to everyone. While Saddler did not achieve this lofty goal, he did develop many "Radio Stage" techniques widely imitated in later years.

Opera was also an important part of Chicago radio. One of its most powerful stations, the Westinghouse Corporation's KYW actually began as an outlet for the Chicago Opera Association. That troupe, like its local predecessors, was perpetually on the verge of insolvency. Productions were expensive and the audiences small. The board of directors had given control to Mary Garden, in hopes that her popularity as a star would draw crowds. When the KYW staff contacted her, she suggested broadcasting the entire opera season. KYW agreed, and strung ten microphones around the stage of the Auditorium Theater. A director, seated in the audience, held a switching box in his lap and selected the appropriate microphones for each part of a performance. The popularity of the series was enormous, but it helped sell more radio sets than opera seats. Although the Opera Association folded, to be replaced by the Civic Opera, Mary Garden had achieved an important milestone both in the arts and in broadcasting.

Chicago's location in the center of the nation allowed it to play yet another important role in the development of radio. Even before 1925 radio technicians realized that the signals of the stronger stations reached across the country. Sometimes stations shared the same wavelength or bled into each other's frequency quite by accident. By 1923 some stations had worked out agreements whereby they took turns on the air. This development, along with the emergence of syndicated chains of stations and extremely popular stars promoted the network idea. This trend toward consolidation resulted in the founding of the National Broadcasting Company in 1925. Within a few years its executives had worked out a plan to syndicate shows to be broadcast nationwide. Chicago, because of its superior facilities and location in the Central Time Zone, became the operations center of the network. Programs transmitted from Merchandise Mart studios would be aired only one hour later in New York and a few hours earlier in San Francisco. Until more sophisticated facilities allowed NBC to consolidate both its mechanical and its business activities in the new Rockefeller Center, Chicago was the focal point of American radio.

Operating from the WMAQ studios, NBC assembled a talented collection of actors, writers, and studio personnel. The development of radio "personalities" paralleled the star system of Hollywood, creating a market for weekly serials. Many of these radio personalities continued to perform in Chicago long after the network's headquarters had left. "The Shadow," "Ma Perkins," "Lum and Abner," "Fibber McGee and Molly," and "Vic and Sade" went out to listeners all over the country. The most famous of them all, however, was "Amos 'n' Andy." This series, started at WGN in 1926, was originally called "Sam and Henry." Within two years it was so popular that WMAQ lured the stars, Freeman Gosden and Charles Correll, to its studio. Its owner, the *Daily News*, began making electrical transcriptions of the program and sold them to thirty-five other stations. When the NBC network purchased WMAQ it also purchased the rights to the program. Although "Amos 'n' Andy" presented an unfortunate stereotype of black Americans, in its time it was the most beloved program on radio.

Chicago's central location also made it a leader in distributing an innovative music called Jazz to America. During World War I the federal government, fearful of the corrupting influence of brothels on military personnel, closed the Storyville district, New Orleans's equivalent to Chicago's Levee. This left many of the Crescent City's best musicians without jobs. Many moved north with the rest of the wartime migration and found employment in small cafes on Chicago's South Side. Here, artists like King Oliver, Louis Armstrong, and Jelly Roll Morton made Chicago an important center for a new and uniquely American artform.

But Chicago was far more than just a city where many Jazz stars lived. It also helped make them nationally famous. These innovative musicians became the mainstay for one early radio station that was heard throughout the Midwest. In 1924 two wealthy brothers, H. Leslie and Ralph Atlass founded WBBM and promoted Jazz. At first their "sensuous" music brought in little advertising revenue, but eventually Jazz caught on, and WBBM prospered. Meanwhile, the Chicago recording industry had discovered the new music. The city was fortunate to have the most sophisticated recording equipment outside of New York, and several small companies, including Paramount and Okeh, supplied discs to the growing ranks of enthusiasts. The most successful of these entrepreneurs were the Kapp brothers, David and Jack. They transformed the profits from a modest Jazz music store into a recording company that eventually became the giant Decca Records.

The Method

Becoming deeply involved in the early history of the movies and radio was characteristic of Chicago. Since the last half of the nineteenth century Chicagoans had started to realize that finding a way to make creative talent known was almost as important as creativity itself. Thus, in Chicago's very early years, the way the Art Institute brought the arts to the people was as significant to many contemporaries as Mrs. Potter Palmer's collection of French Expressionists. The same was true of Lorado Taft, whose public sculpture was most significant, and Theodore Thomas, who not only brought music to large numbers of Chicagoans, but also was credited with inspiring other major cities such as Philadelphia to support symphony orchestras.

What was, of course, unique about movies and the radio was the way that mechanical reproduction enabled new popular artforms to be heard and seen by audiences almost anywhere. Thousands of small towns once culturally isolated except for newspapers and magazines now enjoyed the latest medium of creative expression. The radio went one step beyond that. Farmers could listen to the opera or almost any other form of entertainment while they milked their cows. All this still depended to a great extent on cities. Yet, like mail-order houses, the new media broadcast Chicago's cultural influence far and wide.

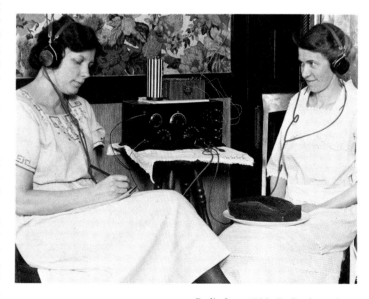

Radio fans, 1923. Radio changed America's leisure habits. Here, listeners snack on "radio cake," made according to a recipe broadcast by a Chicago station.

Scandinavian Padlocks.

Padlock, iron case, painted red, detached shackle, two keys, good substantial lock, like cuts 455–475, excepting has open key hole, and nearly square key,

8252 No. 10, size 2½x1½, each, 35c, per doz. $3 78
8253 No. 12, size 3½x1¾, each, 65c, per doz.   7 04
8254 No. 13, size 3½x2, each, 72c, per doz.   7 78

Padlock, iron case, painted wine color, with swinging shackle, two flat keys. This is the best lock made, burglar-proof and water-proof, exactly like cut.

Nos. 455–475.

8255 No. 455, size 2½x1½, each, 55c, per doz $5 94
8256 No. 475, size 3½x2, each, 85c, per doz. 9 18

Postage on Padlock No. 10.................. 8c. extra.
Postage on Padlock No. 12.................15c. extra.
Postage on Padlock No. 13.................21c. extra.
Postage on Padlock No. 455................ 8c. extra.
Postage on Padlock No. 475...............21c. extra.

Carpet Sweeper.

8269   "THE JEWEL."

The Jewell Carpet Sweeper is the best sweeper made; it is perfectly noiseless, easy to operate, and simple in construction. The dust pans are so arranged that by a simple "twist of the wrist" on the top of the sweeper, the pan revolves and the dust drops out. Price, $2.00 each; $21.00 per doz.

White Mountain Potato Parer.

DIRECTIONS: The potatoes should be washed free from dirt, grit or sand, put on as near the centre as possible; and potatoes over three inches long should be cut in half, and the thickest end put on the fork.

The White Mountain Potato Parer is the only machine ever made that will not only pare a potato much better than it can be done by hand, taking off a thiner paring from every shape or kind of potato, but will go into and clean out the eyes, and altogether at a saving of at least twenty per cent. It is free from the objections made to the old style of rattle-trap, geared parers; is solid and substantial, cannot get out of order, and so cheap as to be within the means of everybody. Almost any of the Potato Parers seem as if they might do the work better "next time," but the "White Mountain" *does it now.* Every machine warranted as represented.

8270 Price, each, ... 70
   "   per dozen..................... 7 56
Sample Parer, by mail, postage paid........... 1 00

Combination Apple Parer, Slicer and Corer.

CORE   APPLE SLICED

8271 The most complete and useful article of the kind ever made. It will pare, slice and core an apple at the same time, or will do either one of them separately, by adjusting the knives; it is very simple in construction, so that a child can use it, never is out of repair; it makes no waste, is more economical than paring by hand. Price, 70c.
   Six for $4.00, twelve for $7.56.

Extra by mail, including postal case, 45 cents each.

OBSERVE CASH DISCOUNTS ON PAGE 4.

Cherry Stone

272 Cherry Stoner, best known, round and plump. Price 65

Pot Cleaners

Pot Cleaner or Wire Dish Clo
venient and popular utensil ext
ettles can be cleaned of grease e
one there is no dirty dish rag to w

273 Pot Cleaner, round wire small.
274 Pot Cleaner, round wire large.

COPP

Sizes 8, 9, 10 and 12 refer to th
engths in each size. We sell them
rivets in each pound.

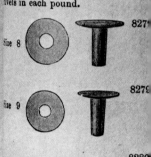

827
Size 8
8279
Size 9
8280
Size 10
8280
Size 12

Burrs.   Rivets.

The copper

Use Jno. Clark, Jr. & Co.'s Best Six-Cord Spool Cotton.

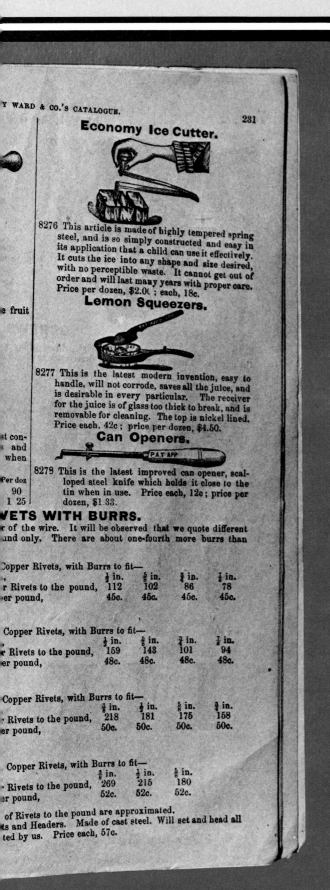

Economy Ice Cutter.

8276 This article is made of highly tempered spring steel, and is so simply constructed and easy in its application that a child can use it effectively. It cuts the ice into any shape and size desired, with no perceptible waste. It cannot get out of order and will last many years with proper care. Price per dozen, $2.00; each, 18c.

Lemon Squeezers.

8277 This is the latest modern invention, easy to handle, will not corrode, saves all the juice, and is desirable in every particular. The receiver for the juice is of glass too thick to break, and is removable for cleaning. The top is nickel lined. Price each, 42c; price per dozen, $4.50.

Can Openers.

8278 This is the latest improved can opener, scalloped steel knife which holds it close to the tin when in use. Price each, 12c; price per dozen, $1.33.

VETS WITH BURRS.

of the wire. It will be observed that we quote different and only. There are about one-fourth more burrs than

Copper Rivets, with Burrs to fit—

	½ in.	⅝ in.	¾ in.	⅞ in.
Rivets to the pound,	112	102	86	78
per pound,	45c.	45c.	45c.	45c.

Copper Rivets, with Burrs to fit—

	½ in.	⅝ in.	¾ in.	⅞ in.
Rivets to the pound,	159	143	101	94
per pound,	48c.	48c.	48c.	48c.

Copper Rivets, with Burrs to fit—

	⅜ in.	½ in.	⅝ in.	¾ in.
Rivets to the pound,	218	181	175	158
per pound,	50c.	50c.	50c.	50c.

Copper Rivets, with Burrs to fit—

	⅜ in.	½ in.	⅝ in.
Rivets to the pound,	269	215	180
per pound,	52c.	52c.	52c.

of Rivets to the pound are approximated. ts and Headers. Made of cast steel. Will set and head all ted by us. Price each, 57c.

Merchandising: Selling New Styles to the Nation

Chicago has frequently been depicted as a materialistic town, one far more concerned about money than beauty. Eastern critics berated Chicago architects for involving themselves with such crass projects as commercial buildings, instead of concentrating their talents on cathedrals and universities. Yet the fact remains that Chicagoans had—and knew that they had—a tremendous impact on the tenor of everyday life. This was scarcely an accident, for the city sold enormous quantities of goods to millions of Americans. While certain of these goods were produced elsewhere and merely retailed from Chicago, many others actually were made there or, at least, showed the direct influence of Chicago. In any event, Chicagoans have helped determine the tastes of a nation.

Montgomery Ward & Co. catalog, 1882. This mail order catalog brought store-bought goods to isolated rural Americans.

Marshall Field and the Department Store

The story of Marshall Field & Co. began in pre-Civil War Chicago with a series of short-lived partnerships in the dry goods business. This pattern was common. Budding entrepreneurs, usually from the East, would pool their resources to establish a business. They would be moderately prosperous for a few years, but then one of the partners would become dissatisfied and sell out, perhaps investing in something else. An enterprising young clerk would buy up the available share of the business, and the company would change its name. It was in just this way that young Marshall Field, a native of Massachusetts, began as a salesman for Cooley, Wadsworth and Company in 1856 and ended up eight years later as a partner in Farwell, Field and Company.

The company underwent two more ownership changes in as many years. In the closing days of the war, Potter Palmer, who in 1852 had established the city's finest dry goods store, sold his firm to Field and his chief bookkeeper, Levi Z. Leiter. Palmer, who had branched out into real estate, needed to cut his business commitments for reasons of health. He retained a token interest in the dry goods business, and Field and Leiter were happy to have the use of his name. The new partnership, Field, Palmer and Leiter, advertised itself as "Successors to P. Palmer." Within a year, however, Palmer sold his remaining share and his name was dropped.

Field, Leiter and Company was the forerunner of Marshall Field & Co. as we know it today. Starting in 1866 with dry goods and notions, the firm gradually added new lines of merchandise. The destruction of the store in the Great Fire of 1871 and its subsequent relocation in a larger building allowed room for expansion. For example, furs, carpets, and gentlemen's furnishings were added in 1874 and a line of imported goods, first introduced just before the Fire, was amplified. Although Field's competitor, E. J. Lehman of The Fair Store, claimed credit for introducing the department store idea to Chicago, Field stocked the best mass-produced goods, and promised to obtain, on special order, anything he did not stock. This service yielded little if any profit, but it did help Field determine what ought to be added to the regular stock. Field also subscribed to the policy of "buying light," making small but frequent wholesale purchases. Rapid turnover made room for the latest fash-

ions, and furthermore the store could experiment with its stock assured that it would not end up with a large inventory of unpopular goods.

Field and Leiter really operated two kinds of stores, wholesale as well as retail, and both affected style and taste throughout a large area of the Midwest. Potter Palmer had converted his basements to wholesale trade as early as 1859, and his successors had kept up and enlarged that end of the business. The pair understood the problems of the small-town merchant, who either had to accept goods sight-unseen or travel all the way back east to make his wholesale purchases. In 1872 Field and Leiter relocated their wholesale trade in a separate building, and in January 1885 Field contracted with the famed Boston architect Henry Hobson Richardson to design a brand-new wholesale house. This seven-story structure, which covered a full square-block on the west edge of the Loop, embodied an interior light-court so that country merchants could better see the wares. Leiter, however, had more faith in the wholesale trade than Field, and disputes over the balance between the two activities ultimately resulted in the breakup of their partnership, in 1881. Field kept a wholesale division, nevertheless, and under the leadership of John G. Shedd it prospered for many years. In this manner Marshall Field of Chicago influenced the way that small-town Americans dressed and decorated their homes.

While the high quality of Field's merchandise was a persuasive advertisement in itself, the company also ran ads in many local magazines and newspapers. The crowds who flocked to the store each day were greeted by a doorman and by clerks who were schooled in the art of public relations. Eventually, after completing a new building, Field added a customer library, children's playrooms, a tea-room, writing rooms, a stenographic service, and telegraph and telephone offices. These services permitted women, who made up the majority of Field's customers, to take care of nearly all their errands in this one building. A complete delivery service enabled women to shop without worrying about how to tote their purchases home, and it also allowed the store to begin stocking larger items such as furniture. Because of this delivery service, Field's was able to retain the patronage of the city's wealthier citizens, who began moving to North Shore suburbs in the late nineteenth century. A telephone order to Field's brought a prompt response from a uniformed delivery man.

Marshall Field & Co. wholesale store, advertising card, c1890. Henry Hobson Richardson designed this building, located in the block bounded by Adams, Quincy, Franklin, and Wells. It was demolished in 1930.

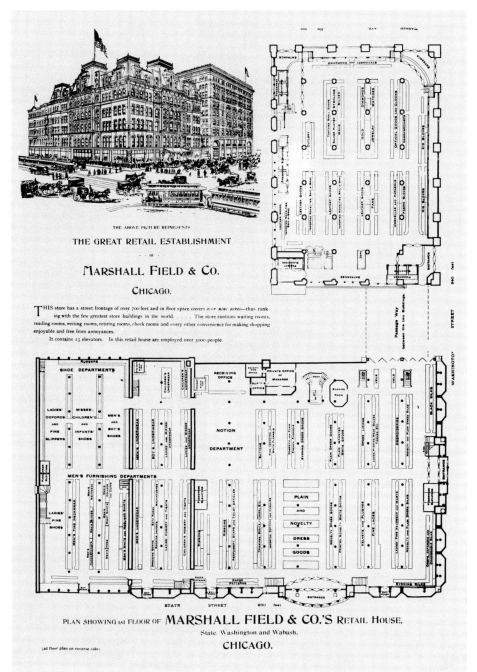

PLAN SHOWING 1st FLOOR OF **MARSHALL FIELD & CO.'S** RETAIL HOUSE,
State, Washington and Wabash,
CHICAGO.

Marshall Field (1834-1902), c1890. Offering a money-back guarantee on goods purchased at his store, Field revolutionized retail merchandising.

Levi Z. Leiter (1834-1904), c1890. Field's business partner from 1865 to 1881, Leiter left to start his own department store. He commissioned William LeBaron Jenney to design a new building on State Street, for several years the largest department store in America. It is now occupied by Sears, Roebuck and Co.

Marshall Field & Co. State Street store, 1885. Erected in sections, this complex of new buildings became the largest department store in the world.

Carpet display, Marshall Field & Co., Inland Architect and Builder, September 1887. Field's had fifteen carpet and rug departments.

Department store windows, c1900. Chicago's building technology, especially the metal frame, allowed architects to turn the ground-floor exterior walls into large display windows.
Marshall Field & Co.

Aaron Montgomery Ward (1844-1913), c1890. Although not the originator of mail order selling, Ward transformed the concept into a respectable and successful industry.

IOWA FARMERS INVESTIGATE MONTGOMERY WARD & CO.

Iowa farmers investigate Montgomery Ward & Co. 1908 catalog. Mail order merchandisers often had to overcome the suspicions of farmers about "city-slickers." Sears and Ward both made use of testimonials to substantiate their claims of honesty and quality.

Montgomery Ward & Co. catalog tube, late 1890s. Farm families often received the latest revision of Ward's catalog in a tube such as this.

The wholesale trade of Marshall Field & Co. was one mode of influencing small-town and rural styles of the last century. Another Chicagoan perfected a competing system of merchandising which likewise influenced the hinterland, mail-order selling. By bringing "the store" to the village or farm, merchants in the big city could provide a larger variety of goods than any country general store could, and at lower prices.

The idea of selling from afar was in its infancy when young Aaron Montgomery Ward arrived in Chicago. Ward had been born in New Jersey in 1843, and after an unsuccessful apprenticeship in the manual arts, had started working in a store. At the age of twenty-three he headed for Chicago, where he obtained employment with Field, Leiter and Company. He soon left that job because of low pay and went on the road as a salesman. Because his territory included hundreds of small towns, he became very familiar with the buying habits of rustics. He noted their dependence on local merchants who extended credit as a means of retaining patrons that might otherwise have been driven away by high prices. Ward also understood the nature of rural hostility to the city, where invisible commodities markets determined prices and railway barons set their exorbitant rates.

Ward realized that thousands of miles of railway extended out in all directions from Chicago. If he could travel to hundreds of towns as a salesman, why not ship things there by rail? And so in 1872 he opened a small office in Chicago's McCormick Block and issued his first mail-order catalog, a simple sheet listing household goods of interest to farm families. To enlarge his market, Ward formed a loose affiliation between his company and the Patrons of Husbandry, better-known as the Grange. The Grange combined the functions of a fraternal organization with those of a legislative lobby. Its membership numbered in the hundreds of thousands, and when Ward became the official Grange supply-house, he found himself so swamped with orders that he had to move again and again to larger headquarters.

Montgomery Ward had been in business eight years when the man who would become his major competitor began his career. Richard Warren Sears was then a telegrapher and station agent in an obscure Minnesota town. His job left him a great amount of free time, so as a sideline he began a small business selling produce to friends in the city. One day, so the story goes, Sears' station received a shipment of watches that had been sent on approval to a local salesman. The addressee refused to accept them. Instead of sending them back, Sears purchased them himself. Adding a small markup, he persuaded fellow station agents along the Minneapolis and St. Louis Railroad to become his salesmen. That was in 1886, and it marks the beginning of the Sears Watch Company. Sears soon moved to Chicago and added new lines of merchandise; by the late 1890s he was competing directly with Ward.

Both companies concentrated heavily on expanding their markets, stressing their natural competitive advantages: no salesmen to pay, no wholesalers to mark up prices. They both bought in volume, and, because neither operated retail stores initially, they could steer clear of any high rent district. By charging a token sum for their catalogs, promotional costs were kept at a minimum. A strictly cash policy eliminated the problem of searching out deadbeats and trying to collect bad debts. They promised customers that they would not make special deals with selected friends, but did reserve the right to adjust prices to match market fluctuations.

Credibility in merchandising was a constant concern. Country merchants continually warned their customers that mail-order purchasing invited disappointment, or, worse, fraud. Sears and Ward filled their catalogs with illustrations and detailed descriptions, and—because farmers worried about ready-to-wear clothes not fitting—with instructions on how to take body measurements correctly. Both companies guaranteed customer satisfaction. Ward made it a practice to send handwritten replies to all correspondence. Sears sold cheap sets of stereopticon slides showing his own plant; this way, potential customers who were timid or skeptical could get a real look at company operations.

The mail order catalog, or "wish book," was the arbiter of taste in much of rural America. Although they eventually became long and unwieldy, catalogs nevertheless compressed a city's entire shopping district into one five-hundred page volume. Not only did each new edition add more lines of merchandise, it also enlarged the range of selection within each section. The 1902 Sears catalog contained some fifty pages of yard-goods listings, with a choice of hundreds of different patterns and colors. There was a tasteful item of every kind for any budget. Someone contemplating the purchase of a dining room chair, for instance, had a choice ranging from a 45-cent bentwood oak, through the "95-cent Leader," and on up to the $2.95-cent model with a leather seat, "richly carved back," and fancy "fine piano finish." Homebuilders could choose from six different designs in "fancy front doors," while the men's and women's ready-to-wear pages seemed to go on endlessly.

This wide range of choices meant that the hard-to-please buyer was more likely to find something he liked in a catalog than in any small-town store. Mail-order houses had to maintain a judicious balance between the established tastes of rural people and the introduction of novelties. Ward's, for instance, was selling aluminum cooking utensils as early as 1895, and both companies had extensive home photography sections. The latest in kitchen gadgets and kerosene lamps also appeared on these pages. Yet, on the other hand, when company buyers traveled the countryside in search of goods, they were careful to seek out opinions about whether some new style or other seemed too rakish. The final decision was made by the customers, whose orders were, in effect, ballots with votes for or against each piece of goods in the catalog.

Richard Warren Sears (1863-1914), c1900. Sears turned a small watch and jewelry business into a company that soon surpassed Montgomery Ward & Co. in sales.

Alvah Roebuck (1864-1948), c1900. Although Roebuck sold his share of Sears, Roebuck and Co. for $20,000 in 1895, the store still carries his name.
Sears, Roebuck and Co.

Sears stenographic department, c1895. Sears sold dozens of stereopticon sets. This stereo card shows the company employees at work corresponding with customers and filling orders.

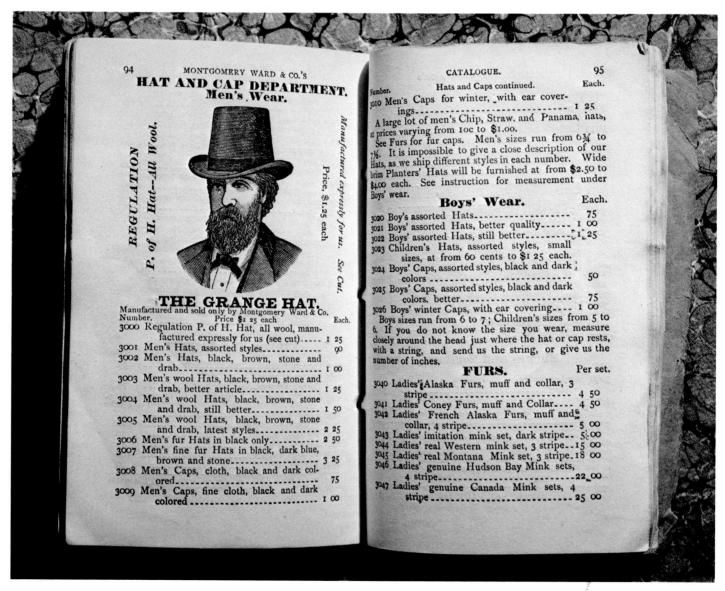

MONTGOMERY WARD & CO.'S
HAT AND CAP DEPARTMENT.
Men's Wear.

REGULATION P. of H. Hat—All Wool.

Manufactured expressly for us. See Cut.

Price, $1.25 each

THE GRANGE HAT.
Manufactured and sold only by Montgomery Ward & Co.

Number. Price $1 25 each.   Each.

3000 Regulation P. of H. Hat, all wool, manufactured expressly for us (see cut)..... 1 25
3001 Men's Hats, assorted styles.............. 90
3002 Men's Hats, black, brown, stone and drab.................................... 1 00
3003 Men's wool Hats, black, brown, stone and drab, better article................ 1 25
3004 Men's wool Hats, black, brown, stone and drab, still better................. 1 50
3005 Men's wool Hats, black, brown, stone and drab, latest styles.............. 2 25
3006 Men's fur Hats in black only............ 2 50
3007 Men's fine fur Hats in black, dark blue, brown and stone...................... 3 25
3008 Men's Caps, cloth, black and dark colored.................................. 75
3009 Men's Caps, fine cloth, black and dark colored.............................. 1 00

CATALOGUE.   95
Hats and Caps continued.   Each.

Number.

3010 Men's Caps for winter, with ear coverings................................ 1 25

A large lot of men's Chip, Straw, and Panama hats, at prices varying from 10c to $1.00.

See Furs for fur caps. Men's sizes run from 6¾ to 7½. It is impossible to give a close description of our Hats, as we ship different styles in each number. Wide brim Planters' Hats will be furnished at from $2.50 to $4.00 each. See instruction for measurement under Boys' wear.

Boys' Wear.   Each.

3020 Boy's assorted Hats................... 75
3021 Boys' assorted Hats, better quality....... 1 00
3022 Boys' assorted Hats, still better......... 1 25
3023 Children's Hats, assorted styles, small sizes, at from 60 cents to $1 25 each.
3024 Boys' Caps, assorted styles, black and dark colors.............................. 50
3025 Boys' Caps, assorted styles, black and dark colors, better................... 75
3026 Boys' winter Caps, with ear covering.... 1 00

Boys sizes run from 6 to 7; Children's sizes from 5 to 6. If you do not know the size you wear, measure closely around the head just where the hat or cap rests, with a string, and send us the string, or give us the number of inches,

FURS.   Per set.

3040 Ladies' Alaska Furs, muff and collar, 3 stripe................................. 4 50
3041 Ladies' Coney Furs, muff and Collar.... 4 50
3042 Ladies' French Alaska Furs, muff and collar, 4 stripe...................... 5 00
3043 Ladies' imitation mink set, dark stripe.. 5 00
3044 Ladies' real Western mink set, 3 stripe.. 15 00
3045 Ladies' real Montana Mink set, 3 stripe. 18 00
3046 Ladies' genuine Hudson Bay Mink sets, 4 stripe.............................. 22 00
3047 Ladies' genuine Canada Mink sets, 4 stripe................................. 25 00

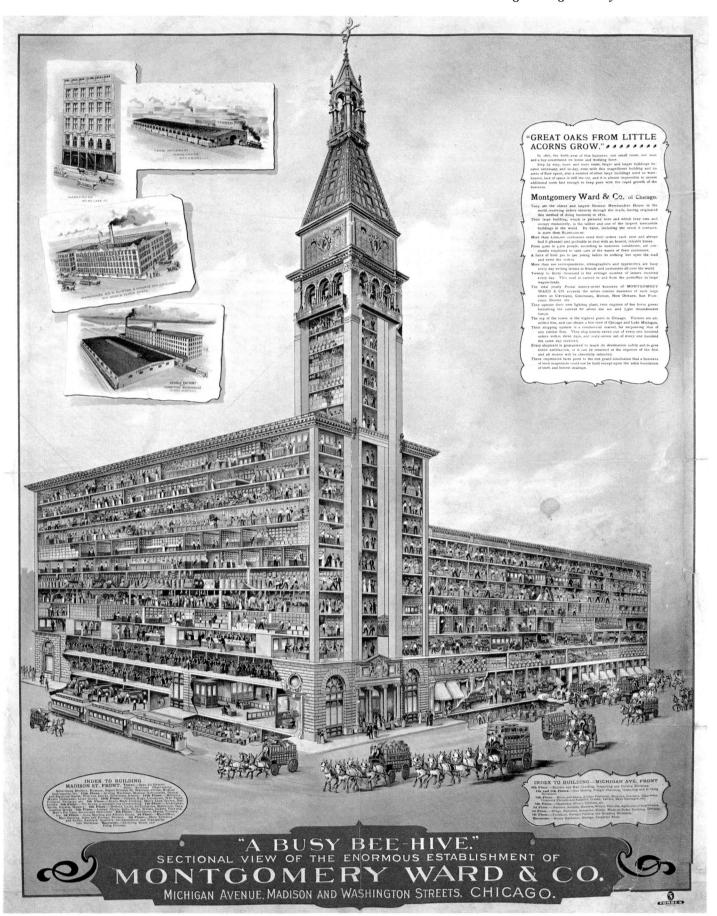

Test for astigmatism. Consumers could test their bodies for various defects, including astigmatism, then order remedies through the Sears catalog.

Test for Astigmatism.

If some of the arms of the above figure appear blacker or more distinct than others it is evidence that your eyes are affected with astigmatism. This trouble, however, is rare, and unless quite severe we will be able to send satisfactory glasses provided the instructions as given above are carefully followed. In severe cases of astigmatism it will be necessary for you to send us an oculist's prescription for the glasses, in which case we will have special cylindrical lenses carefully ground to order for you.

IMPORTANT.—In all cases where spectacles or eye-glasses are to be sent by mail 5 cents extra must be included for postage.

Straight Temple Spectacles
With Round Eye Wire.

Nos. 17500 to 17515.
Postage extra 5c each.

Straight Temple Spectacles are most suitable for those who wear glasses for near work only, and therefore remove them frequently from the eyes.

Clerical or Flat Eye Spectacles.

Nos. 17525 and 17526.
Postage Extra, 5c each.

Clerical spectacles are popular with those who wear glasses for near work only, the shape permitting the wearer to look over the upper edge when viewing distant objects. They are especially convenient for clergymen and other public speakers or anyone whose sight requires glasses for reading but not for distance.
No. 17525 Steel Frames.—Straight temple, clerical or flat eye spectacles, best quality with fine crystalline lenses. Price.................75c
No. 17526 Steel Frames.—Straight temple clerical or flat eye spectacles, best quality and finely tempered. Finest crystalline lenses. Price.................$1.00

Riding Bow Spectacles.

Nos. 17528 to 17540.
Postage extra 5 cents each.

The Riding Bow Spectacles, known also as Hook Bow, are to be preferred in all cases where the glasses are to be worn constantly, or nearly so. The shape of the temples prevents the spectacles falling off, and also keeps the lenses more exactly in the proper position all the time.
No. 17528 Steel Frames. Riding bow temples, good quality, blued. With fine crystalline lenses. Price.................75c
No. 17530 Steel Frames. Riding bow temples, best quality, finely tempered and nickel plated, with finest crystalline lenses. Price.................$1.25
No. 17532 Alumnico Frames. Riding bow temples, broad nose piece, light and well finished. Alumnico is a composition metal similar in weight and appearance to aluminum, showy and warranted not to tarnish. Finest crystalline lenses. Price.................$1.25

Rimless or Skeleton Spectacles.

Nos. 17550 to 17553.
Postage, extra, 5c each.
Rimless spectacles present a very neat and stylish appearance, and for this reason are popular, but owing to the nature of their construction they are necessarily fragile and very easily broken.
No. 77550 Gold filled mountings. Rimless, riding bow temples, broad nose piece, guaranteed for 10 years. Fine crystalline lenses. Price.................$2.20
No. 17552 Solid gold mountings. Rimless, riding bow temples, broad nose piece, solid 10 karat gold. Finest crystalline lenses. Price.................$4.10
No. 17553. Solid gold mountings. Rimless riding bow temples, broad nose piece, solid 14 karat gold. Finest crystalline lenses. Fully guaranteed in every respect. Price.................$5.65

Bi-Focal Spectacles.

Spectacles Showing Split Bi-Focal Lenses.

Spectacles Showing Cemented Bi-Focal Lenses.
Postage, extra, 5c. each.

When glasses for near vision and for distant vision of different strength are needed it is necessary to use bi-focal lenses. These are lenses in which the lower part, used for near work or reading, is made to differ in power from the upper part which is used for distance. We can furnish these lenses in two styles known as the "split" bi-focals and the "cemented" bi-focals.
The Split Bi-focals consist of two half-oval lenses with their straight edges placed together.
The Cemented Bi-focals, which are the latest and

Ordering mail order clothes, c1900. Mail order catalogs included instructions on how to take measurements for ready-made clothing. Some even contained samples of cloth.

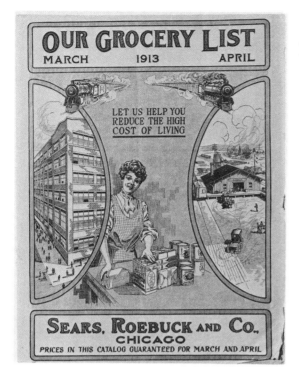

Grocery list, 1913. To bridge the gap between the farm and the city, a rural family could order groceries and even fresh fish from mail order catalogs. Sears, Roebuck and Co.

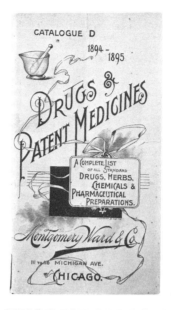

Patent medicine circular, Montgomery Ward & Co., 1894-5. Home remedies were especially popular in rural America, where residents were isolated from doctors.

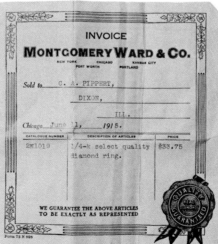

Sears Roebuck and Co., mail order housing ad, c1900. Mail order companies sold thousands of pre-cut balloon-frame houses. These structures left a permanent mark on rural America.

Diamond Ring Guarantee Certificate, Montgomery Ward & Co., 1915. Small-town jewelers joined other merchants in spreading rumors that mail order merchandise was shoddy. To allay fears Ward's offered this guarantee.
Perry Duis

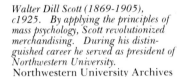

*Walter Dill Scott (1869-1905),
c1925. By applying the principles of
mass psychology, Scott revolutionized
merchandising. During his distinguished career he served as president of
Northwestern University.*
Northwestern University Archives

Delineator *magazine poster, 1903.
The* Delineator *applied Walter Dill
Scott's direct-approach concepts to a
circulation campaign.*
Business Americana Collection,
Smithsonian Institution

While Montgomery Ward, Richard Sears, and Marshall Field demonstrated that sales counters and mail-order catalogs were effective in merchandising and shaping tastes, another Chicagoan was largely responsible for introducing a new style of promotion. Walter Dill Scott had received his undergraduate education at Northwestern University before departing for Europe to study psychology. He took his doctorate in 1900 and returned to his alma mater the following year to begin teaching in its new psychology department. His interest in that science, however, was not confined to abstract experiments. As was the case with many a creative Chicagoan, he saw a practical application for his skills, one that would eventually touch the lives of nearly all Americans.

Scott had studied the mechanisms of human perception. He knew what the eye and the mind noticed, what they picked out of a crowded montage of images. Soon after his return to America, he began exploring the application of psychology to selling. The growth of American business during the late nineteenth century was, in part, the result of intense competition, and firms that had once held non-competitive monopolies now had to scramble to attract customers. Cities became littered with signboards, and the popular press was filled with advertising. Much advertising, however, either went unnoticed or left the reader unconvinced. In the latter regard, often it was not the factual information in the ad that failed, but rather its method of presentation.

Scott's approach to the problem was scientific. He devised experiments to test the reactions of people to visual stimuli, recording thousands of observations about colors, typefaces and sizes, and graphic images. He mailed thousands of questionnaires sounding out feelings toward certain kinds of products and reactions to different sorts of advertising. Then he went to work designing a specific ad campaign to fit a specific product. His theory was that visual images had to be appropriate and that ads had to reach an appropriate audience. He performed one of his most famous experiments for Hart, Schaffner & Marx, a firm that sold well-tailored men's apparel. Scott decided that a distinguished-looking man on horseback suggested a properly balanced image of masculine strength and refinement. The whole idea seemed almost bizarre, and the company was at first reluctant to go along. But eventually it did, and sales increased dramatically.

Scott later became president of Northwestern University, helping to make it one of the nation's major educational institutions. But he also left a great legacy to the business world: six books and over one-hundred articles. He later helped develop the intelligence and aptitude tests employed by the American military in World War I. He also went on to establish a new field of research, industrial psychology. All of this work was significant, but it was his innovative concepts about marketing that helped change the tastes of a nation by bringing new products and new styles to the attention of millions.

Chicago Arts and Crafts: The Settlement

The department store, the mail-order house, and the advertising campaign represented three different means by which Chicago spread its influence. One was urbane and involved the customer on a face-to-face basis. The second was rustic and depended on the U.S. mail service to bridge the distance between buyer and seller. The third involved promoting wants and desires more than specific products themselves. But Chicago was also the scene of another venture in taste-making, one which represented in many ways a rebellion against the others. This was the city's major role in the Arts and Crafts movement.

This crusade for "good taste" had its roots in England. It started essentially as an artistic rebellion. Led by artists and poets like John Ruskin and William Morris, it condemned the depersonalization of mass-produced goods, and especially poor design and the addition of useless and costly ornament of the type so often identified with Victorian styles. Color was used simply to attract attention rather than contribute to beauty in design. Furthermore, the machine had turned the worker into an artistic moron, regardless of the craft talents he or she might possess. Work had become joyless drudgery. Skills handed down through generations faced extinction. Devotees of the English Arts and Crafts movement formed societies to preserve and perpetuate the skills of handwork and to promote a broader appreciation of these skills. The movement started in the late 1860s, and within a decade it had attracted a large following.

During the late nineteenth century the British movement inspired the formation of a counterpart in the United States. Here it quickly became involved in the quest for a unique American art. Many American artists were concerned that their country was merely a cultural satellite which had apparently failed to produce a style or form of art that was not derivative. They wanted to encourage the latent talents of Americans in the arts and crafts, and foster a wider appreciation of the folk arts, which would naturally constitute a major source of any genuine American style. And so, beginning in the 1880s, American artists and their friends began forming small workshops to counteract the grotesque and omnipresent canons of Victoriana.

The Arts and Crafts movement found fertile ground in Chicago, already renowned for its rebellion against "Eastern style." A local designer, Isaac Scott, had produced a variation on the British Eastlake style of furniture; this was a fairly simple design to which was applied handmade, rectilinear trim. Some of Chicago's artistically-inclined residents commissioned Scott to design their furnishings. For instance, when the John J. Glessners built their new home on Prairie Avenue in the mid-1880s, Scott designed the furniture to blend with the Romanesque architecture of Henry Hobson Richardson. Likewise, Chicago's architects were conscious that their skyscrapers were unique. The same self-consciousness that promoted the publication of the *Inland Architect* prompted the city's architect-writers like Louis Sullivan and Frank Lloyd Wright to insist that Chicagoans had devised the first truly American style of building design.

It was therefore not an unexpected event when Chicagoans formed what was probably the first organized Arts and Crafts society in any major American city. The Chicago Arts and Crafts Society was founded on October 22, 1897, at a meeting at Hull-House. Its purposes were clear. It wanted to promote an appreciation of beauty everywhere, especially in the design of everyday items. It wanted to reduce the drudgery of factory work without letting the machines "dominate the workman and reduce his production to a mechanical distortion." It wanted to encourage handicraft work, and to promote its virtues through public exhibitions. Essentially, the society's philosophy was that "Nothing is too insignificant to merit the labor of an artist, and the artistic temperament can express itself in any material."

The society brought together an extraordinary mixture of people. Many Prairie-School architects were very active, including Myron Hunt, Marion Mahony, Dwight Perkins, and Frank Lloyd Wright himself. The Pond brothers, who designed the Hull-House complex and several other settlements, were charter members. Henry Demarest Lloyd, the social critic, joined, as did the *Chicago Herald*'s art critic Lucy Monroe. Big business and high society were represented by Mr. and Mrs. Frederick Delano and by Mrs. P. F. Pettibone, wife of the city's leading printer of legal forms. Herman Winslow was there, and his wife. A manufacturer of ornamental iron, Winslow was Wright's first client. Finally, there was a scattering of artists and academics and a few settlement workers from Hull-House.

Many of those involved in the movement completely abjured the machine age, preferring instead to use hand tools and ancient techniques. The most obvious exception was Frank Lloyd Wright. As a founding member of the society he sympathized at least partially with its assaults on industrialism. The Prairie-School architecture was designed for furniture in the simple, angular Arts and Crafts mode. Yet Wright was certainly not ready to reject the machine outright. The machine had simply been misapplied by the bunglers in control. Wright argued that there was no reason why mass-produced goods should not be beautiful, simple, and practical. While the preservation of folk crafts was undoubtedly important, it was the end-product that was of most crucial importance. Properly applied, the machine could liberate humanity rather than enslave it. "The machine," he pleaded, "does not write the doom of Liberty, but is waiting at man's hand as a peerless tool, for him to use to put foundations beneath a genuine Democracy."

The Arts and Crafts Society remained active for many years. Meetings usually included a short philosophical lecture and a practical demonstration of some craft. The society had a small office in the Woman's Temple, a downtown building designed by Burnham and Root (and which was owned for a time by the Woman's Christian Temperance Union). A few members sold craft-work there. The society also joined in producing exhibitions with the Chicago Architectural Club. And, all the while, its members kept up a stream of newspaper and magazine articles berating manufacturers for turning out merchandise that was expensive and flashy but shoddy and poorly designed.

Frank Lloyd Wright, "The Art and Craft of the Machine," 1901. The text of Wright's famous address was printed in the Catalog of the Fourteenth Annual Exhibit of the Chicago Architectural Club.

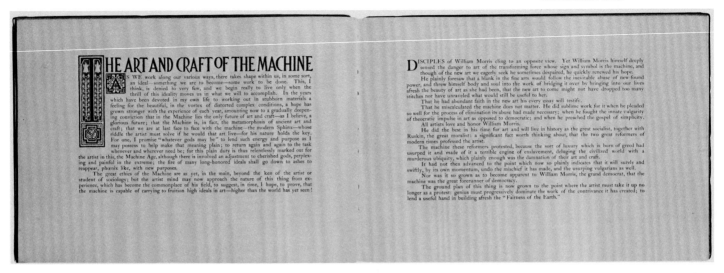

Although many of the organizers of the Arts and Crafts Society were well educated and at least moderately wealthy, they had a special interest in the poor, for they felt the movement had great potential for alleviating the ills of tenements. Simply designed furniture, for instance, could improve the quality of everyday life. Furniture made of oak, without gaudy ornamentation and garish embellishment, was not only cheaper, it was far more durable and less likely to become shabby. In March 1900 the society organized an exhibition at the Art Institute which demonstrated exactly how the principles of good taste were also the principles of practicality, and thus had relevance to the lives of even the most humble of citizens.

Hull-House became a major center for the Chicago Arts and Crafts movement. The first new building added to the complex was an art gallery designed by the Pond brothers. The reproductions of great paintings displayed there provided, according to Jane Addams and Ellen Gates Starr, a little beauty in the drab lives of the poor. Moreover, this was a wholesome recreation that they hoped could compete successfully with saloons, cheap concert halls, and "museums of anatomy." There was also a small circulating collection of reproductions. In tenements on the Near West Side, the work of the great masters could be found hanging against a backdrop of cracked plaster and torn wallpaper. Until the Art Institute opened its fine new building a few years later, there was simply no other way for the indigent to partake of classical beauty.

Eventually Hull-House developed a whole group of crafts shops, from woodcarving to needlework. The most famous was the bookbindery founded by Ellen Gates Starr, who had studied that art in Europe and initially intended to make it her vocation. She ended up practicing the craft avocationally as a part of the Hull-House program, binding a few things to help raise funds, and passing her skills on to interested pupils. Starr remained convinced that such skills allowed people to exercise their creative minds, while at the same time using their hands. Modern industry, she lamented, had artificially sundered the two.

The crafts activities at Hull-House focused on its Labor Museum. Opened in November 1900, this had two functions. One was to illustrate the history of industrial processes, to show how a particular craft evolved and how attendant machinery fit into the historical picture. The second goal of the Labor Museum was to restore the dignity that labor once had and the respect it once commanded. Young children who were a bit ashamed of the folk-art their parents treasured would gain a new understanding. This, in turn, would help bridge misunderstandings between the Americanized generation and the unassimilated generation. Through these exhibits various ethnic groups could appreciate each other's heritage. Although a few exhibitors sold what they produced, the Museum was primarily conceived as an educational experience. Jane Addams realized the difficulty of forcing adults into the discipline of the schoolroom, but, by observing and by doing, first- and second-generation immigrants could learn an important lesson.

Hull-House was only one of many settlements that initiated Arts and Crafts activities. Virtually every one of them set up at least one small shop, while the larger settlements bought kilns, looms, and even presses. There was also a related venture in this field, the Chicago Art Craft Institute. Established in 1900, it viewed these skills in an intensely practical light. Many of the students on scholarships were "young men and women of refinement who have been unexpectedly thrown upon their resources." Such pursuits as cabinetmaking, printing, sewing, and weaving were marketable skills. During its first four years the Institute placed over two hundred graduates in good jobs. Optimistically, it predicted that its graduates would become "the stronghold of the manufacturing interest of the country, the veritable backbone of our artistic industries."

Hull-House potter, photographed by Wallace Kirkland, c1925.
Jane Addams Memorial Collection, University of Illinois at Chicago Circle

Pottery bank, Hull-House, c1900. This bank, made in one of the settlement's craft classes, was located near the front door for contributions.
Jane Addams Memorial Collection, University of Illinois at Chicago Circle

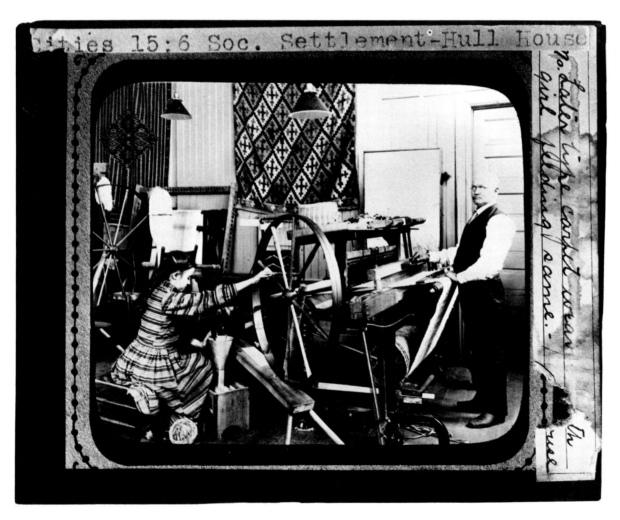

Lantern slide showing a corner of the Hull-House Labor Museum, c1900. Generations, young and old, met here to exchange craft skills and enthusiasm.

Mission furniture, Spiegel, May, Stern Company, 1900. By the turn of the century mail order houses were the major suppliers of Mission-style furniture to the Midwest. Most of it was made of oak, stained brown, and upholstered in imitation leather.

Societies and Salons

The Arts and Crafts movement in Chicago developed at two social levels. There were the philanthropic efforts of settlement houses and the Chicago Art Craft Institute. In addition, there were other efforts that appealed to a middle-class membership. The Industrial Art League was organized in 1899 by Oscar Lovell Triggs, an English professor at the University of Chicago. The League provided instruction in the arts and crafts, worked to establish art libraries, and published a beautifully-designed book on Morris and Ruskin. It also opened a small workshop, the Bohemia Guild, on South Michigan Avenue. Unfortunately, even though George Pullman's son-in-law, Frank Lowden, was its president, and Rabbi Emil Hirsch its vice-president, and even though there were four hundred members in 1903, it went out of existence after only four years.

The Industrial Art League's demise was largely because of its location and because its functions were absorbed by another organization. In 1903 Joseph Twyman, an immigrant English furniture-builder, organized the William Morris Society. This group promoted studios and schools of design. Edmund J. James, the head of Northwestern University, was its first president, and Oscar Triggs succeeded him the following year. Remnants of Triggs's own Industrial Art League later took over the publication activities of the Morris Society, transforming its *Bulletin* into *To-Morrow*, which eventually became a journal of socialist protest.

The other reason for the failure of the Industrial Art League was the founding of several outlying workshops more accessible than a central shop in the Loop. In the spring of 1903 George L. Schreiber bought an old church, equipped it for metal working and potting, and organized the Longwood Art Industry in the suburb of the same name. Payment of a dollar allowed members to use the

shops. Schreiber also grew his own flax and conducted art classes. A similar venture, the South Park Workshop, opened in 1903 also. Located at 5835 Kimbark Avenue in Hyde Park, it took over the equipment that once belonged to the defunct Bohemia Guild.

In addition to these small workshop ventures, Chicagoans developed several kinds of commercial establishments that sold Arts and Crafts goods. The largest was the Tobey Furniture Company. Joseph Twyman, who became the company's chief designer, established a Morris Room and persuaded the management to convert much of its production to Morris chairs and other furnishings of similar design. All items were handmade and fairly expensive, but the customer had the satisfaction of purchasing something out of the ordinary, so-called "New Furniture." As one typical Tobey ad put it:

It is with a pleasant satisfaction that we are able to place before our customers an interesting collection of the "New Furniture." The "New Furniture" is a departure from all established styles—a casting off of the shackles of the past. Extremely simple in design and honest in manufacture, it constitutes a style that is thoroughly practical, not too good for daily use, moderate in price, and is in demand by people of culture and taste.

Such ornament as it bears is incut carving . . . with something from nature as its motive.

The Tobey Company was a major manufacturer compared with the many smaller shops that appeared after the turn of the century. There was the Kalo Shop, which was founded in Park Ridge in 1900, moved to Michigan Avenue in 1908, and to the Fine Arts Building in 1918. The Wilro Shop, likewise located in the Fine Arts Building, produced leather-goods, wardrobe chests, metalwork, and other handmade goods. The Swastica Shop operated in the Marshall Field Building and sold a variety of Arts and Crafts work gathered from across the country. Finally, there were dozens of smaller craftshops that sold whatever was made on the premises.

Selling Good Taste

Grueby Pottery ad, Marshall Field &
Co., c1905. Robert Grueby's work
was considered to be among the best in
the nation. Field's was his exclusive
Chicago outlet.

The Arts and Crafts movement represented a rebellion against the ornate, machine-made goods sold by Field's or Ward's. Yet, ironically, the same methods of distribution spread the idea of Arts and Crafts across a wide area of the Midwest. Field's itself opened a special room devoted to "Mission furniture," the name applied to the simple, geometric Arts and Crafts style. It carried a complete line of Tobey products. During the 1920s Field's opened its own metalcraft shops, which employed many creative craftsmen. Nearly a whole floor of the store was devoted to handmade jewelry and other finely crafted items.

The styles of the Arts and Crafts movement were popularized by two other Chicago institutions. One was the mail-order house. As early as 1902 Ward's was selling a semi-ornate version of William Morris's famous reclining chair, and six years later the catalog carried a complete page of Mission furniture. Durability and simplicity of design attracted the attention of farm families, who often added a Mission table or Morris chair—a stark contrast to the ornate sideboard that often stood at the other end of the room.

Lastly, Chicago was the home of *House Beautiful.* This magazine, founded in December 1896, became the arbiter of good taste in middle-class homes across the nation. It quickly discovered Arts and Crafts, and published many articles about that movement. In addition, its advertising rates were low enough that many of the smaller shops could afford to publicize their products. Ironically, many advertisers employed a subtle appeal to good taste and culture that paralleled techniques perfected by Walter Dill Scott.

It is appropriate that Field's, Ward's, and *House Beautiful* delivered the Arts and Crafts style to the American public, for that was typical of Chicago. Located astride the nation's railway network, it was in a position to influence millions of Americans. Chicagoans quickly discovered that a physical object was much more than "a thing." Its style, its construction and how it was sold represented a series of ideas, and often creative genius. By dint of innovative techniques in merchandising, Chicagoans were able to reach the minds of most of America.

Tobey Furniture Company catalog.
Tobey was one of the nation's largest
manufacturers of Mission-style furniture.

CHIMES

ROBERT
HERRICK

UNDER
THE SKY
LIGHTS
FULLER

FABLES
in
SLANG
By
GEORGE
ADE

BY
BREAD
ALONE

I.K.
FRIEDMAN

THE
CONGO
AND
OTHER
POEMS

VACHEL
LINDSAY

Y 285
L 6423

Culture
Garland

Eugene
Field

SI
GA
DR

MACMILLAN

APPLETONS

STONE
CHICAGO

McCLUR
PHILLIP
& COMPAN

MACMILLAN

B.W.
& CO

Literature: An Urban Awakening

In the exciting atmosphere of late nineteenth-century Chicago, literature became a craft as well as an art. The creativity of local writers was well known. During each of the four decades after 1880 there was at least one "Chicago School" of literature. This term came to signify an urban realism, a frank confrontation with the growth of the city— just as Chicago architecture represented an attempt to come to terms with the physical manifestations of urbanization.

The evolution of Chicago literature as an artform actually took place on two social levels. Each was written by, for, and about a fairly distinct group of people. One was the literature of the genteel middle class, and tended to reflect the realities of business and professional life. The city itself played a relatively minor role, generally serving simply as a backdrop for the complexities of personal and social interaction. Chicago was a symbol more than a subject.

The other literary stratum did not become clearly defined until somewhat later. Its practitioners focused on the changes that urbanization had brought, on the city itself as an exciting saga, a rich quilt of diversity. The realities were often harsh, but Chicago was treated as an ongoing dramatic event that deserved reciting, even celebration. The literature this group produced was more freewheeling, more rebellious, more often calculated to upset propriety. It also provided insights about the lives of workers and immigrants that were rarely to be found in the writings of the other school.

The two schools were not mutually exclusive, however, nor were they invariably hostile to one another. Both had at least one thing in common with all the other creative movements in the city during those years: an abiding interest in presenting ideas to new audiences in original ways. And so it was that their efforts were both a craft and an art.

A shelf of Chicago books. For nearly thirty years Chicago was known for its innovative style and frank realism.

Henry Blake Fuller (1857-1929), bust by Lorado Taft, 1894. The first Chicago novelist to gain national fame, Fuller captured the spirit of Chicago during the Columbian Exposition.

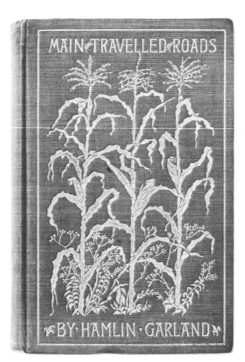

Hamlin Garland (1860-1940). Garland helped develop a distinctive Midwestern literary style.

Cover for Main-Travelled Roads, *1894. Hamlin Garland portrayed rural America in stark, realistic prose.*
Newberry Library

The Early Generation

The first wave of Chicago writers were a varied lot who ended up in the city for diverse reasons. Henry Blake Fuller was exceptional in being a native Chicagoan. Born in 1857, he had been sent to work at an early age by his wealthy father. After a term as a messenger boy and another as a crockery salesman, he managed to steal away to Europe for a short time, and there he discovered his artistic inclinations. Although he returned to manage the family fortune, he soon found himself cheated out of his inheritance. So he spent the rest of his years trying to support himself as a professional writer—never quite successfully, for he had to take a variety of jobs from selling books to newspaper work.

Relatively poor though he was, Fuller enjoyed an active social life, and got to know several other writers. One was Joseph Kirkland. A native of New York, Kirkland had been brought west by his family, and his mother, Caroline, had become one of the first published writers in Chicago or in Illinois. But Kirkland started out in more conventional pursuits, serving as an auditor for the Illinois Central Railroad for a while, and then operating a coal business that was destroyed in the Great Fire. Although he had studied law and been admitted to the bar, Kirkland began devoting himself more to writing, occasionally contributing a piece to some magazine. In 1886 he began work on his first novel. After publishing *Zury: The Meanest Man in Spring County* the following year, he turned his undivided attention to literary pursuits. Other novels followed, and in 1889 Kirkland became literary editor of the *Tribune.* He died only four years later, not long after persuading his friend Hamlin Garland to come to Chicago.

Born near West Salem, Wisconsin, in 1860, Garland had spent his early years on farms in Iowa and Dakota Territory,

and in small-town Wisconsin. He grew to hate the loneliness and drudgery of rural life, so in 1884 he sold his modest accumulation of land and moved to Boston. There, he was befriended by William Dean Howells and began writing about his experiences on the prairie. His *Main-Travelled Roads,* published in 1891, depicted the hardships and disappointments of rural life. Neither this nor three other realistic novels he published during the next two years sold well in the East, however. Even though Howells had predicted that Garland would emerge as the leading realist writer of his day, the young author felt rejected. He decided to try his lot in Chicago, a thoroughly realistic town.

Garland found Chicago amazingly sophisticated. He moved easily into its artistic circles and even started one important literary group himself, the Cliff Dwellers. But the true focus of a genteel cultural life was what became known as the "Little Room." It was named after a place in a ghost novel, a room that appeared and disappeared unpredictably. This small group began meeting in 1892, informally but regularly, after the Friday afternoon symphony concerts. After changing location several times it eventually ended up at the studio of Ralph Clarkson in the Fine Arts Building.

The Little Room attracted a remarkable assemblage of talent. Besides Garland and Fuller, there was Lorado Taft, whose sister had married Garland. There was Anna Morgan, the famous dramatics teacher. There were the Pond brothers, both architects, and Charles F. Brown, the artist. And among the leaders of the set were Lucy and Harriet Monroe. Lucy was the art critic for the *Herald,* and Harriet had become Chicago's most promising young poet. She had published her first verse in 1888 and the following year had presented the dedicatory ode at the opening of the Auditorium Theater. In 1893 she had officially opened the World's Fair with her "Columbian Ode," which brought her worldwide fame. A few years later she published a biog-

raphy of John Wellborn Root, her brother-in-law, a tribute to one kind of artist from another.

Although the Little Room was a varied group, some important figures of that early period were absent. One was Robert Herrick. Born in Cambridge, Massachusetts, in 1868, Herrick was educated at Harvard and had taught at M.I.T. before coming to the new University of Chicago in 1892. He established that institution's English program, but devoted himself mainly to writing. Although his novels were indictments of middle-class values, the security of a university position gave his life a stability that few of his contemporaries enjoyed.

Garland continued to write his novels of rural realism, while Herrick and Fuller turned to the businessmen who seemed to epitomize the transformation of Chicago after the Fire. Herrick's *Memoirs of an American Citizen* (1905) was a pseudo-autobiography of E. V. Harrington, a meatpacking baron, a story of unbridled ambition that conveys an image of Chicagoans as a collection of savages in celluloid collars. Here, as in *The Web of Life* (1900), a novel about a doctor who lacked the drive to succeed, Herrick showed his disdain for the city as a place that distorted the best of human qualities and subverted everything to gain. Fuller, meanwhile, was somewhat more ambivalent toward Chicago. His *With the Procession* (1895) was a sympathetic study of a family of older wealth striving but failing to keep up "with the procession"—to stay abreast of the newly-rich. The *Cliff-dwellers* (1893) was Fuller's attempt to treat the skyscraper, which he hated, as a symbol of modern ruthlessness. People entering "The Clifton" became "business machines." Fuller, however, at least regarded the city as an interesting place. While Herrick very seldom described Chicago itself, Fuller seemed fascinated—albeit in some morbid sense—by the drama of the streets. He went to great lengths to create a vivid image of a traffic jam or the rainy-day smells of immigrant hordes in the Public Library.

Chap-Book *poster, 1895. Competition for a growing middle-class clientele helped foster the development of Chicago poster art.*

Genteel Journals and a Critic

While most of the Little Room group wrote about businessmen and other people of power and influence, theirs was still a small and somewhat elitist group. Even the newspaper writers such as the Monroes and Fuller were cultural critics whose self-appointed role was to "improve" Chicago and bring it up to some hypothetical standard. In 1897, for instance, Fuller wrote an *Atlantic Monthly* article on "The Upward Movement in Chicago." Couched in tones that fluctuated between apology and boosterism, this cultural survey inveighed that "We are obliged to fight—determinedly, unremittingly—for those desirable, those indispensable things that older, more fortunate, more practiced communities possess and enjoy as a matter of course." Chicago, in other words, was emerging from "a struggle for bare necessities" into a plane of achievement that represented "a propulsion of a new and vigorous Western type past the plane of mere acquired culture."

The Little Room group employed books and literary magazines as their principal means of reaching readers. A leading journal was *The Dial,* founded and edited by Francis Fisher Browne. Born in Massachusetts, Browne had gone west after service in the Union army. A printer by trade, he had purchased an interest in a short-lived local magazine that failed during the depression of the 1870s. Browne then went to work as an editor at a local publishing house, Jansen, McClurg and Company, and in 1880 he persuaded his employers to let him start a new literary journal. *The Dial* resurrected the name once used by two defunct eastern predecessors. It contained notices of new books, brief reviews, and articles on the fine arts. Though conservative in its outlook, when it published articles about Chicago it applauded the efforts of local people who were dispelling the image of an unsophisticated, overgrown village. *The Dial* seldom attracted more than a thousand subscribers, yet its high editorial standards garnered the undying support of a wealthy band of followers.

By the turn of the century Chicago had emerged as a center for the publication of innovative periodical literature, the form of which could often be as important as the content. There was, for example, the *Chap-Book,* started by Herbert S. Stone, son of the publisher of the *Chicago Daily News.* While the first issues emanated from Cambridge, Massachusetts, Stone moved the editorial offices to Chicago in August 1894. With his friend H. I. Kimball he established a publishing house, their intention being to promote their books and introduce new authors through the periodical, naturally taking advantage of cheap postal rates.

The *Chap-Book,* however, soon took on an intrinsic significance. It attracted critical commentaries by writers who regarded contemporary literature with disdain, and the editors made no attempt to tone down their scathing reviews. The *Chap-Book*'s format was artistically creative, as were the promotional posters sent out to newsstands. The latter were elaborate, colorful, and so distinctive that they sometimes attracted more interest than the magazine itself: how typical it was for Chicagoans to put Toulouse-Lautrec on a piece of cardboard! The posters did help sell magazines, though, pushing the circulation of some issues over 50,000, and normally keeping it above 20,000. It soon spawned imitators. As the editors noted, "Its habits of free speech produced a curious movement among the young writers of the country. There was scarcely a village or town which did not have its little individualistic pamphlet frankly imitating the form and tone of the *Chap-Book.*"

Unfortunately, by 1898 the imitators had helped put the *Chap-Book* in financial trouble. While circulation declined only slightly, advertising revenue fell off drastically. Stone and Kimball had wanted to attract ads from other publishers, but the devastating reviews they had run in the *Chap-Book* prompted what amounted to a boycott. On July 15, 1898, the *Chap-Book* folded. Stone and Kimball continued to publish books by Chicago authors, however, and they also remained in the periodical field, concentrating their efforts on *House Beautiful,* which they had taken over in 1897. Three years later Stone established *House Beautiful* as a separate company.

The Little Room group represented one concept of the writer's role in urban society. But this was not the only one. By the 1890s there was also emerging in Chicago a school less concerned either with middle-class life or uplift than with attracting a wider audience. Though starting out contemporaneously with the Little Room, this school ultimately proved much more influential and popular. It produced a literature that dealt with the everyday lives of ordinary Chicagoans, who, in turn, constituted its patrons. It was gutsy, almost proletarian, both in style and content.

The work of Eugene Field represented a step in this direction. Born in St. Louis in 1859, Field had been fortunate enough to receive a college education. Early in life he had decided to become a newspaperman, had spent some years in Denver, and was already famous when he came to work for the *Chicago Daily News* in 1883. He was an essayist and a poet, and combined those talents with a quick wit. His work had a biting humor that proved deadly to any sort of pretentiousness. "Sharps and Flats," as his column was called, was a whimsical flood of short poems, which he often facetiously attributed to embarrassed civic leaders. Often his own freehand drawings adorned his pieces. One of his spoofs described a "folding bed for cultured Chicagoans," which, when closed, appeared to be a bookcase—available in poetry, drama, or fiction. Each volume, however, was hollow, and actually served as a drawer. Field also lampooned the Theodore Thomas orchestra for a particular program in which it played five pieces in 150 minutes—rapid, yes, but not as fast or efficient as a Chicago packinghouse. The latter, Field observed, could process 450 hogs in the same amount of time.

Field cultivated an amazing capability for communicating with the average reader. An ardent baseball fan and an excellent bowler, he could devote an entire column to oft-told fishing tales, and make them all sound fresh and original. He also became well known for his children's poetry. Generations of boys and girls grew up hearing "Wynken, Blynken, and Nod" and "Little Boy Blue" without ever knowing that those familiar verses first appeared in a newspaper column. The gentle ribbing he gave Chicago's intelligentsia and his mass appeal clearly put Field at odds with the Little Room group. Yet he was not truly a rebel. He spoke in the vernacular but was no revolutionary. He did not launch any sustained attack on genteel poetry or literature. There is a remote possibility that he might have done so, though probably not—he was too much the cheerful practical joker—and in any event his prolific pen was stilled by sudden death in 1895. Genuine rebellion came from a younger group of writers and poets who were less comfortable with society. This group wrote in a realistic mode, but its work derived from a different set of experiences. Speaking primarily through the competitive mass-circulation magazine and the daily press, this second generation of writers had an intimate familiarity with the city in all its facets.

Eugene Field (1850-1895), working at home, 1893. An essayist, poet, and wit, Field combined these talents in his "Sharps and Flats" column for the Chicago Daily News.

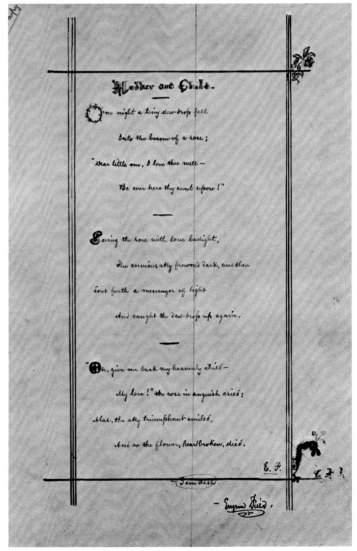

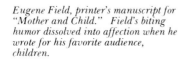

Eugene Field, printer's manuscript for "Mother and Child." Field's biting humor dissolved into affection when he wrote for his favorite audience, children.

McClurg's bookstore bulletin, 1905.
A. C. McClurg & Co. was for many years the largest book dealer in America.

Arkansaw Traveler, *1891. Edited by Opie Read, the* Arkansaw Traveler's *style often reflected a folksy "Chicago style" humor.*

The development of a publishing industry receptive to innovation was an essential antecedent to Chicago's literary creativity. That tradition dated back almost to the beginning of the city. There were a number of short-lived and undistinguished periodicals published in small-town Chicago during the early 1840s. Many were political, yet one was not—the *Gem of the Prairie,* begun in 1844. While the style of its poetry and prose was decidedly rough, it became a financial success, so much so that eight years later it was transmuted into the Sunday edition of a new daily newspaper, the *Chicago Tribune.* Thus, even at this early date, crude efforts at producing creative literature became entwined with the day-to-day reporting of news and with commercialism. The potential readership in the town was so small that literature had to become a sort of stepchild to advertising. For instance, W. W. Dannenhower included poetry and fiction in his bookstore flyer, while *Sloan's Garden City Monthly* started as a vehicle for promoting patent medicines, and *Chicago Magazine: The West As It Is* was primarily in the business of selling engraved portraits.

These literary beginnings may seem tawdry, yet they were inevitable in a town under the imperial domination of the East. With the exception of the *Lady's Western Magazine,* published by Benjamin F. Taylor, literary content was secondary. None of the local magazines made much of an effort to create new literary forms. Rather, their editors brought old traditions along with them on their westward migration. Innovations did not come until the 1860s and 1870s, and, even then, they initially affected not content but the way that literature was distributed.

The development of the railroad helped transform Chicago's role as a literary center. As the lines reached into the countryside, they created the means for a regional interchange of culture between city and farm. The expansion of trading territory brought the Midwest in close contact with the publications as well as the products of Chicago. These attracted talented young men and women from farms, who, in turn, instilled Chicago's publishing industry with fresh ideas. The result was a flurry of new ways to package and sell literature. At the end of the Civil War a group of Chicagoans saw that the railroad network could be used to distribute magazines. In 1866 they founded the Western News Company, and that organization helped sustain a number of new Chicago publications. For example, the *Western Monthly,* started in 1865, was renamed the *Lakeside Magazine* by new owners who redefined its purpose. Not only would it be written for Chicagoans, it would help interpret and "sell" the city to the entire region and perhaps even the nation. This publication also introduced Chicagoans to the idea of combining the production of books and periodicals in a single company. The Lakeside Press also did much to elevate standards of printing and book design in Chicago.

Other kinds of publications soon appeared on Chicago and Midwestern newsstands. The *Little Corporal,* started in Evanston in the late 1860s, was one of the first regional children's magazines. The Lakeside Library of the 1870s pro-

Chicago Public Library, 1870s. Chicago's first public library building, a water tank, was called the "Rookery" because it attracted hundreds of nesting birds. When Burnham and Root constructed a new building on the site in 1886, they kept that name.

duced cheap reprints of classics. Another periodical of note was the *Chicago Ledger,* published by William D. Boyce, best known for introducing the Boy Scout movement into the United States. Boyce's *Ledger* became commonplace in farmhouse parlors. The first and most successful of the mail-order magazines (and, coincidentally, founded the same year as Montgomery Ward's, 1872), the *Ledger* was a "family magazine" that avoided controversial questions and concentrated on light moralistic fiction.

Chicago produced two important humor magazines. *Carl Pretzel's Forum,* started in 1873, originated what became known as "Chicago-style" humor, direct and warm, folksy and human. Commentators often contrasted it to what they termed "New York cynicism." This type of humor was also present in the *Arkansaw Traveler,* which was started in Little Rock in 1882 but moved to Chicago five years later. Under the direction of Opie Read, one of America's foremost humorists, it was specifically aimed at railway

travelers, and sold on trains across the nation. Thus, in yet another way Chicago's location at the heart of the American rail network helped shape the cultural life of the city.

The development of a publishing industry concerned about mass consumption was important in establishing Chicago as a major literary center. But the city also had to develop a reading audience of its own. Many small clubs and literary societies appeared during the last half of the nineteenth century, and these provided a forum for the discussion not only of published works but also unpublished manuscripts. Chicago had a number of bookstores, and McClurg's became the nation's largest book jobber. There were also private libraries, especially in the years before the Great Fire, although these were naturally limited to people of wealth and education. To develop a truly lively literary tradition Chicagoans had to find ways to reach the poor and the foreign-born, two groups that in sheer numbers were rapidly becoming predominant.

One of Chicago's most important triumphs in this realm was the belated creation of a Public Library that deliberately set out to help expand the community of readers. Prior to 1871 the general public enjoyed only a limited access to book collections in a few philanthropic reading rooms. Although the agitation for a public library dated from the 1830s, it took the Great Fire to bring the Illinois General Assembly to the rescue. A new state law, passed in 1872, established a Library Board empowered to raise funds through taxation. The proponents of this act had been so concerned about potential opposition that they consulted the nation's leading authorities and framed the most detailed and specific public library law in the country. Indeed, this Illinois law became the model for new and revised statutes in many other states.

From the beginning, the Chicago Public Library regarded itself as a service institution rather than a scholarly retreat. It opened on January 1, 1873, with 2,800 volumes. By May of the following year the collection had grown to 17,355. What proved most significant about this collection was the large proportion of foreign-language books. This was partly accidental, for citizens in several European countries donated books to Chicago as a sort of cultural relief program. Soon after the Fire, a member of the Library Board traveled abroad and brought back nine thousand volumes in six modern languages. By 1884 further acquisitions had brought the foreign-language holdings to nearly a quarter of the total. Not until the great expansion of American publishing in the 1890s did that percentage begin to decline.

Those foreign-language volumes played an important role in the extension of Chicago's library facilities. In 1884 the Library Board realized that its building in the Loop was becoming more remote from the growing communities of immigrants, so it established a "delivery station," the first of several scattered throughout the city. These had no permanent collections or card catalogs; rather, they transmitted book requests downtown and books back out to the neighborhoods. To accommodate customers the library issued finding lists and bibliographies on a variety of subjects.

The delivery stations, located in space rented from shopkeepers or in settlements such as Hull-House, proved enormously popular. In 1887 the Library Board noted the progress of a station at 531 West 18th Street in Pilsen:

> The work of a new station, No. VII, is quite remarkable. It is located nearly three miles from the Library, in the midst of a settlement of Bohemians who are a laboring people and seldome come to the part of the city where the Library is situated. Before the establishment of this station only 2.8 per cent of the books issued at all of the stations were in the Bohemian language. The issue of books at this station is not larger than any other; and the proportion of books in the Bohemian Language issued at all the stations has risen to 12.12 per cent. Many books in the English, German and other languages are also issued at this station, which would not have reached the community except for the establishment of this station.

As the children of immigrants became Americanized and learned English, the importance of foreign-language books in the Public Library gradually dwindled. But the presence of such a service was an early indication of the way that Chicagoans viewed culture: success was measured in terms of reaching out to large numbers of people.

Fuller, Garland, Herrick, and their circle of friends had constituted the foundation of Chicago's literary tradition. The appearance of Eugene Field had provided a necessary component of gentle, humorous criticism. But the Denver transplant proved that a newspaper drew inspiration from the mundane and must appeal to wide audiences to be successful. Efforts too closely keyed to uplift in the manner of Henry Fuller or *The Dial* proved unpopular. Newspaper fiction might embody subtle moralisms, but the style had to be clear and the presentation straightforward. This was not exactly a matter of appealing to the lowest common denominator, yet it is true that members of the "second school" largely lacked the financial independence of the first, had worked their way up from the bottom, and knew the city as few others did. Much of the fiction they produced was shaped by their experiences in the city.

A favorite mode of presenting literary journalism was the daily column, a mainstay of all of the larger newspapers. Editors tried out promising staff writers, and from time to time one of them managed to capture the public fancy. This was how each of the two young men who became Chicago's most famous columnists got their start. The two came from very different backgrounds. One, George Ade, was born in 1866 in an isolated little place called Kentland, Indiana. The other, Finley Peter Dunne, was born the following year in a middle-class Irish Catholic neighborhood on Chicago's West Side. Ade had the benefit of a college education at Purdue, while declining family fortunes terminated Dunne's formal schooling with his high school graduation. Despite their very different origins, however, these two writers created a distinctive style of humor, one that spoke to Chicago and about it as well.

Dunne began work on the *Chicago Telegram* in June 1884 at the age of sixteen. He had not been at that paper long when he received an offer from the *Daily News*. His new job was to write pithy barbs about the day's events for the editorial page. Soon he graduated to sportswriting, covering baseball. By 1887 he had already developed a reputation for his subtle humor—quite the opposite of his colleague Eugene Field's bombastic wit. In 1888 his savvy as a reporter earned him a chance to become city editor of the rival *Times*, but a shakeup in the management left him unemployed. After a year with the *Tribune*, he moved to the *Herald*, and finally to the latter's sister paper, the *Chicago Evening Post*. After that, Dunne began to spend less time on the street and more time putting his wit down on paper. At first this was confined to the editorial page. The *Post* had a strong intellectual and literary bent, however, and humorous opinions were not out of place. By 1892 he had also begun to do an occasional column, saying his piece through the medium of a saloonkeeper he had invented. Gradually this character began to assume an Irish dialect and on October 7, 1893, Martin J. Dooley was born—"Mr. Dooley," ultimately a legend.

Working behind his bar out on "Archey Road" (Archer Avenue), Mr. Dooley had something to say about almost every aspect of urban life. At first he kept to Chicago and its prominent people. Like Eugene Field, he could deflate the the most outrageous pretentions with a single well-chosen adjective. Later, after Dunne's work started getting nationwide syndication, Mr. Dooley's philosophical discourses ranged on into national and international affairs. Yet there remained an essential neighborhood provincialism about the pieces that reduced the most complex issues to matters of simple logic. "Shakespeare, th' Bible, and' Mike Ahearn's histhry iv Chicago" achieved parity. Dunne's innocence and lack of cynicism was typical of the city's humorists, however, and these were the same traits that characterized the work of a writer for a rival paper, George Ade.

Ade's vehicle for humorous commentary had also derived from his experiences as a street reporter. He had gone everywhere for the *Record* (a new name given the morning edition of the *News*), and he knew the saloons and the justice-of-the-peace courts as well as the cultural pursuits and club-life of the wealthy. He was always eager to comment on what seemed the most mundane aspects of everyday life. Finally, in 1893, Ade settled upon "Stories of the Streets and of the Town," a daily column of bemused observations about the ordinary. While his characters were fictionalized, they were patterned on the real-life concerns of Chicago's "little people:" a young office-worker wonders whether the skyscraper going up nearby will block out the sunlight coming in his window; a middle-class family's lawn party is ruined by indigent neighbors gawking hungrily through the fence. Hobos to nabobs, Chicagoans of every description provided material for Ade, and their diversity reflected the multiform patchwork of the city.

After a few years, Ade decided to cast certain of his characters in more-or-less regular roles—Doc Horn and Pink Marsh, for instance. Pink Marsh was a black bootblack somewhere downtown. As had happened with Dunne's Mr. Dooley, Ade's pieces proved so appealing that they were collected in paperback anthologies with the general title *Stories of the Streets and of the Town.* His work was also syndicated, and published between hard covers for sale in the nation's bookshops. Fame and fortune came to both Ade and Dunne as America adopted a Chicago reading habit and imbibed the streetcorner realism of its new generation of writers.

The newspaper writers of Chicago formed their own little group in 1889. It met informally in the back of Henry Koster's saloon in an alley near the *News* and the *Herald.* Named the "Whitechapel Club" after the scene of "Jack the Ripper's" murders, its members were a casual lot who drank heavily and pulled endless macabre practical jokes on each other. The saloon was decorated with skulls and blood-stained Indian blankets. Its membership included, through the years, both Ade and Dunne, as well as Alfred Henry Lewis, whose exposés of patent medicines would later make him famous. There was Opie Read, the humorist, and Brand Whitlock, who later became the reform mayor of Toledo, but was then a young reporter on the *Herald.* They were an unusual group, these men who formed a club that represented a zestful affirmation of urbanism, an acceptance of the city for what it was. Their

Finley Peter Dunne (1867-1936), c1900. Bridging the gap between journalism and literature, Dunne's syndicated column reflected a "Chicago style" humor. His "Mr. Dooley" became a national favorite.

George Ade (1865-1944), c1898. Ade's syndicated column, "Stories of the Streets and of the Town," was based on the ordinary experiences of average Chicagoans.

place was a distilled essence of Chicago; quite unlike the Little Room, ethereal and altogether aloof toward the city. Members gradually drifted away to other jobs in other cities, but the spirit of the Whitechapel Club remained.

The next major celebrant of the Chicago experience and purveyor of curbstone realism was actually a member of the Little Room. But I. K. Friedman was decidedly a maverick. Born in Chicago in 1870, Friedman might well have developed into the spokesman for an intellectual elite. He held an undergraduate degree from Michigan and had attended graduate courses in philosophy at the new University of Chicago. But instead of pursuing the comfortable career he might have, he chose instead to go to work for the *Daily News.* Special assignments took him into the city's slums, and he drew upon his experience, plus that of his own family in the city's Jewish ghetto, to create a series of sympathetic fictional vignettes of slum life. Some of these he expanded into books. His first, *The Lucky Number,* appeared in 1896. Making effective use of the city's street jargon, it told of thieves and beggars who assembled in a gambling saloon called "The Lucky Number." His *Poor People* (1900) depicted the social life and genuine humanity of slum dwellers, while *The Autobiography of a Beggar* (1903) was set in a flophouse during an electoral campaign by "No-Car-Fare O'Brien." Friedman later became one of the city's leading socialists.

Friedman's background was a bit unusual. More typical was Theodore Dreiser. Born in 1871 in Terre Haute, Dreiser grew up in a miserable broken home. His father was an alcoholic, and in an attempt to escape from poverty his mother moved to Chicago with young Theodore. City life, the ethnic diversity, and the beer garden outside the window of their flat fascinated Dreiser; he returned to Indiana with his mother, but when he was sixteen he ran away, back to Chicago. He went through a succession of jobs, from bill collector to newspaper reporter. He learned at

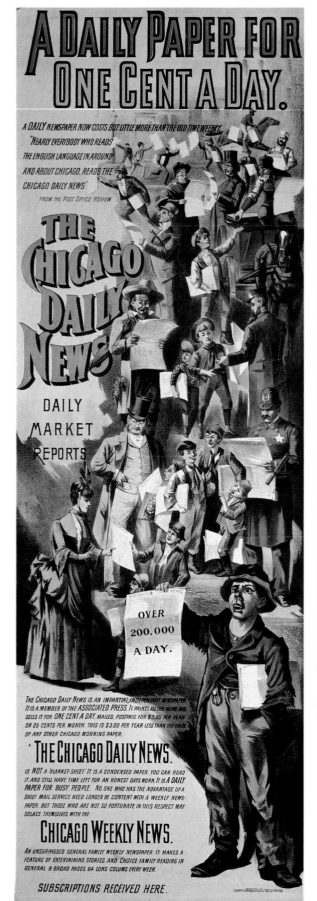

"Mr. Dooley on the Recall of Judges,"
by Finley Peter Dunne, 1912.   The
new judicial system inaugurated in
Chicago in 1906 was not perfect, and
Dunne could not resist saying so.

Chicago Herald *poster, 1890.*
Artist Will Denslow created this exam-
ple of popular throw-away art.

Chicago Daily News *poster, 1881.*
Chicago writers depended on the broad
readership represented in this poster.

PART II. EDITORIAL.

The Chicago Sunday Tribune.
THE WORLD'S GREATEST NEWSPAPER

PART II. EDITORIAL.

APRIL 14. 1912.

MR. DOOLEY ON THE RECALL OF JUDGES
BY FINLEY PETER DUNNE

"He's apt to think he's still on the bench an' hand ye a punch."

"When he sint a man down th' road f'r forty or fifty years he always give him such a dhressin' down that th' pris'ner was glad to get away where he'd be safe."

"A-RRE ye in favor iv th' in—th' whatd'ye-call-it—an' th' rifirindum an' th' recall?" asked Mr. Hennessy.

"Am I in favor iv what?" said Mr. Dooley.

"Iv th' init—th' in—" Mr. Hennessy tried again.

"Niver mind tellin' me," Mr. Dooley interrupted. "I know what ye mean be th' faces ye're makin'. No, I'm not. I'm not in favor iv ayether iv these glorious principals that has been handed down to us f'rm our Swiss ancestors. Man an' boy I've voted f'r fifty years f'r pollytickal issues that I cuddent undherstand, but I dhraw the line whin they hand me issues that I can't aven pronounce. I've been a free thrader, although ivrything I read proved to me that if I got me foolish wishes I'd be rooned through th' products iv th' pauper labor iv Europe poorin' in an' floodin' ye out iv ye'er job. That bribe iv two twinty-five a day that ye cajole out iv th' steel thrust f'r takin' a healthy amount iv exercise wud go, an' whin it wint down wud fall this splindid commercial intherprise that I've built up. So I voted f'r free thrade. An' me frind Silo, th' thruck farmer, who knew he was bein' crushed be th' tariff, voted to go on bein' crushed. It was all right. If he won th' tariff stayed an' if I won it was increased, an' there we were with nawthin' to throuble us between illictions.

"But these new issues ar-re diff'rent. Suppose I say I'm f'r thim. 'Ar-re ye f'r th'—as ye said—an' th' so-an'-so?' says th' judge iv illiction, 'I am,' says I in a ringin' voice. 'I wud die f'r thim,' says I. 'Thin spell thim,' says th' judge iv illiction. An' I faint with shame.

"But th' recall is betther. I can pronounce that without premachurely agein' me face. Besides 'tis a fine issue. Ye don't have to get a college pro-fissor to take a pointer an' a diagram an' explain it to th' other ign'rant voters. They know all about it. They've been votin' f'r it f'r years. Put in simple language it is: 'We're tired iv him. Throw him out.' Nawthin' is more raisonable thin that an' nawthin' will go home quicker to th' gin'rous heart iv th' people iv this gr-reat counthry. Supposin' some fellow goes to th' ligislachure as a frind iv th' people an' th' on'y want iv his old chums that can get to see him a month afther he's at th' capitol is th' janyal prisidint iv th' gas comp'ny. Well, wan day ye see his wife go by in an autymobill an' ye say: 'Don't ye think Higgins has got enough? Let's put th' law on him.' So we go down to Springfield an' we say: 'Bill, ye're such a good fellow that we can't do without ye. We miss ye'er smilin' face on th' scow. Ye must be with us again. An' to show ye how kind we feel to'rds ye we've found ye'er old pick an' shovel an' brought thim to ye.' An' wan iv us takes him be th' hair an' th' other be th' heels an' we throw him out iv th' window. An' that's th' recall.

"It suits me th' best iv all th' issues iv th' year. There's nowhere I hate to see th' same old face thin with its feet up on th' desk iv a pollytickal office. An' they ain't anny rule iv life betther thin this, that whin ye put a man on a perch an' he don't sing th' way we want, bump him off.

"Am I in favor iv recallin' th' judges, too? Ye bet I am. Well, maybe I wuddent recall thim exactly. A judge that's been on th' bench anny lenth iv time is poor comp'ny in a crowd. If he says, 'It's a fine day,' and ye say 'It ain't,' he's apt to think he's still on the bench an' hand ye a punch. Whin a man gets what Hogan calls th' joodicyal timper it means he's cross all th' time. So p'rhaps I wuddent haul thim back to publick life. But I'd pretind I was goin' to. Ivry wanst in a while I'd give thim a dark look as much as to say: 'An' I'll get ye, too, me good fellow if ye don't brace up. An' I'm th' boy that can do it.' An' aither a while whin I said 'How d'ye do?' to him he might say somethin' more janyal thin 'Thirty days.'

"Ye see, 'tis this way. Ye mind little Levy that was ilicted judge. He was th' junyor mimber iv th' firm iv lawyers that done all th' lagal wurruk in th' common council f'r Garrity, th' big contrhactor. I guess he wasn't much good in th' office, so Perkins, his boss, made a judge iv him. He was a pleasant man durin' th' campaign, an' there was a frind iv mine that wint crazy about him. His name was Dougherty. Dougherty cuddent say too much about his frind Judge Levy. He begun callin' him Judge two months before th' iliction. 'There's a man that'll make a mark f'r himsilf,' says he. 'He's got th' fine constitutional mind,' he says. 'An' a pleasant man an' a frind iv th' poor an' downthrodden,' he says. Well, Dougherty ilicted him, or annyhow thought he did, an' th' judge leaped upon th' bench. I guess he made a good judge. Whin he sint a man down th' road f'r forty or fifty years he always give him such a dhressin' down that th' pris'ner was glad to get away where he'd be safe. His interpretations iv th' constitution was gr-rand. 'Tis funny about th' constitution. It reads plain, but no wan can undherstand it without an interpreter. This here frind iv Dougherty's thranslated th' ol' constitution into Yiddish, low German, Fr-rinch, Rooshyan, an' arly English.

"Annyhow, it was Dougherty's good luck to have a case before him. If I iver go into coort th' polis'll have to take me in in chains. I'm a gr-reat reader, an', as Hogan says, familyarity with decisions broods contimpt iv coort. But Dougherty didn't know, an' whin he'd stepped into a hole in th' flure at th' facthry an' broke his leg he got a lawyer an' sued Flannigan, th' owner. Th' lawyer told Dougherty that th' laste Flannigan wud have to do to square himsilf was to give him th' facthry an' a pair iv goold crutches to hop to an' fr'm his autymobill on. Dougherty got so proud over this here sudden flood iv wealth that there was no talkin' to him. If ye ast him what he was doin' he wud say, 'Lookin' afther me lawsuit,' as much as to say, 'Runnin' me bank.'

"Well, sir, th' case come to thrile an' Dougherty wint to th' coorthouse. He thought his old frind seemed near sighted, f'r whin Dougherty thried to wave his hankerchief at him his honor motioned to th' coort attendant. Durin' th' examination this binivolent monarch dhrew pitchers on a pa-paper, but he showed two or three times that he remimbered Dougherty be sayin', 'Speak up, me man,' or 'Answer th' question or I'll lock ye up.' Fin'lly whin all th' ividence was in th' judge motioned th' coort polisman to throw Dougherty out, an' thin spoke as follows: 'This here case started Dougherty again Flannigan, but it's now me again congress, an' I give th' verdick f'r mesilf, an' if I had congress here I'd sind it to jail f'r passin' a law in favor iv this here polthroon. I've half a mind now to g-r-ther th' bailiff to pinch th' house iv reprisintatives, th' sinit, an' th' prisidint that signed th' law an' put thim in th' basteel.' Th' constitution says they had a right to, says Dougherty's lawyer. 'Eighty days f'r contimpt iv coort,' says his honor. 'If th' constitution says so it niver meant it. What did the constitution say? I don't know, but undher th' decision iv Lord Justice Poke in th' Eighth Elizabeth, a man in Dougherty's job was th' same as a horse an' he can't've changed. Who iver heerd iv a horse collictin' damages? It wud be conthry to all th' rules iv law an' property,' says he. 'D'ye mean to say I'm th' same as a horse?' says Dougherty. 'That is ye'er status,' says the coort. 'Thin,' says Dougherty, 'if I've got a broken leg Flannigan has a right to shoot me an' I'd betther be goin', an' he broke another leg on th' stairs, but he sued th' county an' recovered damages.

"Don't I think a poor man has a chanst in coort? Iv coorse he has. He has th' same chanst there that he has outside. He has a splindid, poor man's chanst. Annyhow, he ought to stay out iv coort onless he's done somethin' pleasant to get himsilf there. It's no place f'r him or f'r anny man, rich or poor, to go fortune huntin'.

"An' do I think th' judges'll iver be recalled? Faith, I do not. Wud ye lave anny wan recall me if ye was a judge? I see mesilf doin' it. Whin th' popylace thried to whistle me back to practice law on th' third flure I'd call th' bailiff over an' say: 'James, get out th' handcuffs.' Ye can bet that th' first law recallin' th' judges will be pronounced onconstitutional be th' entire joodicyary iv th' counthry be a risin' vote an' with three hearty cheers. If I was a judge I wud know that a law throwin' me out iv a job was onconstitutional at wanst, ex post facto, ex propria vigore, an' de juribus non dispytandam, as Hogan says. An' I wuddent have to get th' constitution out iv th' safe to decide it ayether. I'd decide it accoordin' to me grocery bill.

"No, sir, ye'll live a long time before ye iver see judges recalled. But it don't do anny harm to scare thim. It don't do annybody anny harm to scare thim wanst in a while. They've f'rgotten we're outside. We'll make a noise, an' whin they say, 'Ar-re they goin' to haul me out?' we'll yell, 'Judge, put ye'er head out iv th' window. There ar-re people out here. That's it—people, not lawyers. We don't objick to ye'er makin' laws, but don't make thim on'y f'r lawyers. Cut out a few pattherns that will fit us, too. We don't want manny, but we'd like a few simple wans that we can wear to keep off th' cold. An' if ye haven't time f'r annything excipt a harness that we ar-re not iddycated enough to put on, f'r hivens sake let us make some laws f'r ourslves that plazes our low tastes. We don't want laws to wear in coort. We want thim to wear outside.'"

"What is this English common law I read about?" asked Mr. Hennessy.

"It's th' law I left Ireland to get away f'rm," said Mr. Dooley. "If it's pursooed me over here I'll go to Chiny."

"An' wan iv us takes him be th' hair an' th' other be th' heels an' we throw him out iv th' window. An' that's th' recall."

129

Ben Hecht, 1001 Afternoons in
Chicago, *1923.*
Newberry Library

first-hand not only the miseries of slum life, but also the corruption that pervaded politics and business at all levels, high
and low. His first published pieces were newspaper accounts of crime and tenement miseries. His later works,
novels read by a fascinated public, dealt with the same
themes.

Dreiser's novels shocked conventional sensibilities. *Sister
Carrie* (1900) was based on the experiences of his own sister,
who actually was kept by a salesman and ran away with a
saloon manager who had absconded with his employer's
money. His later trilogy, *The Financier, The Titan,* and *The
Genius,* was a study of corrupted ambition, thinly-veiled but
obviously based on the life of Charles T. Yerkes, Chicago's
traction baron. While Dreiser detested its businessmen, he
was clearly in love with the city itself. In its diversity
Chicago was dramatic and stimulating, even intoxicating,
and Dreiser cast his portraits of city scenes in tones that captured all this as never before and probably never since.

Other young writers saw Chicago as a refuge from the
dreariness of the small town. Sherwood Anderson walked
away from a fairly prosperous business in Elyria, Ohio, to
pursue a hungry existence in a North Side rooming house.
Anderson's novels, such as *Windy McPherson's Son* (1916),
were a commentary on the sad fate of small-town failures.
In 1908 Floyd Dell came from Davenport, Iowa, and after

several other jobs ended up with the *Chicago Evening Post.*
That paper had created a separate *Friday Literary Review* in
1909, and Dell became its editor in 1911. Later he published the *Moon Calf* (1920) and the *Briary Bush* (1921), both
based on his experiences in the local bohemia. Meanwhile,
another young writer named Ben Hecht had come to town
from Wisconsin.

The new writers and their friends gathered in a small intellectual enclave down in Hyde Park. After the closing of the
Columbian Exposition the severe depression of the 1890s
had left a number of nearby stores vacant. Attracted by
cheap rents, writers and artists began to move in and establish studios. They summered at the Indiana Dunes and
talked endlessly about the arts. Quite unlike the followers
of the Little Room, they clearly regarded themselves as reb-
els against the canons of conventional literature. Perhaps
the most important manifestation of this spirit was embodied in a magazine, *The Little Review,* begun in 1914 under
the editorship of Margaret Anderson. It was controversial
from the very beginning. Anderson published writers who
attacked anything and everything sacred, and she challenged the censorship laws by serializing James Joyce's *Ulys-
ses.* The movement the *Little Review* represented was clearly
the forerunner of the Greenwich Village bohemianism of
the 1920s.

Theodore Dreiser (1871-1945), c1895. A controversial author, Dreiser's first novel, Sister Carrie *(1900), evoked a storm of public criticism for its frank treatment of marital infidelity.*
Theodore Dreiser Collection, University of Pennsylvania Library

John T. McCutcheon, "The Traction Magnate's Dream," 1908. McCutcheon captured the feelings of thousands of average Chicagoans in this cartoon.

Sherwood Anderson (1876-1941), 1922. A latecomer to Chicago's literary bohemia, Anderson had been a successful advertising writer.

Minnie's flat, as the one-floor resident apartments were then being called, was in a part of West Van Buren Street inhabited by families of labourers and clerks, men who had come, and were still coming, with the rush of population pouring in at the rate of 50,000 a year. It was on the third floor, the front windows looking down into the street, where, at night, the lights of grocery stores were shining and children were playing. To Carrie, the sound of the little bells upon the horse-cars, as they tinkled in and out of hearing, was as pleasing as it was novel. She gazed into the lighted street when Minnie brought her into the front room, and wondered at the sounds, the movement, the murmur of the vast city which stretched for miles and miles in every direction.

From Theodore Dreiser,
Sister Carrie, 1900.

Where Carrie Meeber's sister Minnie lived, West Van Buren Street near Union Park, 1913.

The automatic piano in the penny arcade whangs dolorously into a forgotten tango. The two errand boys stand with their eyes glued on the interiors of the picture slot machines—"An Artist's Model" and "On the Beach at Atlantic City." A gun pops foolishly in the rear and the 3-inch bullseye clangs. In a corner behind the Postal Card Photo Taken in a Minute gallery sits Dutch, the world's leading tattooer. Sample tattoo designs cover the two walls. Dragons, scorpions, bulbous nymphs, crossed flags, wreathed anchors, cupids, butterflies, daggers and quaint decorations that seem the grotesque survivals of the mid-Victorian schools of fantasy. Photographs of famous men also cover the walls—Capt. Constantinus tattooed from head to foot, every inch of him; Barnum's favorites, ancient and forgotten kooch dancers, fire eaters, sword swallowers, magicians and museum freaks.

From Ben Hecht, *1001 Afternoons in Chicago,* 1923.

Chicago's Tenderloin, State Street between Van Buren and Congress, c1912.

A Chicago ice handler, c1900.

Ice Handler

*I know an ice handler who wears a flannel shirt with pearl buttons
     the size of a dollar,
And he lugs a hundred-pound hunk into a saloon icebox, helps him-
     self to cold ham and rye bread,
Tells the bartender it's hotter than yesterday and will hotter yet to-
     morrow, by Jesus,
And is on his way with his head in the air and a hard pair of fists.
He spends a dollar or so every Saturday night on a two hundred
     pound woman who washes dishes in the Hotel Morrison.
He remembers when the union was organized he broke the noses of
     two scabs and loosened the nuts so the wheels came off six differ-
     ent wagons one morning, and he came around and watched the
     ice melt in the street.
All he was sorry for was one of the scabs bit him on the knuckles of the
     right hand so they bled when he came around to the saloon to tell
     the boys about it.*

From Carl Sandburg, *Chicago Poems,* 1916.

*The grimy lattice-work of the drawbridge
swung to slowly, the steam-tug blackened
the dull air and roiled the turbid water as it
dragged its schooner on towards the
lumber-yards of the South Branch, and a
long line of waiting vehicles took up their
interrupted course through the smoke and
the stench as they filed across the stream into
the thick of business beyond: first a yellow
street-car; then a robust truck laden with
rattling sheet-iron, or piled high with fresh
wooden pails and willow baskets; then a
junk-cart bearing a pair of dwarfed and
bearded Poles, who bumped in unison with
the jars of its clattering springs; then,
perhaps, a bespattered buggy, with reins
jerked by a pair of sinewy and impatient
hands. Then more street-cars; then a
butcher's cart loaded with the carcasses of
calves—red, black, piebald—or an express
wagon with a yellow cur yelping from its
rear; then, it may be, an insolently venture-
some landau, with crested panel and top-
booted coachman. Then drays and om-
nibuses and more street-cars; then, pre-
sently, somewhere in the line, between the
tail end of one truck and the menacing
tongue of another, a family carry-all—a
carry-all loaded with its family, driven by a
man of all work, drawn by a slight and
amiable old mare, and encumbered with
luggage which shows the labels of half the
hotels of Europe.*

From Henry Blake Fuller,
With the Procession, 1895.

Rush Street Bridge, 1902.

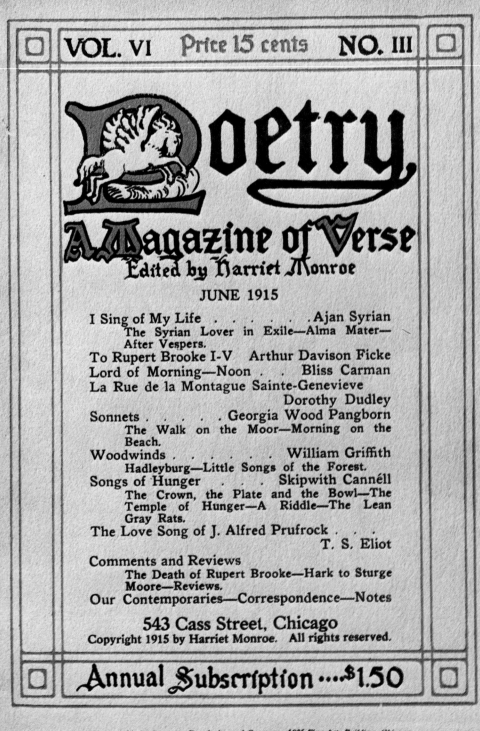

VOL. VI   Price 15 cents   NO. III

Poetry

A Magazine of Verse

Edited by Harriet Monroe

JUNE 1915

543 Cass Street, Chicago

Annual Subscription $1.50

Published monthly by Seymour, Daughaday and Company, 1025 Fine Arts Building, Chicago.
Entered as second-class matter at Postoffice, Chicago

Poetry, *June 1915.   Harriet Monroe's* Poetry *magazine introduced many controversial works to the American public, including "The Love Song of J. Alfred Prufrock," by T. S. Eliot.* University of Chicago Library

New Bards for Chicago

The new experience of curbstone realism also influenced Chicago's poets and even modified the precepts of those who had survived from the old Little Room group. In 1911 Harriet Monroe founded *Poetry*. Launching a new journal, unlike simply publishing something in the newspapers, demanded investment capital. Because Monroe had turned to old friends like Henry Blake Fuller, some critics expected *Poetry* to be a throwback to the genteel spirit of the Little Room. She proved them wrong. The journal introduced numerous young poets whose startling meter and rhyme broke many conventions.

Poetry attracted a large audience and proved to be an effective medium for a rebellious "Chicago School" of poets. But, even more important, it provided an outlet for poets from all over the Midwest. Edgar Lee Masters, already famous for his *Spoon River Anthology*, contributed a few pieces, relatively minor. But his fellow writer from downstate Sangamon County, Vachel Lindsay, produced his greatest work in *Poetry*. A failure as a pre-medical student and as an artist, Lindsay sold volumes of his poems to survive. In January 1913 he published "General William Booth Enters Into Heaven" in *Poetry,* and the following year he contributed "The Congo," with its heavy beat that proved most distressing to critics who thought poetry should be something delicate. Nevertheless, it made Lindsay famous. Another major poet who began making his reputation in *Poetry* was T. S. Eliot, born in St. Louis, whose "The Love Song of J. Alfred Prufrock" was published in 1915.

Finally, there was the work of a young socialist newspaperman who became the most important and famous of literary journalists. Carl Sandburg was born in 1878 in Galesburg, Illinois, the son of an immigrant Swedish blacksmith who toiled in the shops of the Chicago, Burlington and Quincy Railroad. Young Carl was forced to terminate his formal education at the eighth grade in order to help support his family. At the age of seventeen he left home and went on the road. Working his way westward, he lived a hobo's life, supporting himself at odd jobs. When twenty he volunteered for service in the Spanish-American War. After his return home, he entered Lombard College in Galesburg, although he had never even attended high school. For four years he worked as a janitor to pay for his schooling. Then, just before he was about to graduate, he again took to the road.

This time he went east, and while he was in New York he decided on a career. During his army days he had been a special correspondent for his hometown newspaper, and he cited that experience to land a job with the *New York Daily News*. After two years as a police reporter, he returned to Galesburg and became a fireman, then worked for a magazine in Chicago, and for three successive newspapers in Milwaukee. While in Wisconsin he developed a firm attachment to the Socialist Party, which rewarded him with the job of personal secretary to Emil Seidel, who was elected mayor in 1910. After that, and after another short stint with a Milwaukee paper, Sandburg returned to Chicago.

Harriet Monroe (1860-1936), 1906. Miss Monroe, who wrote odes to dedicate the Auditorium and the Columbian Exposition, is best known for founding Poetry *magazine.*

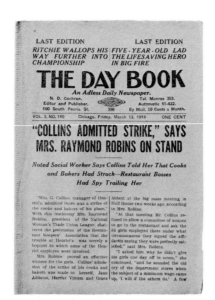

Carl Sandburg's typescript for "The Windy City." Sandburg published this frank appraisal of Chicago in Harriet Monroe's Poetry magazine. University of Chicago Library

The Day Book, 1914. While this small "adless" newspaper survived only a few years, its reporters, including Carl Sandburg, unearthed corruption that other papers thought too controversial to publish.

Vachel Lindsay (1879-1931), c1919. Like Edgar Lee Masters, Lindsay spent his formative years in Chicago. His poems, "The Congo" and "General William Booth enters Heaven," were noteworthy for their compelling rhythm. University of Chicago Library

Carl Sandburg (1878-1967), c1920. Sandburg drew upon his experience as an itinerant journalist to create a stark Midwestern realism. In his later years he published a massive biography of Abraham Lincoln.

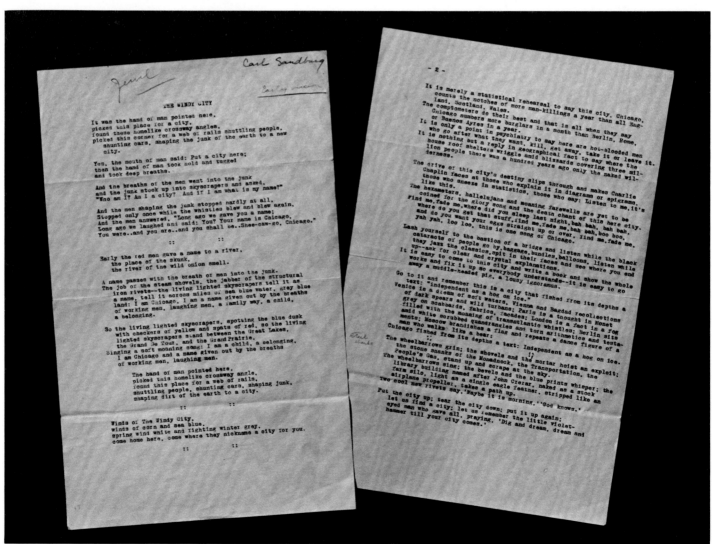

By 1912 Sandburg's life had begun to take shape. At thirty-four years of age, he had already held a lifetime of jobs. While his experiences had confirmed his socialist leanings, he still could work for *System,* a business-efficiency journal in which many of Walter Dill Scott's articles had appeared. But, as so often before, he soon moved on, first to the Socialist *Chicago Evening World,* and then to a strange little daily called *The Day Book.* This was a Scripps paper, published in a small pocket-size format and selling for a penny. It was filled with news of official corruption, the organized crime then incipient, and miscellaneous misconduct by the wealthy. Sandburg stayed with the *Day Book* until it folded in 1917, continuing to do free-lance work on a favorite topic, workingmen's hazards and industrial safety.

During these important transitional years Sandburg also emerged as a promising poet. What he set to line and meter reflected his own life and the working-class world in which he had immersed himself. His most important early poem was "Chicago," published in 1914 in Harriet Monroe's *Poetry.* Characterizing the city as "Hog Butcher for the World," he shocked genteel readers both with its form and content. *The Dial,* by then a fading reflection of Chicago literary taste, complained that "The typographical arrangement of this jargon creates a suspicion that it is intended to be taken as some form of poetry . . . ." But Sandburg knew which economic forces had really built Chicago, and as a young man alone in the city he had known what it was like to encounter painted women under streetlamps. He had seen conditions in these sweatshops, and, while at the *Day Book* in 1915, he covered a garment workers' strike. Thus, when he wrote poetry about tired shopgirls on the Halsted streetcar, he was speaking from experience. For the next decade his poems continued to reflect the world he knew.

After the *Day Book* folded Sandburg went to Hearst's *Chicago Herald-American,* but Henry Justin Smith, managing editor of the *Daily News,* soon lured him away. Here, finally, was a place that Sandburg liked, and he stayed until 1932. He continued to report labor news, and to espouse "Parliamentary Socialism," a gradualist stance. Meanwhile, during the War, he had begun to notice another problem in society, the situation of blacks in the North. His labor reporting had drawn his attention to the wartime migration northward and his historical interests had made him sensitive to the problem of racism. Just as he was beginning an investigation of the Black Belt, the infamous 1919 Riot had broken out. He covered that tragic episode for the *Daily News,* and his accounts appeared on the front pages. Afterwards he published his articles as a book, *The Chicago Race Riots.* Virtually every point he made in that book was later substantiated by a state investigation.

Jane Addams writes Harriet Monroe, 1911. Chicago's creative people often exchanged ideas. In this letter Jane Addams is asking Harriet Monroe's opinion of a budding young poet. University of Chicago Library

The Traditions in Perspective

The Chicago literary tradition was not without its ironies. The two schools of writing were fairly distinct. One seemed to be in constant distress over the misconduct of Chicago's upper crust. The writers of the Little Room—with the major exception of Friedman—were distraught by the displacement of proper old families by the crass *nouveau riche.* But greedy parvenus were scarcely the only thing to lament. The city harbored an agglomeration of unpleasantries from horrendous traffic jams to hordes of unwashed immigrants who jammed the Public Library. In his articles surveying Chicago's cultural scene, Fuller had gone far out of his way to condemn the skyscraper. In his novel it became the very symbol of greed.

The anomaly lay in the fact that the second group of writers included many whom poverty had forced to abandon even the garret for a job on the streets. They became bill collectors or newspapermen. Here they came into direct contact with the miseries of the metropolis. Newspapers thrived on stories of misfortune, and any reporter was continually confronted with the failures of urban civilization. Yet, out of this situation came a literature that was fundamentally affirmative. A Dreiser or a Sandburg could decry poverty or labor strife and then write odes to cities of big shoulders.

The Chicago writers, whether they belonged to the Little Room or read the *Little Review,* found direct means of communicating with readers. It might be through *The Dial* or the *Chap-Book,* or through novels or newspapers. Perceptive Chicagoans realized that they could avail themselves of truly fresh and significant literature for a penny or two. But, then, it was hardly unusual for Chicagoans to partake of the avant-garde through mass-consumption media.

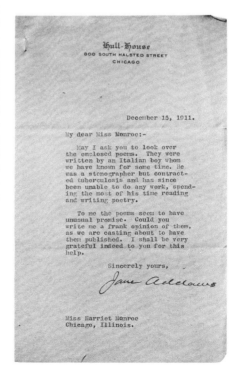

Epilogue

The Chicago creators were an unusual group. Their willingness to issue bold challenges against accepted cultural norms branded them as brash, almost reckless. They were interrelated in diverse ways. Some were actually intermarried, such as John Root with Harriet Monroe's sister, and Hamlin Garland with Lorado Taft's. There were salons of varying degrees of gentility, from the Little Room to the 57th Street colony and the Whitechapel Club. The Chicago creators attended the symphony and belonged to the Art Institute. Many artists had studios in the Fine Arts Building, as did the architect S. S. Beman. Hull-House benefitted from their support and served as Frank Lloyd Wright's forum for his famous speech on the "The Art and Craft of the Machine." Jane Addams sent the work of promising neighborhood poets to Harriet Monroe, and Lorado Taft judged artwork done at the settlements. The Chicago creators were a self-conscious cultural elite, yet they realized that the success of their work depended on their ability to make it available and comprehensible to the general public. Sometimes they were motivated by philanthropic ideals, but just as often by materialism. In a city where cultural continuity from the East was disjunctive, the "merchants of the new" (as Mencken called them) found a welcome audience.

It was a sad fact, nevertheless, that by the time Mencken wrote his famous article recognizing Chicago's cultural importance, its first great era was drawing to a close. Although some institutions remained intact, others seemed to dissolve. In architecture, most of the giants were gone by 1920. Root died in 1891 and Burnham in 1912. Adler terminated his partnership with Sullivan in 1895 and five years later he was dead. Sullivan's career went into a steep decline after the turn of the century. The plans for the Schlesinger and Mayer store were largely complete by 1899, and afterward Sullivan was reduced to designing small-town banks, beautiful but not very profitable for him. Largely in an attempt to revive his reputation, he turned to writing. Holabird and Roche continued for several years into the post-Versailles decade, but Frank Lloyd Wright's Chicago practice almost disappeared after he ran off with the wife of a client.

In literature, Chicago's leadership waned largely because most of the authors had left town by the early 1920s, some going to Greenwich Village, some to Europe to join the "Lost Generation." Their periodicals did continue—*The Little Review* until 1929 and *Poetry* to the present. Film makers left after discovering the climatic advantages of southern California. And Chicago's era at the center of radio also was brief. NBC moved to Rockefeller Center, nearer the source of advertising revenues. Most radio serials did, however, continue to emanate from Chicago. The Arts and Crafts movement gradually died out, although Marshall Field's opened its own silver shop in 1920. The Municipal Art League continued into the postwar decade, but it, too, declined in vitality.

Nevertheless, the end of this first great era of creativity did not mark the final eclipse of Chicago as a cultural entrepôt. During the Depression of the 1930s Chicago architects began experimenting with stark modern forms, and the arrival of refugee architects from Germany in 1939 signaled the rebirth of the Chicago architectural tradition. Novelists like Saul Bellow and poets like Gwendolyn Brooks added new ethnic and racial dimensions to Chicago realism. In recent years there have been other significant creative enterprises, from Second City and vibrant satirical comedy to a group of artists known for their bold experimentation.

The term "Chicago School" has become a cliché. In nearly every realm of creative endeavor Chicago has made a bold contribution, either in content or in the presentation of new ideas to wide audiences. Chicago has always thrived on a unique blend of innovation and popularization. No doubt it will continue to do so.

This bibliography is necessarily brief and selective. Space does not permit the citation of more than a handful of primary sources, obscure articles, or unpublished dissertations. Most material listed here is available in public libraries and, of course, at the Chicago Historical Society.

There have been few previous historical surveys of creative Chicago. One standard work, Hugh D. Duncan, *Culture and Democracy* (Totowa, N.J.: Bedminster Press, 1965) is concerned more with the democratic philosophy of Chicago's creative leadership than with its accomplishments. Also, it omits such important figures as Lorado Taft and Theodore Thomas. A recent volume, Kenny Jackson Williams, *In the City of Men: Another Story of Chicago* (Nashville: Townsend Press, 1974) is a bit more comprehensive and readable, but it lacks a central theme and is, at times, vague and verbose.

Chicago's architecture has been the subject of several excellent studies. Carl Condit's writings, especially *The Chicago School of Architecture* (Chicago: The University of Chicago Press, 1964), have led the way in making Americans aware of Chicago's heritage. Thomas Tallmadge, *Architecture in Old Chicago* (Chicago: The University of Chicago Press, 1941), recently reissued in paperback, is a venerable study that takes the story down to the 1890s. Frank Randall, *History of the Development of Building Construction in Chicago* (Urbana: The University of Illinois Press, 1949) is a detailed, street-by-street guide.

Biographies of individual architects are a mixed bag. Donald Hoffman, *The Architecture of John Wellborn Root* (Baltimore: The Johns Hopkins University Press, 1973) is a model study, an improvement upon Harriet Monroe's 1896 biography, *John Wellborn Root, Architect* (facsimile edition, Park Forest, Illinois: Prairie School Press, 1966). Hugh Morrison, *Louis Sullivan: Prophet of Modern Architecture* (New York: W.W. Norton & Company, 1935) is the best work on Sullivan. There is a growing literature on Frank Lloyd Wright. Grant Manson, *Frank Lloyd Wright to 1910: The First Golden Age* (New York: The Reinhold Publishing Corp., 1958) is the best so far on his early years, and Robert Twombly, *Frank Lloyd Wright: An Interpretive Biography* (New York: Harper & Row, 1973) is the best general biography. H. Allen Brooks, *The Prairie School* (Toronto: University of Toronto Press, 1972) is a superb survey, which should arouse the reader's interest in *The Prairie School Review*, an excellent journal on Chicago architecture. As yet there are no substantial published biographies of William LeBaron Jenney, Dankmar Adler, or Holabird and Roche.

There is little consensus about the talents of Daniel Burnham. A bitter Louis Sullivan claimed that he was a successful back-slapper-businessman but a pedestrian architect. Thomas Hines, *Burnham of Chicago: Architect and Planner* (New York: Oxford University Press, 1974) is a generous corrective to that view, while David Burg, *Chicago's White City* (Lexington: The University Press of Kentucky, 1976) also lauds Burnham. Burg has provided a much-needed scholarly study of the Columbian Exposition, put-

ting that event in proper historical perspective. Although DaCapo Press has issued a reprint of the 1909 Plan of Chicago, other information about planning is harder to find. Victoria Ranney, *Olmsted in Chicago* (Chicago: Open Lands Project, 1972) is a fine pamphlet on the way Olmsted left his mark on Chicago. Stanley Buder's *Pullman* (New York: Oxford University Press, 1966) is an excellent study of the industrial community. James Birrell, *Walter Burley Griffin* (Brisbane: University of Queensland Press, 1964) is an able study, but focuses primarily on Griffin and Mahony in Australia.

There are a number of good studies of Chicago reformers. James Findlay, *Dwight Moody* (Chicago: The University of Chicago Press, 1969) is the best on Moody. On Frances Willard, her own autobiographical works are still the most useful source, though Joseph Gusfield, *Symbolic Crusade* (Urbana: The University of Illinois Press, 1953) is an interesting interpretation by a sociologist. Jane Addams was her own best publicist, and *Twenty Years at Hull-House*, available in various editions, is an American classic. Allen Davis, *American Heroine* (New York: Oxford University Press, 1973) is not always complimentary. Davis and Mary Lynn McCree edited *Eighty Years at Hull-House* (Chicago: Quadrangle Books, 1969), a fascinating collection of first-hand accounts. Louise Wade, *Graham Taylor: Pioneer for Social Justice* (Chicago: The University of Chicago Press, 1964) is a very important book. Taylor himself wrote two books about Chicago Commons. There are biographies of Margaret Dreier Robins, Agnes Nestor, Florence Kelley, Julia Lathrop, and Mary McDowell. Other reformers, unfortunately, have not been as well studied.

Books on the history of educational theory, such as Robert Cremin, *The Transformation of the School* (New York: Alfred A. Knopf, 1961), put the ideas of Dewey and Parker in proper perspective. Richard Storr, *Harper's University* (Chicago: The University of Chicago Press, 1967) covers the early years of The University of Chicago. Anthony Platt, *The Child Savers* (Chicago: The University of Chicago Press, 1969) describes the crusade against juvenile delinquency. Herman Kogan, *The First Century: The Chicago Bar Association, 1874-1974* (Chicago: Rand McNally & Company, 1974) includes an interesting chapter on court reform. Roi Ottley, *Lonely Warrior* (Chicago: Henry Regnery Company, 1955) is a highly readable biography of Robert Abbott. Allen Spear, *Black Chicago* (Chicago: The University of Chicago Press, 1967) attempts to survey the development of the Chicago black community before 1920.

There are few good books on Chicago arts. Scholars have virtually ignored the history of The Art Institute, although the forthcoming book by Helen Horowitz is expected to fill this void. There is no published biography of Lorado Taft, and the standard work on Thomas, Charles E. Russell, *The American Orchestra and Theodore Thomas* (Garden City, N.Y.: Doubleday, Page & Company, 1927) is uncritical. In contrast, Ronald Davis, *Opera in Chicago* (New York: Appleton-Century, 1966) is a sophisticated cultural study. Otherwise, the story of music in Chicago remains buried in unpublished sources and obscure publications. Ellis A. Johnson, "The Chicago Symphony" (M.A. thesis, The University of Chicago, 1951) is concise and most useful, while no serious researcher should fail to consult the Theodore Thomas Scrapbooks at the Chicago Historical Society and an important article by George P. Upton, "Music in Chicago," *New England Magazine*, n.s. 6 (December 1892), pp. 477-94. A venerable volume, Philo Adams Otis, *The Chicago Symphony Orchestra: Its Organization and Development: 1891-1924* (Chicago: Clayton F. Summy Co., 1924) is valuable. Readers should also consult the various editions of Theodore Thomas's autobiography.

Researchers interested in Chicago as an art center must also rely on old or unpublished sources. Lucy Monroe, "Art in Chicago," *New England Magazine,* n.s. 6 (June 1892), 411-32, is extremely valuable, as is Ernest Poole, "Art and Democracy: How the Chicago Art Institute Reaches the People," *The Outlook* 85 (March 23, 1907), pp. 665-74. The outstanding work on art is by Eugenia Whitridge, "Art in Chicago: The Structure of the Art World in a Metropolitan Community" (Ph.D. dissertation, The University of Chicago, 1946), which contains a substantial historical section.

Public art is another subject about which little has been published. For the story of the Municipal Art League, one must consult its annual reports. There is a useful article on the Ferguson Fund, L.M. McCauley, "Municipal Art in Chicago: A Civic Renaissance Planned for the Western Metropolis," *The Craftsman* 9 (December 1905), pp. 321-40. Lorado Taft wrote an excellent review of Chicago statues in his "The Monuments of Chicago," *Art and Archeology* 12 (October 1921), pp. 120-27. One should also consult "Lorado Taft and the Western School of Sculptors: A Group of Men and Women Who Are Finding a New and Vital Expression in Art by Recording the Simplest Phases of Life and Work," *The Craftsman* 14 (April 1908), pp. 12-25. The Chicago architect Peter Wight reviewed the plans for Taft's most ambitious work in "Apotheosis of the Midway Plaisance," *Architectural Review* 28 (November 1910), pp. 335-49. There is an outstanding summary of the sculptor's life in Lewis Williams, "Lorado Taft: American Sculptor and Art Missionary" (Ph.D. dissertation, The University of Chicago, 1958).

Generally, the popular arts have fared better than the fine arts. William Grisham has published several articles on the Chicago film industry, especially on the Essanay and Ebony companies. Kalton LaHue has skillfully assembled a volume of articles, *Motion Picture Pioneer: The Selig Polyscope Company* (South Brunswick, N.J.: A. S. Barnes and Company, 1973.) Erick Barnow, *A Tower in Babel* (New York: Oxford University Press, 1966), the standard history of radio in America, makes frequent mention of Chicago. On the popular performing arts, there are several unpublished works. George Mitchell, "The Images of the City in the American Film, 1896-1928" (Ph.D. dissertation, The University of Chicago, 1971) is a fascinating look at the urban drama. There is also a useful summary of the film industry in George Scheetz, "The Chicago Film Industry: The Beginnings to 1918," an unpublished manuscript in the library of the University of Illinois at Urbana.

Historians discovered Chicago merchandising some years ago. Although Montgomery Ward lacks a substantial historical treatment, there is a detailed study of Sears, Boris Emmet and John Jeuck, *Catalogues and Counters: A History of Sears, Roebuck & Company* (Chicago: The University of Chicago Press, 1950). Robert W. Twyman, *History of Marshall Field & Co., 1852-1906* (Philadelphia: University of Pennsylvania Press, 1954) is a model corporate history, and Lloyd Wendt and Herman Kogan, *Give the Lady What She Wants* (Chicago: Rand McNally & Company, 1952), also about Field's, is a product of skilled research.

The Arts and Crafts movement is a new field of research. David Hanks, "The Midwest," in Robert Judson Clark, *The Arts and Crafts Movement in America* (Princeton: Princeton University Press, 1972) is a pioneer effort whose major shortcoming is its failure adequately to treat the relationship between the settlement houses and the movement. The best sources of information on the Arts and Crafts movement are the original ones. Various pamphlets in the Chicago Historical Society, such as *The Chicago Arts and Crafts Society* (n.p., n.d.), are most useful. One phase of the movement is the subject of "The Hull-House Book Bindery," *The Commons* 6 (June 1900), pp. 21-22. See also "Some Work of the Arts and Crafts Society," *Brush and Pencil* 3 (December 1898), pp. 148-52. There are numerous articles in other issues of the *Brush and Pencil* as well as in *House Beautiful* and *The Craftsman.*

Chicago literary figures have been popular subjects for years. Bernard Duffey, *The Chicago Renaissance in American Letters* (East Lansing: Michigan State University Press, 1956) covers the nineteenth century uplifters. Dale Kramer, *Chicago Renaissance* (New York: Appleton-Century, 1966) is a capable survey of the later writers before 1930. Lenox B. Grey, "Chicago and the Great American Novel" (Ph.D. dissertation, The University of Chicago, 1935) is often used but seldom cited by scholars. Virtually every literary figure of note has been the subject of scholarly study. There are some exceptions, however, among them Ben Hecht, I.K. Friedman, and George Ade. Worse, few studies treat the way writers reach large audiences, the major exception being Hugh Duncan, *The Rise of Chicago as a Literary Center from 1885 to 1920* (Totowa, N.J.: Bedminster Press, 1964).

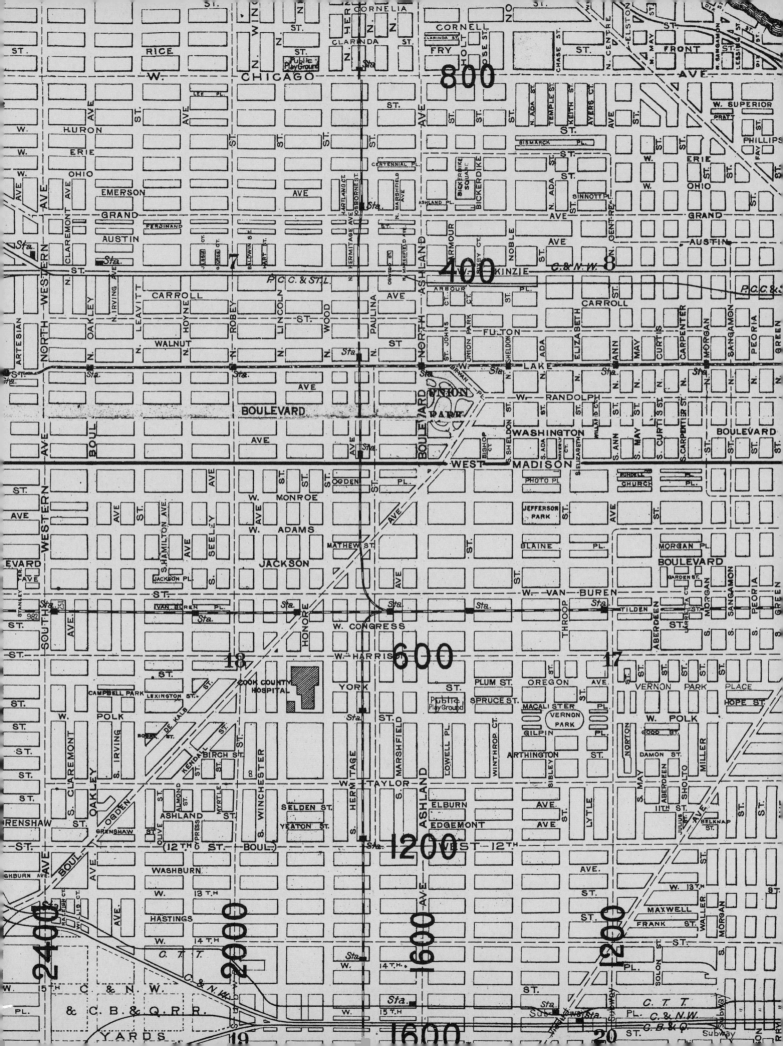